Raced to Death in 1920s Hawai'i

THE ASIAN AMERICAN EXPERIENCE

Series Editors
Eiichiro Azuma
Jigna Desai
Martin F. Manalansan IV
Lisa Sun-Hee Park
David K. Yoo

Roger Daniels, Founding Series Editor

A list of books in the series appears at the end of this book.

Raced to Death in 1920s Hawai'i

Injustice and Revenge in the Fukunaga Case

JONATHAN Y. OKAMURA

UNIVERSITY OF ILLINOIS PRESS
Urbana, Chicago, and Springfield

1 2 3 4 5 C P 5 4 3 2 1
∞ This book is printed on acid-free paper.

Library of Congress Cataloging-in-Publication Data
Names: Okamura, Jonathan Y., author.
Title: Raced to death in 1920s Hawai'i : injustice and revenge in the Fukunaga case / Jonathan Y. Okamura.
Description: Urbana : University of Illinois Press, 2019. | Series: The Asian American experience | Includes bibliographical references and index. | Identifiers: LCCN 2019002214 (print) | LCCN 2019005382 (ebook) | ISBN 9780252051449 (ebook) | ISBN 9780252042607 (cloth : alk. paper) | ISBN 9780252084430 (pbk. : alk. paper)
Subjects: LCSH: Fukunaga, Myles Yutaka. 1909-1929—Trials, litigation, etc. | Trials (Murder)—Hawaii—History—20th century. | Discrimination in criminal justice administration—Hawaii—History—20th century. | Japanese Americans--Legal status, laws, etc.—Hawaii—History—20th century. | Hawaii—Race relations—History—20th century.
Classification: LCC KF224.F85 (ebook) | LCC KF224.F85 O39 2019 (print) | DDC 345.969/02523099693—dc23
LC record available at https://lccn.loc.gov/2019002214

For Kekuni Blaisdell

Contents

Preface

Perhaps I was fated to write this book. For more than twenty years until 2010, when I began the research for *Raced to Death*, I lived with my wife and daughter in the shadow of the grave of Myles Fukunaga. After being hanged in 1929 for murdering a young Haole or White boy, Gill Jamieson, Fukunaga was buried in the Japanese cemetery in Mōʻiliʻili, a predominantly Japanese American community in Honolulu before World War II. I was familiar with the Fukunaga case since the mid-1970s and lectured regularly about it in my Japanese in Hawaiʻi course. But I did not consider writing a book about the case because I thought I would have to be able to read Japanese so that I could determine what the Japanese language newspapers in Honolulu had written about it. However, when I began my research on the case at the Archives Collection of the University of Hawaiʻi Hamilton Library, I learned that those newspapers had numerous articles and editorials in English about it, as did the Honolulu daily newspapers. At that point, I knew that I could and wanted to write a book about the Fukunaga case, and *Raced to Death* is the first to be written about it.

I was especially attracted to the Fukunaga case because of its racial dimensions and my theoretical and research interests in race and ethnicity. As I argue, these racial elements extend well beyond the fact that Fukunaga was Japanese American and his victim was White and affirm the larger racial significance of the case, especially concerning the racial injustices inflicted upon Japanese Americans and other non-Haoles. *Raced to Death* also expands on some of the arguments regarding the historical significance of race that I presented in my previous book, *From Race to Ethnicity: Interpreting Japanese American Experiences in Hawaiʻi* (2014). The Fukunaga case concretely demonstrates the primacy of race as the foremost organizing principle of social relations in Hawai'i, especially before World War II, and how it enforced the dominant boundary between Haoles and non-Haoles.

As with my previous books, I need to extend my grateful appreciation to a number of friends and colleagues who kindly read chapter drafts and met with me to discuss their questions and concerns. Ibrahim Aoude and Noel Kent, my longtime friends in the Department of Ethnic Studies at UH Mānoa, shared their vast knowledge and racial and class perspectives on Hawai'i history in their discussions with me about the chapters they reviewed. A more recent department friend, Brian Chung, provided his insights on contemporary race and colorblindness in his reading of the introductory chapter. Also at Mānoa, Warren Nishimoto and Michiko Kodama-Nishimoto, recently retired from the Center for Oral History, each read a chapter and offered very helpful comments, especially in presenting trial testimony. Lois Yamauchi of the UH Department of Educational Psychology gave very useful advice on the chapter concerning Fukunaga's insanity. As with my two previous books on race and ethnicity in Hawai'i, Franklin Ng, recently retired after forty years at California State University, Fresno, carefully read and discussed his questions and concerns with me regarding several chapters. The two anonymous reviewers of my book manuscript approached by the University of Illinois Press both provided very constructive comments and suggestions for revision, which I greatly appreciate.

At the University of Illinois Press, Dawn Durante, senior acquisitions editor, was always supportive and encouraging of my book project since I first contacted her about it and promptly responded to all my questions and concerns, even while traveling.

I also am thankful for the generous research assistance a number of individuals provided. James Cartwright and Sherman Seki of the Archives Collection at the UH Hamilton Library were very helpful to me in providing daily access to the files on the Fukunaga case during the summer of 2010. At the Hawai'i State Archives, I especially appreciate the assistance of Gina Vergara-Bautista, who located the folders from the vast papers of Governor Lawrence Judd that contained the information I was interested in. While I was a visiting professor at Sophia University in Tokyo in spring 2014, Keaki Matsudaira was my most diligent research assistant who found articles on the Fukunaga case published in Japanese newspapers and translated them into English for me. I was fortunate to have Dr. Mariko Iijima as my faculty sponsor at Sophia who, as director of the Institute of American and Canadian Studies, invited me to give a lecture on my research on the Fukunaga case in 2015. At UH Mānoa, I had two hardworking student assistants who made my research much easier to complete. Kenith Scott conscientiously made copies of too many newspaper articles I requested him to find at the Microfilm Collection at Hamilton Library, while Lily Chen carefully reproduced the lengthy legal briefs, trial transcripts, and other legal documents related to the Fukunaga case.

I am very pleased to dedicate this book to the late Richard Kekuni Akana Blaisdell, who was an emeritus professor of the John A. Burns School of Medicine of the University of Hawai'i and a longtime leader of the Hawaiian sovereignty movement. Kekuni, as he was known to everyone, passed away at age ninety in February 2016, and it was a very easy decision for me to dedicate this book to him because of his unceasing advocacy of justice for his Native Hawaiian people. I met Kekuni in 1987 shortly after I returned to Hawai'i after teaching in the Philippines for three years, and it did not take very long for me to become friends with him. Over the years, I was especially gratified that my daughter Mika, who first met Kekuni when she was two years old, also developed a friendship with him, and Kekuni once accepted her invitation to speak at the University of California, Davis, when she was an undergraduate student. As a sovereignty leader, Kekuni was the primary organizer of *Kapakaukau* (the roundtable), which sought independence for Hawai'i, and the convener of the Kanaka Maoli People's Tribunal in 1993, which critically marked the one-hundredth anniversary of the overthrow of the Hawaiian monarchy. At the UH School of Medicine, which he joined in 1966, he was an early advocate of the health needs and concerns of Native Hawaiians and a beloved and inspiring teacher and later mentor of his many students. But I will always remember Kekuni primarily for personifying aloha, which he generously extended to everyone he encountered, together with his warm, friendly smile and *honi* (touching noses) greeting.

Research Methods and Sources

The research for this book was primarily conducted by reviewing primary sources pertaining to the Fukunaga case and secondary sources related to the case and to historical race in Hawai'i. Archival materials included numerous newspaper articles and editorials published in the *Honolulu Star-Bulletin* and *Honolulu Advertiser* and in the English-language sections of the *Hawaii Hochi* and *Nippu Jiji* Japanese newspapers in Honolulu. I accessed those materials at the Archives Collection and the Microfilm Collection at the University of Hawai'i Hamilton Library. I also read from the Archives Collection the official transcripts of jury selection for Fukunaga's trial and of the trial itself, the legal motions and appeals submitted by Fukunaga's attorneys following his death sentence, the reply briefs to those motions filed by the prosecuting attorneys, and the court rulings on those appeals. In addition, I reviewed documents related to the case in the official papers of Governor Wallace R. Farrington and Governor Lawrence M. Judd at the State Archives. And last, through the research and translation services of my research assistant, I read how the Fukunaga case was reported in the *Tokyo Asahi Shimbun* newspaper as it transpired. By reviewing these numerous and varied primary materials, I was able to cross-check and evaluate their accuracy with each other and with secondary sources on the Fukunaga case.

Figure 1: Gill Jamieson. Photo courtesy of the *Honolulu Star-Advertiser*.

Raced to Death in 1920s Hawai'i

Introduction

On the morning of September 18, 1928, when ten-year-old George Gill Jamieson said goodbye to his mother Lulu while leaving their home in affluent Mānoa for the exclusive Punahou Academy, he did not know that he would never see her again.[1] Within a few hours, Gill, as he was called by his parents, would be brutally bludgeoned to death in Waikīkī after being kidnapped from his school. His soon-to-be-captured killer, Yutaka Fukunaga, was a nineteen-year-old nisei, or second-generation Japanese American. Myles, as he called himself, had lived until recently with his impoverished immigrant parents and six younger siblings in downtown Honolulu in a rented house. That Tuesday morning, he awoke in a room he had just rented in a downtown tenement hotel, the Serene Rooms, occupied by young workers like himself, but he had other plans for that day than going to work. A bright but unhappy and lonely youth who claimed books were his only "friends," Fukunaga had twice tried to kill himself earlier in the year. He was also insane, according to two competent observers of his actions and statements.

How did young Gill Jamieson, a thoughtful and cheerful child, become Fukunaga's intended victim? What could have driven Fukunaga to commit such a violent act against Gill that everyone who knew him said was totally inconsistent with his quiet if not meek personality? A partial explanation is that Gill's father Frederick was a vice president of the Hawaiian Trust Company, which managed the leasing of the cottage the Fukunaga family was renting. After a dispute about $20 in overdue rent owed by his parents, Fukunaga developed an irrational desire for revenge and a "hatred" for the company, which led him to select Gill as his murder victim after learning that the boy's father was a Hawaiian Trust executive. In committing his crime, Fukunaga copied the infamous Leopold and Loeb kidnapping and murder of a teen-aged boy four years earlier in Chicago. Apprehended four days after killing Gill and collecting $4,000 in ransom money from the Jamiesons, Fukunaga readily admitted his guilt to the police. He was quickly put on trial, convicted of first-degree murder, and sentenced to be hanged, all in a little more than two weeks after his capture. But legal appeals of his conviction, which went ultimately to the U.S. Supreme Court and were based on arguments that he had not been given a fair trial and a full psychiatric examination, delayed his execution for more than a year until November 19, 1929.

Raced to Death is not a "true crime" story or a belated effort to provide justice to Myles Fukunaga and his relatives in Hawai'i by demonstrating that he was unjustly hanged for murder given his likely insanity. Instead, it is primarily concerned with the larger racial significance of the case by illuminating what it reveals about how race operated in Hawai'i in the 1920s, particularly in enforcing the hierarchical relations between Haoles (Whites) and non-Haoles. The period from 1920 to 1930 was an especially critical decade for Japanese Americans that began with their leading the first multiethnic plantation strike on O'ahu, which cost the planters $12 million in losses. At more than 40 percent, Japanese Americans were by far the largest and perceived as the most politically, economically, and culturally threatening group to continued Haole supremacy. Rather than an individual act, Fukunaga's killing of Gill was viewed by Haoles as a heinous murder by a Japanese American that disrupted the racial order, which had to be immediately restored through his speedy conviction and execution. As I argue, the Fukunaga case makes abundantly clear that race was the dominant principle of social organization in Hawai'i, which structured highly unequal relations between Haoles and non-Haoles. The case hence demonstrates that the territory was a racially unjust and colonized society ruled by a Haole settler oligarchy in which race determined the relative status of groups and their individual members in employment, wealth, education, political power, and justice before the law.

While it is beyond question that Fukunaga killed Gill Jamieson, given his willing admission, it also is clear that he was "raced" to his death.[2] I use race with two different but related meanings in this book. First, I argue that the reason Fukunaga was so quickly convicted and sentenced to be hanged is because he was, in the language of that time, of the "Japanese race." Instead of being viewed and treated by the police, prosecution, court, press, and public as an individual without regard to race, Fukunaga was racialized by all of them and could not escape being seen as anything but Japanese. As such, for Haoles he had to suffer the severest penalty provided by the law because he had brazenly murdered one of their own. Second, I contend that Fukunaga was raced or rushed to his death sentence insofar as Haoles, desirous of immediate revenge, wanted him found guilty and executed as quickly as possible. This all-consuming objective explains the speed with which Fukunaga's trial was started and concluded, especially his defense of nineteen minutes provided by his court-appointed attorneys, who called no witnesses on his behalf.

The Fukunaga case unfolded during the same decade when the first representations of Hawai'i as an exceptional, if not unique, "racial melting pot" and "racial paradise" were being advanced by University of Hawai'i sociologists and the Honolulu daily newspapers. Even earlier at the 1915 Panama-Pacific International Exposition in San Francisco, territorial government officials and other island promoters portrayed Hawai'i as "a conflict-free world where everyday barriers of race were somehow transcended," a veritable racial "fantasy reinforced in music and film."[3] Despite being easily contradicted by the deeply embedded racial inequality and biologically based racism in the territory, this idealized imagery was consistently affirmed by the editors of the Honolulu dailies throughout the Fukunaga case. They maintained that the "racial harmony" of the islands was being threatened by the efforts of Fukunaga's largely Japanese American supporters to obtain a new trial for him. These supporters contended that his being denied a fair trial and his hasty death sentence were the result of racial discrimination because he was Japanese. I refer to the initial representations of Hawai'i as a racial melting pot and paradise as "emergent multiculturalism" because they later developed into the false depiction of the islands as a "multicultural model" for other racially and ethnically divided societies. The Fukunaga case reveals these highly divergent understandings of the meaning and significance of race among Hawaii's constituent groups and the reasons for them. These differing views regarding what race means and its salience in society continue to the present, as is evident in competing racial projects that seek hegemony as the racial "common sense" in America, which is currently colorblindness.[4]

The ultimate outcome of the Fukunaga incident starkly challenged the racial harmony and racial paradise representations of Hawai'i by demonstrating how race operated to maintain simultaneously Haole domination and non-Haole oppression. Nonetheless, that did not stop Haoles from arguing that Fukunaga was treated by the courts as an individual without consideration of his being of the "Japanese race" and hence had received a fair and impartial trial. Thus, another major racial revelation of the Fukunaga case is the "incipient colorblindness" asserted in public discourse by the press, prosecution, judges, and government officials, despite Fukunaga being racialized as Japanese. I specify this supposed colorblindness as incipient because it obviously was not the dominant racial ideology in Hawai'i or the continental United States in the 1920s, when biologically based notions of race and racism, including eugenics, prevailed. Nonetheless, claiming colorblindness in the prosecution and conviction of Fukunaga was a strategic means for the dominant Haoles to counter the charges shortly made by the Japanese American community that he had been victimized by the "two systems of justice" in Hawai'i—one for Haoles and the other for non-Haoles. Race theorists Michael Omi and Howard Winant assert that colorblindness is "largely an ideological framework for the effacement of racial consciousness,"[5] and it hence "denies that race should inform perceptions, shape attitudes, or influence individual or collective action."[6] In the 1920s as at present, colorblindness maintained White supremacy by denying the significance of race through the denial of racial difference in the experiences and status of Whites and non-Whites. Haoles maintained that Fukunaga's treatment by government authorities and the outcome of his trial were the same as if he had been a Haole himself. In the contemporary situation, race scholar Eduardo Bonilla-Silva contends that colorblindness, as the leading racial ideology in America, is a form of racism, which is advanced to justify persisting racial inequality and White power and privilege.[7]

The colorblindness professed in the Fukunaga case can also be considered incipient because it appears to be one of its first significant public manifestations in the territory, given that the Hawaiian kingdom after the imposition of the "Bayonet Constitution" in 1887 became blatantly race conscious. Called such because King Kalākaua was forced by elite Haoles to accept it under threat of violence, the new constitution established a high property requirement that precluded the great majority of Native Hawaiians from running and voting for office, allowed male "nonsubject residents" of American and European ancestry to do so, and prohibited male subjects of Asian ancestry from doing both.[8] Before the Bayonet Constitution, the Hawaiian kingdom can be regarded as constitutionally colorblind insofar as it provided citizenship without consideration of race, including to persons, such as Chinese and Japanese, who were not of Native Hawaiian ancestry.[9]

Who was considered Haole needs clarification because the term did not and presently does not equate with the racial category White as understood in the continental United States. In the Hawaiian language, Haole initially referred to a foreigner, and, since the first group of them in Hawai'i following contact were Europeans and White Americans, the term came to be applied to them. Prior to statehood in 1959, Haoles constituted the dominant political and economic group, as is evident in their control of territorial government through the Republican Party and of the economy through the Big

Five companies (see chapter 1). However, the social construction of race in Hawai'i meant that not all Europeans and Whites were considered Haole; the notable exception were Portuguese who, unlike in the continental United States, were not racialized as White. Their nonacceptance as Haole can be attributed to Portuguese recruitment and employment as plantation workers beginning in 1878, especially since three-fourths of them were illiterate peasants from the Azores and Madeira islands.[10] Since most Portuguese were working class, while most Haoles were of middle-class status or higher, this significant class difference limited Portuguese from being accepted as Haole. As emphasized by sociologist Evelyn Nakano Glenn, "the term 'haole' came to have a specific class as well as racial meaning in contrast to an ethnically diverse laboring class,"[11] which consisted predominantly of non-Haoles.

In this way, the full benefits and privileges of Whiteness were reserved for those viewed as Haole, which is indicative of how restrictive the racial boundary between Haoles and non-Haoles was. For this reason, I refer to the racial setting as separating Haoles and non-Haoles, rather than Whites and non-Whites, because of the different meanings these racial categories as socially constructed had in Hawai'i. Sociologist of race Moon-Kie Jung has observed that "whiteness has been, above all, a racial formation that presupposed and reproduced relations of inequality and domination between 'whites' and their racial others."[12] However, in Hawai'i by the 1930s in the aftermath of the Massie-Kahahawai murder case (see below), Haoles had become the racial (and cultural) other to non-Haoles as the latter constructed and asserted a shared local identity based on their common racial and class differences with Haoles.

As for Haole supremacy in Hawai'i, it consisted of the racist ideology held and advanced particularly by those from long-resident elite families that they were "born to rule" and to dominate and control the territory by virtue of their inherent racial superiority.[13] Thus, in 1920 a representative of the Hawaiian Sugar Planters' Association (HSPA), Royal M. Mead, in public testimony before the U.S. House of Representatives unabashedly proclaimed: "I do not think that there is any contest as to who shall dominate; the white race, the white people, the Americans in Hawaii are going to dominate and will continue to dominate—there is no question about it."[14] Besides the assertion of continued Haole supremacy, the declaration is noteworthy for its racial equation between being White and being American, which was a particularly widespread assumption during that period. Haole supremacy defined themselves "as the only real Americans in Hawaii,"[15] although by the early 1920s most Japanese were American by birth. During the same decade, in-migration from the continental United States, especially of military personnel, resulted in more than doubling the White population in the islands, which became much more diverse in terms of class.[16] These newcomer Haoles were even more actively racist toward non-Haoles than were their longer-resident elite counterparts. While not viewing themselves as born to rule like the latter, they certainly considered themselves racially entitled to some of the same economic, political, and social privileges under Haole settler colonialism.

Obscuring Haole supremacy as the dominant racial ideology in Hawai'i, both emergent multiculturalism and incipient colorblindness were strategically deployed by Haoles to refute the salience of race in the accelerated conviction and death penalty given to Fukunaga. The former was primarily advanced by the *Honolulu Star-Bulletin* and the *Nippu Jiji* Japanese newspaper in their criticisms that Japanese American community efforts, led by the *Hawaii Hochi* Japanese paper, to obtain a new trial for Fukunaga threatened the "racial harmony" of Hawai'i. The *Star-Bulletin* and the *Honolulu Advertiser*, the *Nippu Jiji*, the prosecuting attorneys, and judges invoked incipient colorblindness in their respective arguments that Fukunaga was tried and convicted as an individual without regard to his being Japanese American. In the contemporary situation, colorblindness and multiculturalism, as variants of postracialism, are both similarly employed to maintain the racial status quo of White power and privilege and to explain away persisting racial inequality and racism in their common claims of a postracial America, despite contradicting each other as policy and practice.[17]

In *Raced to Death*, I also discuss how the Fukunaga incident is closely related to the much-better-known Massie-Kahahawai case, which began almost exactly three years later on September 13, 1931.[18] The twenty-year-old White wife of a navy lieutenant stationed at Pearl Harbor, Thalia Massie claimed that she had been raped by five local men, including Joseph Kahahawai, who was later kidnapped and killed by Massie's husband, her mother, and two navy sailors. This case, in which race and racism also played decisive roles in its ultimate outcome, is arguably one of the most pivotal episodes in the racial history of Hawai'i after U.S. annexation in 1898. In the concluding chapter, I provide a fuller comparison of the Fukunaga and Massie-Kahahawai cases than has been advanced previously, especially of their closely related racial aspects. The comparison shows how Haole elites used some of the same political and legal tactics, which they had utilized in the Fukunaga case, to usurp the criminal justice system in the Massie-Kahahawai case so they could obtain the legal results they wanted. But before those two cases, Haoles had already learned in the 1920s that they could subvert the law by unlawful means in conspiracy cases involving Japanese and Filipino labor leaders in order to have them imprisoned, as discussed in chapter 1. Challenging Haole supremacy, these union leaders, including Noboru Tsutsumi and Pablo Manlapit, organized multiplantation sugar strikes in 1920 and 1924 that cost the planters to lose millions of dollars. I thus argue that the Fukunaga case was a major element in a trajectory of racial injustice against non-Haoles, which extended from before to after it occurred, as the dominant Haoles sought to maintain their political and economic control over the territory. I now turn to a discussion of how the case has remained a compelling issue for both scholars and the general public ninety years after it disrupted the racial order of "the paradise of the Pacific."

The Fukunaga Case in the Racial History of Hawai'i

The case has been the subject of scholarly analyses since its occurrence to the present, and I review most of them below in the order of their appearance. The first academic study of the Fukunaga incident was issued less than a month after he was sentenced to death by Lockwood Myrick Jr., a University of Hawai'i philosophy professor.[19] His lengthy paper concerned with Fukunaga's short life and mental status is discussed in chapter 5. Suffice it to state here that Myrick concluded that Fukunaga was legally, and not just mentally, insane when he killed Gill Jamieson because he was subject to a compelling force he could not withstand.

Proceeding to the 1960s, many of the leading historians and sociologists of Hawai'i have written about the case, although not extensively. In *Hawaii Pono*, historian Lawrence Fuchs cites the incident as an example of how Kinzaburo "Fred" Makino, publisher of the *Hawaii Hochi* newspaper, "defied prominent Honoluluans and called for a fair trial" after Fukunaga received the death sentence.[20] Born in Japan in 1877 to a British father and a Japanese mother, Makino immigrated to Hawai'i in 1899 to join his eldest brother and started the *Hochi* in 1912.[21] Fuchs also notes "deep internal division" within the Japanese American community between the supporters of Makino, who was a steadfast advocate of the constitutional rights of Japanese Americans, and the followers of Rev. Takie Okumura and Yasutaro Soga, publisher and editor of the rival *Nippu Jiji* newspaper. Makino and the *Hochi* led the campaign by the Japanese American community to obtain a new trial for Fukunaga, while Soga and the *Nippu Jiji* strongly opposed that initiative and supported his execution, consistent with their accommodationist stance to deal with Haole efforts to subordinate Japanese Americans.

Historian Gavan Daws in the other well-known history of Hawai'i, *Shoal of Time*, has more pointed observations than Fuchs does about the Fukunaga case. Like the editors of the *Honolulu Star-Bulletin* and *Honolulu Advertiser*, who denied that race had played any role in Fukunaga's conviction and death penalty, Daws asserts, "Fukunaga was tried, convicted, and hanged not as a representative of his race, but as a sad and solitary criminal."[22] Oblivious to the ongoing anti-Japanese movement (see chapter 1), Daws would have us believe that being Japanese American was irrelevant in Fukunaga's accelerated trial, conviction and death sentence, as though he was treated the same as a Haole would have been. By dismissing the significance of race, Daws affirms what I referred to above as incipient colorblindness in the Fukunaga incident. Similar to many other commentators about it, Daws follows with observations of the Massie-Kahahawai case, remarking that "once her [Massie's] story became known the polite conventions and limited agreements that made it possible for men of different races to live together more or less comfortably were rendered meaningless."[23] As one of the renowned expert historians of Hawai'i, Daws appears to lack an understanding of its racial history in the 1920s and 1930s during which Haoles and non-Haoles could hardly have been described as living "comfortably" with one another. As reviewed in chapter 1, the extended strikes by Japanese and Filipino plantation workers in 1909, 1920, 1924, and 1937 do not provide evidence that they found much comfort in their lives under Haole supremacy. The "polite conventions" that Daws notes probably referred to the deference, if not submissiveness, that non-Haoles were expected to show Haoles in their interpersonal interactions with them but ignored collective assertions of resistance and advocacy, such as the plantation strikes.

The major work on the Fukunaga case for several decades was a chapter titled "Reaping the Whirlwind" by American studies scholar Dennis Ogawa in his *Jan Ken Po: The World of Hawaii's Japanese Americans*.[24] One of Ogawa's principal contentions concerns Fukunaga's supposed motives for killing Gill Jamieson, including "to bring honor to his parents."[25] Even with his highly disturbed mind, Fukunaga did not engage in the mental gymnastics required to believe that committing a violent murder would somehow be a way for him to bestow honor on his parents. Ogawa further argues, "In March of 1928 . . . , Myles had attempted suicide but failed miserably. But what was worse, by his actions he had shamed his parents and he felt a need to achieve honor, thus redeeming himself in their eyes. He must do something to help them out of their state of abject poverty. He must earn enough money to send his parents back to Japan where they so earnestly desired to go."[26] After he was apprehended, Fukunaga did say to the police and press that one of his main reasons for kidnapping and killing Gill was because he wanted to obtain ransom money to finance his parents' return to Japan. He also gave as another primary reason for his crime his desire to die, having failed in two suicide attempts in early April (and not March). But nowhere in his three statements to the prosecutors, police, and press did Fukunaga mention as a motive to achieve honor and to redeem himself before his parents because by his suicide attempts he had brought shame to them. Furthermore, his parents were not even aware that he had tried to kill himself because the Japanese doctor they took him to see diagnosed Fukunaga as suffering from neurasthenia, a nervous condition. Ogawa also claims that Fukunaga "had committed a violent act to prove his manhood."[27] Again, Fukunaga's own reasons for his crime do not reveal such a desire to be achieved through violence, nor do his three statements indicate that he felt a general need to validate his masculinity.

Ogawa also presents an explanation of why the Japanese American community sought a full psychiatric examination of Fukunaga to determine if he was sane or not after he was sentenced to be hanged.[28] As he contends, "The logic behind the Japanese community's insistence that Myles was insane was very basic. If Myles . . . were truly sane, then the implication was that any Japanese could commit such a brutal crime. If he were insane, however, the community's . . . responsibility for the boy's criminal nature would be absolved. What was at stake wasn't only the fate of Myles Fukunaga, but the image of the Japanese American community." In truth, this argument had been presented forty-five years earlier by the *Hawaii Hochi*, which should have been acknowledged.[29]

Like Daws, sociologist Andrew W. Lind, the foremost scholar of historical race relations in Hawai'i, also discusses the Fukunaga and Massie-Kahahawai cases together.[30] These "two dramatic incidents," according to Lind, "illustrate how delicately balanced the public attitude of racial toleration actually was and how easily it could be disturbed, and as readily restored." Rather than racial tolerance being balanced between Haoles and non-Haoles, it was more the case that the former constrained the actions of the latter through restrictive laws, practices, and social norms, including the "polite conventions and limited agreements" mentioned by Daws, thus providing a semblance of racial tranquility. Furthermore, racial tolerance was hardly reestablished after the two cases because non-Haoles began to join together to pursue their common working-class interests through labor organizing in order to challenge Haole supremacy (see Conclusion). The Massie-Kahahawai case was especially a catalyst for permanent change in the racial hierarchy.

Lind continues that the Massie-Kahahawai case resulted in analyses of what distinguished Hawaii's perspectives on race and race relations, and he identifies as "one of the most incisive" that advanced by the first sociologist of the territory, Romanzo Adams.[31] In his 1934 essay on "The Unorthodox Race Doctrine of Hawaii," Adams asserts that it consisted of "mores of racial equality" and hence was "unorthodox from the standpoint of white people" in the continental United States.[32] Obviously, equality did not distinguish the relations among Hawaii's races historically and to the present. Contrary to Lind's claim, Adams does not even mention either the Fukunaga or Massie-Kahahawai cases in his article on Hawaii's unorthodox race doctrine, very likely because they both grossly contradicted his primary argument concerning racial equality. Even earlier, due to its high rate of interracial marriage, Adams had described Hawai'i as a "racial melting pot," which was one of the first scholarly representations of island society as a site of especially tolerant and harmonious race relations,[33] or what I referred to above as emergent multiculturalism.

Political scientist Roland Kotani also reviews the Fukunaga and Massie-Kahahawai incidents together in a chapter of his book published in commemoration of the one-hundredth anniversary of Japanese immigration to Hawai'i in 1985.[34] Drawing primarily from the above noted works by Ogawa and Myrick, Kotani argues that "conditions of poverty and discrimination . . . were the real culprits in the kidnapping and murder of Gill Jamieson" and that Fukunaga was "driven to insanity and murder by the miserable conditions of his life."[35] However, those same wretched, impoverished, and seemingly hopeless circumstances were faced by tens of thousands of nisei youth who, nonetheless, were not driven insane or compelled to commit murder by them. Fukunaga had his own psychological demons, which were exacerbated by the specific depressing experiences and conditions of his life, that led him to carry out his vicious crime. Being poor and discriminated against cannot provide a sufficient explanation of Fukunaga's homicidal behavior; otherwise, an epidemic of such violence would have erupted among nisei and other Japanese, who shared that same oppressive situation with him.

Of the numerous historians and social scientists who have reviewed the Fukunaga and Massie-Kahahawai cases in conjunction with each other, Kotani has contributed the longest discussion, devoting a full chapter of his book. However, he discusses the incidents separately, and only in a short concluding paragraph does he consider them together as events "which brought the Islands' 'melting pot' to a boil." Kotani concludes, "Local residents could not help but be struck by the contrast between the fate of Myles Fukunaga . . . , who was executed for his crime, and the fate of Mrs. Fortescue and Lt. Massie, members of a Haole elite who carried out lynch law with impunity and received a sentence of one hour in the governor's office."[36] While a huge difference certainly is evident in the outcome for the defendants in their respective homicide trials, it also is clear that the two principal local persons in the cases—Fukunaga and Kahahawai—as non-Haoles shared a similar fate in both being raced to death.

Historian Gary Y. Okihiro in *Cane Fires: The Anti-Japanese Movement in Hawaii, 1865–1945* makes a brief but insightful comparison between the execution of Fukunaga and the limited internment of Japanese, aliens and U.S. citizens, in the territory after the attack on Pearl Harbor.[37] He contends that internment "served mentally to imprison even those" who were not confined, "having the same chilling effect" on Japanese Americans as Fukunaga's hanging had. As I argue, the Japanese American community understood that the quick conviction and execution of Fukunaga were directed to them as a warning not to upset the racial order as he had, and therefore they were chilled, if not frozen, into nonaction in the plantation labor movement, which they had led since the turn of the century.

In *No Sword to Bury: Japanese Americans in Hawai'i during World War II*, historian Franklin Odo presents oral history recollections about the Fukunaga incident from former members of the Varsity Victory Volunteers.[38] The "Triple-V" was a voluntary labor battalion formed by Japanese American former Reserve Officer Training Corps (ROTC) students at the University of Hawai'i after the Pearl Harbor attack. One of them, Ted Tsukiyama,[39] recalled, "The whole Japanese community was in a state of tension and anxiety. . . . There was a feeling of community shame among Japanese that a Japanese person would have done something so terrible as this. There was great *haji* [shame], . . . and, of course, rather unthinkable that someone from this lowly ethnic status, would dare to pull off an act such as demand ransom and then go and kill a scion of a Big Five family."[40] Tsukiyama's memories of how he and the Japanese American community felt as news of Fukunaga's horrendous crime spread indicate their keen awareness of its racial aspects. He especially highlights how the Japanese American community experienced a collective sense of shame and guilt as a result of the Jamieson killing, despite not being personally involved in any way. The shared nature of these feelings reveals much about how Japanese Americans viewed themselves in their strained relations with other groups. If a Haole teenager had murdered a Japanese American boy, it is doubtful that Haoles would have felt "community shame" to the same extent that Japanese Americans did. It certainly was not evident when Haole men killed Japanese men or when they murdered Joe Kahahawai.

So it is that many of the foremost historians and social scientists of Hawai'i society have discussed the Fukunaga and Massie-Kahahawai cases in close relation to one another from the 1960s onward. This juxtaposition is certainly understandable since both incidents evidence blatant racial injustice, and they occurred less than four years and less than four miles from each other in Honolulu. But rather than proceeding forward in time from the Fukunaga to the Massie-Kahahawai case, I trace the former incident back to events beginning in 1920 and delineate a trajectory of racial injustice against non-Haoles. More thoroughly than others have provided previously, I compare, in this book's conclusion, the Fukunaga and Kahahawai cases and the relation between them by focusing on their closely connected racial dimensions.

Besides scholarly writings about the Fukunaga case, it lives on in people's memory and knowledge, at least in Hawai'i, through popular media sources. The local print press regularly brings up the incident every several years, such as a 2015 *Honolulu Star-Advertiser* article about a walking tour of Mo'ili'ili, a Japanese American community before World War II, which features a stop at Fukunaga's grave.[41] Guided "crime" tours, advertised online, are another way the Fukunaga case is remembered and point to how it is primarily represented in the popular media—as a "true crime" story rather than as a highly racialized and therefore compelling event in Hawai'i history. Websites, such as "Crime in the 1920s" and "The Kiawe Killer," provide basic information about Fukunaga's crime, conviction, and execution but generally ignore its racial elements. Nonetheless, those online sources along with local news articles attest that the case still resonates with meaning and significance for the general public ninety years after it occurred. This remembering and retelling of the Fukunaga case occur precisely because of its troubling racial aspects, much as the Massie-Kahahawai case is still recalled and written about.[42] Both tragic events remind Hawaii's people of their racially conflictual past and why they should not believe in the glorified and idealized portrayals of their racial history, as represented in its multicultural reinterpretation.

Looking Ahead

Raced to Death argues that the Fukunaga case was a principal component in a trajectory of racial injustice that prevailed from the 1920s to the 1930s against other non-Haoles, who had defied Haole oligarchical rule. The close relation of the case to the major racial conflicts of that time confirms its larger racial significance. After chapter 1, the others follow in roughly chronological order as the case evolved with the abduction and killing of Gill Jamieson, Fukunaga's trial and death sentence, and the unsuccessful efforts led by the *Hawaii Hochi* to obtain a new trial for him. The concluding chapter provides a comparative analysis of the case with the Kahahawai case.

Chapter 1, "The Racial Setting of Hawai'i in the 1920s," situates the Fukunaga incident in the larger racialized context of island society during the decade in which the anti-Japanese movement peaked before World War II. It begins by discussing Haole political and economic racialized power in Hawai'i, which resulted from their making and enforcing race as the dominant organizing principle of social relations. Another prominent feature of the racial setting was the anti-Japanese campaign, which sought to subordinate Japanese Americans because they were considered the most dangerous threat to Haole settler colonial control. Hence, as a Japanese American charged with murdering a Haole boy, Fukunaga was hardly viewed and treated in colorblind mode as an individual without regard to race but was subject to its omnipresent power to subjugate. The chapter also discusses previous racial injustices against Japanese and Filipino labor leaders and striking workers in the 1920s who, like Fukunaga, had upset the racial hierarchy, in their case by organizing plantation unions and strikes. It concludes that the racial setting of Hawai'i was demarcated by an uneven racial divide between Haoles and non-Haoles because, among the latter, Native Hawaiians had much greater political access, although not necessarily political power.

Chapter 2, "Kidnapping, Killing, and Racial Profiling," encompasses the first four days of the Fukunaga case, from Tuesday through Friday, starting with the abduction and homicide of Gill Jamieson. It reviews why and how Gill, as the young son of a Hawaiian Trust Co. executive, became Fukunaga's intended victim, even though he only learned of the boy's existence a few hours before killing him. Also discussed are the rapid elite Haole response to the crime, led by the Honolulu Chamber of Commerce, the immediate immense publicity given to the kidnapping by the Honolulu daily newspapers, and the massive manhunt that was quickly organized to search for Gill and his assumed abductors. Those developments probably led Fukunaga to assume that he would soon be captured, so he decided to make a last visit on Friday to the plantation town where he had distinguished himself as a student, which resulted in his arrest the next day. The chapter also describes the taking into custody and interrogation of numerous Japanese American young men, who were racially profiled as suspects in the crime. Among them was the Jamieson's former chauffeur, Harry Kaisan, who was beaten by the police in futile attempts to force a confession from him and was nearly framed for the murder.

Chapter 3 on "Capture, Confession, and Court" reviews the next four days in the case, from Saturday through Tuesday, and highlights the speed with which it proceeded in the criminal justice system after Fukunaga was caught. The major events considered include his apprehension as a result of spending a $5 bill from the ransom money, his immediate admission of guilt to the police, and the publication in the newspapers of highly incriminating statements he made starting that same night, virtually guaranteeing his conviction. The chapter analyzes the official transcript of his police interrogation, which came to be referred to as his "confession," that provided detailed information about his crime and his reasons for committing it. It also notes the responses of the Japanese American community to Gill's killing and Fukunaga's arrest, including those from the Japanese newspapers in their editorials and articles. In addition, the chapter reviews Fukunaga's prompt indictment and arraignment in court for first degree murder and appointment the next day of his two attorneys. That same day they recommended to the presiding judge that Fukunaga's trial begin the following Monday, thus moving the case quickly along but giving them very little time to prepare their defense of him.

Chapter 4, "Racial Bias and Injustice in Jury Selection and Trial," begins with a review of one of the major racial injustices in the Fukunaga case—the voir dire examination of the prospective jurors for his trial. The great majority of those who were selected for the jury stated under oath that they had formed an opinion about Fukunaga's guilt or innocence but claimed they could set it aside and provide him a fair trial. Given the publication of Fukunaga's admission to killing Gill Jamieson, it is extremely unlikely that the opinion of those jurors was that he was innocent. Nonetheless, Fukunaga's attorneys did not use their challenges to have them and other biased jurors removed because most of them were members of the privileged Haole class in Honolulu. Thus, the racial bias in selecting the jury concerned the inclusion of such predisposed Haoles by the defense attorneys rather than the exclusion of non-Haoles. Racial injustice continued with Fukunaga's trial, as is evident in the rush to have him convicted and executed as soon as possible. This haste is readily discernible in the exceptionally brief defense his attorneys provided, calling no witnesses on his behalf. In addition, on the first day of the two-day trial, they committed their worst blunder by stipulating that Fukunaga killed Gill, without offering an insanity or other defense to exonerate him. Furthermore, questions from the prosecution and testimony from some of their key witnesses demonstrate how Fukunaga was racialized as Japanese rather than being tried as an individual without consideration of his race.

"The Insanity Question," the subject of chapter 5, considers a lingering issue in the case because of the abbreviated ninety-minute mental examination Fukunaga received from three court-appointed psychiatrists instead of the ten-day evaluation required by Hawai'i law. The chapter reviews the written findings of two other independent analysts of Fukunaga's mental condition—Prof. Lockwood Myrick Jr. of the University of Hawai'i and Dr. Joseph C. Thompson, a U.S. Navy medical officer based at Pearl Harbor. Both of them maintained that Fukunaga was mentally insane when he killed Gill Jamieson and suffered particularly from dissociation of personality, although neither was permitted to interview him. In his detailed study, Myrick went further than Thompson and concluded that Fukunaga was legally insane because he was compelled by a force he could not resist—his desire for vengeance against the Hawaiian Trust Co.—which drove him to kill Gill. Besides the inability to differentiate between right and wrong, being compelled by such a force was another criterion for being considered legally insane, according to the territorial Insanity Act of 1925. Thus, yet another racial injustice exacted against Fukunaga was the failure of the prosecuting and defense attorneys, the judge at his trial, and the three psychiatrists who examined him to acknowledge this factor of compelling force.

Chapter 6 on "Aftermath of Death Sentence: Racial, Legal, and Community" covers the period after Fukunaga was given the death penalty to more than a year later after his last legal appeal had failed. These legal initiatives included a motion for a new trial filed a week after he was sentenced to be executed and subsequent appeals requesting the same to the territorial Supreme Court, the Ninth U.S. Circuit Court of Appeals in San Francisco, and the U.S. Supreme Court. The chapter also discusses the public assertions of colorblindness in the Fukunaga case by the Honolulu daily newspapers, the *Nippu Jiji*, and the presiding judge in his trial, which all sought to deny the decisive role race had played in his conviction and death sentence. In addition, it outlines the advocacy efforts by the Japanese American community organized by the *Hawaii Hochi* to obtain a new trial for Fukunaga and the opposition to that campaign led by the press, including the *Nippu Jiji*. During this period, the *Hochi* presented and elaborated on its argument that "two kinds of justice" prevailed in Hawai'i by comparing Fukunaga's death penalty with the noncapital punishment given to Haole convicted murderers. Last, the chapter reviews Fukunaga's execution, funeral service, and an outdoor public gathering convened by the *Hochi*, the latter two events attracting thousands of sympathizers and participants because Fukunaga's hanging had transformed him into a martyr among Japanese Americans.

The concluding chapter, "Fukunaga and Kahahawai," provides a more extensive racial comparison between the two cases and the close relation between them than has been advanced previously. It argues that like Fukunaga, Joe Kahahawai, as a Native Hawaiian racialized as Black, was also raced to death after being falsely accused of raping Thalia Massie. Thus, race was the decisive factor in both of their deaths—in the execution of Fukunaga and the lynching of Kahahawai. Based on their previous experience with non-Haole defendants, by the time of the Fukunaga trial, the dominant Haoles knew they could manipulate the criminal justice system to secure the objective they wanted—his hanging. So it is not surprising that less than three years later they would subvert that same system to have the ten-year sentences of the four convicted killers of Kahahawai commuted to one hour. The discussion demonstrates how the racial injustices perpetrated against Fukunaga are apparent in both earlier and later such violations against other non-Haoles, who were viewed as contesting Haole oligarchical rule. Thus, the racial significance of the Fukunaga case is evident in its illuminating the primacy of race to maintain Haole supremacy and non-Haole oppression, despite the claims of colorblind justice and multicultural harmony supposedly prevalent in Hawaiʻi. The conclusion also discusses the most recent public assertions of colorblindness and multiculturalism in the islands, which continue to be deployed to sustain the racial and ethnic status quo of inequality and domination, as they were ninety years ago.

1. The Racial Setting of Hawai'i in the 1920s

Myles Fukunaga committed his crime during the decade in which anti-Japanese racism in Hawai'i reached its apex prior to World War II as a direct response to Japanese leadership, participation in, and community support of the 1920 sugar strike. This labor militancy followed a little more than a decade after Japanese had organized the first multiplantation strike in 1909. That strike further fueled the anti-Japanese movement, which elite Haoles had initiated in the 1900s to maintain their economic, political, and cultural subordination of Japanese after it became evident that they intended to remain permanently in Hawai'i. Other non-Haole groups, including Native Hawaiians, Filipinos, Portuguese, and Chinese, were subject to Haole determination to continue their racial supremacy in the territory as an oligarchy of planters, merchants, and politicians.

This chapter situates the Fukunaga case in the larger racial context of Hawai'i in the 1920s by demonstrating how race operated to maintain Haole domination over non-Haoles. As the primary principle of social organization, race enforced the exclusion and oppression of non-Haoles in economic, political, legal, and cultural arenas, resulting in a highly unequal, racialized society. Thus, rather than being prosecuted as an individual without regard to race, Fukunaga was treated as a non-Haole who had violently disrupted the racial order by killing a Haole boy and therefore was hanged. This chapter discusses other racial injustices inflicted upon Japanese and Filipino labor leaders and workers earlier in the 1920s because they had challenged the racial hierarchy by conducting multiplantation strikes against the planters and the Big Five companies (see below), which reigned over the economy. It begins with a discussion of Haole political and economic power, which they acquired by ousting the Hawaiian queen, Liliʻuokalani, from her throne.

Haole Racial Rule

Not satisfied with their dominance over Hawaiʻi under the Bayonet Constitution, Haoles fully established their rule by overthrowing the Hawaiian monarchy in 1893 with the military support of the U.S. minister in Honolulu. The overthrow was led by Americans, many of whom were also citizens of the Hawaiian nation, who wanted political control of the islands to ensure the financial security of their economic investments, including the plantations and mercantile businesses. When President Grover Cleveland refused to accept Hawaiʻi as a territory because he considered the overthrow an "act of war," elite Haoles established the Republic of Hawaiʻi for four years until 1898. The islands were annexed that year by the United States through a joint resolution of Congress instead of a treaty that would have required sixty votes in the Senate, which may not have been forthcoming.[1] Fuchs contends that subsequent Haole domination of Hawaiʻi was maintained through a "web of oligarchy" to the extent that "no community of comparable size on the mainland was controlled so completely by so few individuals for so long. Rarely were political, economic, and social controls simultaneously enforced as in Hawaii. . . . For forty years [1900–1941], Hawaii's oligarchy skillfully and meticulously spun its web of control over the Islands' politics, labor, land, and economic institutions, without fundamental change."[2] But Haoles first had to deal with the major problem of being vastly outnumbered by non-Haoles.

Following annexation, under U.S. law Native Hawaiians became the largest group of American citizens, a majority of voters until 1924, and a plurality until 1938.[3] In the first elections in 1900 they reasserted their political power, albeit in a U.S. settler colony, by capturing nearly three-fourths of the seats in the new territorial legislature, with all of the Native Hawaiians belonging to the Home Rule Party.[4] Openly anti-Haole, this party sought to restore the Hawaiian queen back to power and was represented and supported predominantly by Native Hawaiians. They also elected one of their own, Robert W. Wilcox, as Hawaii's first nonvoting delegate to Congress. He had led two rebellions against Haole-dominated governments, including in 1895 against the Republic of Hawaiʻi, and so was unacceptable to Haoles. After only one term, Wilcox lost his reelection bid in 1902 to Prince Jonah Kūhiō Kalanianaʻole, who was supported by Haole Republicans, even though as a twenty-four-year-old, he had participated in the 1895 "Wilcox Rebellion" and so was imprisoned for almost nine months.

Haoles constituted just one-sixth of the new territorial legislators, most of them Republican, although that was three times greater than their 5.4 percent of the population.[5] They quickly realized that U.S. colonial rule over Hawai'i, which they had desired, had huge political disadvantages for them, particularly America's enshrined principle of one man, one vote. They therefore sought to establish a political alliance with Native Hawaiians by offering them patronage jobs in the territorial and county governments in exchange for their votes for Haole Republican candidates and for Native Hawaiians to seek office as Republicans rather than as Home Rulers.[6] Haoles also promised they would support Prince Kuhiō for election as Hawaii's delegate to Congress. Of *ali'i,* or noble, ancestry, Kūhiō attended Punahou School and was later educated in California and England. He served as congressional delegate from 1903 until his death in 1922, during which he introduced the bill that created the Hawaiian homelands.[7] The political compact between Haoles and Native Hawaiians was remarkably successful for the former and by 1905 resulted in their more than doubling their representation in the legislature to almost 40 percent and exceeding that figure during most of the two decades before World War II.[8] As historian Tom Coffman remarks, "With the American-Hawaiian alliance in place, a long slumber descended, during which the white elite extended its control of the territorial political institutions as well as the territorial economy."[9]

While Native Hawaiians made up a majority of legislators until the mid-1930s, those belonging to the Home Rule Party plummeted to a lone representative by 1905 and to none ten years later because most of them joined the dominant Republicans.[10] Thus, the political division between Haoles and at least Native Hawaiians during the 1920s and 1930s was not as oppressive as was the racial hierarchy on the plantations and in the wider economy since it did allow for their substantial participation in the territorial legislature. But by joining the Republican Party with Haoles, the political power that Native Hawaiians otherwise could have wielded through their majority representation was dissipated. As Coffman observes, by allying themselves with Haole Republicans, "Hawaiians secured additional government patronage jobs but considerably less than controlling political power, let alone economic power."[11] Nonetheless, the alliance with Haoles did have some political benefits for them; in 1927 Native Hawaiians held 46 percent of the appointed executive positions and a majority of the elective offices and judgeships.[12]

As for patronage jobs, in 1927 Native Hawaiians occupied 55 percent of clerical and other government positions, and in 1930 more of them were judges, lawyers, and teachers than those from any other racial group, including Haoles.[13] However, they generally experienced little occupational mobility from unskilled and semiskilled work during the two decades before the war. In 1930, 40 percent of Native Hawaiian males worked as laborers, while another 22 percent of "Part Hawaiians" were similarly employed, and only 4.1 percent of the former and 6.7 percent of the latter were professionals.[14] Haoles continued to dominate the latter category, as is evident from the 17 percent of their men who were professionally employed, while only 4.4 percent were laborers, which was the lowest percentage by far of all the racial groups.[15]

In terms of political party, the Haole-led Republicans controlled both houses of the territorial legislature from 1903 until the "Democratic Revolution" of 1954, when the Democrats gained ascendancy. During the 1920s and 1930s, Republicans greatly outnumbered Democrats among territorial legislators with the Democrats holding on average only about six of the forty-five seats each legislative session.[16] This average includes the fourteen Democrats elected in 1932, representing a tremendous gain from the three elected two years earlier. They may very well have benefited from a non-Haole backlash vote against the Republicans and Governor Lawrence M. Judd, who earlier in the year had commuted the sentences of the four convicted killers of Joe Kahahawai (see Conclusion). But this huge increase in Democrats was short-lived, particularly in the House of Representatives, where the party soon returned to its more typical representation of two or three members after the 1938 election. Another base of Haole political power in the 1920s until statehood in 1959 was the office of the territorial governor, who was appointed by the U.S. president. As a general practice, Republican presidents appointed Republicans from Hawai'i as governor, and the same rule prevailed among Democrats.

With regard to the political status of other groups, they were severely disadvantaged by their extremely limited number of American citizens of voting age until the 1930s. Another major restriction was the racist U.S. citizenship laws that prohibited Asians from becoming naturalized citizens until during or after World War II. In 1930 the proportion of registered voters from different racial groups in Hawai'i was, in descending order: Native Hawaiians (38.1 percent), Haoles (23.3 percent), Portuguese Americans (15.8 percent), Japanese Americans (13.4 percent), and Chinese Americans (8.4 percent).[17] Not having arrived in large numbers until the 1910s, Filipino Americans constituted less than 1 percent of registered voters in 1930, and not until 1954 would one of them be elected to the territorial legislature. The first Chinese Americans (two) to serve in the legislature were elected in 1928, and they had increased to only four by the outbreak of World War II. As for Japanese Americans, the second-generation nisei did not become of age in significant numbers until the 1920s. Thus, not until 1930 were Japanese Americans (four) elected to the legislature; by the time of the war, seven of them were legislators, all Republicans.

Although Portuguese Americans were the third-largest group of voters, the social construction of Haole identity restricted acceptance of them, despite their being of European ancestry. Before World War II, Portuguese Americans occupied an intermediate status on the plantations and in the wider society above that of non-Haoles but below that of Haoles. While Haoles virtually monopolized top management and professional positions on the plantations, Portuguese Americans had greater access to supervisory and skilled jobs, such as *luna* (field overseer) and carpenter, than did Japanese and Filipinos. Nonetheless, in 1930, 30 percent of Portuguese working males were still classified as laborers, while only 2.6 percent were professionals, more than fifty years after they began immigrating to Hawai'i.[18] Thus, while they were considered White for purposes of naturalization as U.S. citizens, Portuguese were not fully accorded Haole status and identity, unlike other Europeans in Hawai'i. The presumed difference between Portuguese Americans and Haoles as distinct "races" was given official recognition in territorial government census categories that distinguished between "Portuguese" and "Other Caucasians."[19] In short, Portuguese Americans were viewed not just as racially different but as racially inferior to Haoles, but so was everyone else.

As for Haole domination of the economy, it was effected through the Big Five companies that were established beginning in the mid-nineteenth century as Honolulu stores, except for Alexander & Baldwin. The other companies were American Factors, Castle & Cooke, C. Brewer & Co., and Theo H. Davies & Co., and they all acted as agents for the plantations by purchasing their raw sugar for sale to refineries on the West Coast.[20] By the 1920s the Big Five managed nearly 90 percent of the sugar shipped from Hawai'i, which resulted from their earlier formation of the Hawaiian Sugar Planters' Association to foster cooperation among them.[21] Big Five reign over the economy extended well beyond the sugar industry and included banking, transportation, public utilities, tourism, insurance, manufacturing, and wholesale and retail trade.[22] To ensure Haole control, the companies were connected by interlocking directorates and by marriage between members of their principal families. Needless to say, the Big Five were staunch supporters of the Republican Party and advocates of Haole interests in the territory.

Due to Haole economic and political oligarchical power, a close relation obtained between race and class during the pre-World War II period; nonetheless, race prevailed over class as the foremost principle of social organization in Hawai'i. Its ascendancy is most evident in labor organizing on the plantations in which separate unions and strikes by Japanese and Filipino workers, as in 1909, 1920, 1924, and 1937, with Portuguese joining neither group, was the general rule, despite their common working-class status. Besides the divide-and-control policy of the planters, the racism among Japanese, Filipino, and Portuguese laborers also kept them from collaborating with each other and from recognizing their shared class interests as workers. Nevertheless, class in Hawai'i and elsewhere should not be regarded as somehow more fundamental than race since the latter, rather than being an "epiphenomenon of class," "can no more be reduced to an economic matter than it can to a cultural or national one," as Omi and Winant assert.[23] Accordingly, Jung observes of race, class, and nation in prewar Hawai'i that "race was the fulcrum, as it hinged the other two"[24] and hence was more significant.

Thus, during the prewar period the conflict between the Haole planters and non-Haole workers was primarily attributable to race rather than class because interracial class consciousness was muted. Nonetheless, in its intersection with race, class reinforced the inequality and difference generated and maintained by race. As an organizing principle of social relations in Hawai'i, class became more salient starting in the late 1930s with the unionization of dock workers by the International Longshoremen's and Warehousemen's Union, which led to its organizing of sugar and pineapple workers and the first multiracial plantation strike in 1946. Jung argues that alteration by Hawaii's "working-class interracialism" of "the conceptual relationship between class and race was not that race subsided in significance but that it no longer 'cut at right angles to class.'"[25] After the war, then, class gained in consequence, while race and the prevailing racial hierarchy declined in importance; however, they were not replaced by class but by ethnicity as the leading principle of social organization by the early 1970s.[26] But decades before then, Haoles had to deal with the Japanese racial menace.

The Anti-Japanese Movement

Under the Haole oligarchy, a dominant feature of the racial setting of Hawai'i in the 1920s was the ongoing anti-Japanese campaign.[27] This racial project was the organized effort by the territorial government, the planters and Big Five companies, and the military, all primarily Haole institutions, to subjugate Japanese Americans because they were viewed as the greatest threat to continued Haole supremacy.[28] Racism was certainly intrinsic to the anti-Japanese movement, but Haole racism against Japanese Americans differed from that directed toward all other racial minorities in Hawai'i. It viewed and represented them as sufficiently capable, rather than inherently inferior, in some activities, such as labor organizing, to constitute a serious challenge to their rule. For Haoles, anti-Japanese racism was based on their fear that Japanese Americans were not innately inferior, hence the threat they posed to them.[29]

Haole racism against Japanese Americans was succinctly captured in *Temperament and Race* by University of Hawai'i clinical psychology professor Stanley Porteus and Marjorie Babcock.[30] Their book purported to be a study of the character and psychological features of six racial groups in Hawai'i, including Japanese Americans, Native Hawaiians, and Filipino Americans, but notably not Haoles. A major portion of the data for their research came from a survey of twenty-five elite Haoles, sixteen of whom were plantation managers, while the others were plantation doctors, head social workers, and teachers. They provided their ratings of the six racial groups on various traits, such as "planning capacity," "resolution," and "self determination." Reflecting their view of Japanese Americans as hardly inferior, the Haole raters gave them the highest composite score of 85.5 on a 100-point scale, the top score presumably what Haoles would have received if they had been rated.[31] Summarizing the above and other findings on Japanese Americans, Porteus and Babcock described them as "intensely race-conscious, ready to combine for any purposes of group advancement, aggressive . . . when self-interest is in question."[32] Rather than being based on "objective" psychological data, these alleged characteristics of Japanese Americans can be easily traced to their leadership and participation in the recent 1920 strike. Thus Porteus and Babcock, invoking a biological notion of race, concluded that their results "all point to the fact of superior endowment in the Japanese over all the other races studied."[33] Racializing Japanese Americans as the principal threat to Haole dominance, the anti-Japanese movement sought to subordinate them, especially in political, economic, and cultural arenas.

Haoles considered Japanese Americans as politically threatening because they were widely suspected of being loyal to Japan and, conversely, disloyal to the United States. Instead of inferiority, Jung argues that the crux of "anti-Japanese racism concerned national loyalty" insofar as "Japanese were constructed as an inscrutable people beholden racially, and therefore inherently, to their nation of origin."[34] Hence, rather than a labor conflict, the 1920 strike was represented by the territorial government, the planters, and the press as a conspiracy between Japanese plantation workers and the empire of Japan to seize control of Hawai'i.[35] The dual citizenship of most Japanese Americans, which they acquired when their parents registered their birth with the Japanese Consulate in Honolulu, was severely criticized as demonstrating their political allegiance to Japan. Japanese also were seen as a political threat since their Hawai'i-born children would eventually become the largest group of voters, and Haoles feared they would take over the territorial government from them. At 43 percent of the population in 1920, the mere size of the Japanese American community was viewed with alarm by Haoles because they greatly outnumbered them and continued to increase with immigration and the high birth rate of Japanese women, such as Fukunaga's mother with her seven children.

As for being an economic threat, Haoles perceived Japanese Americans as such because they organized large and costly plantation strikes and thereby endangered the financial viability of the dominant sugar industry and the Big Five companies. Japanese Americans were also chastised for leaving the plantations for urban areas, as Fukunaga's family did in 1925, to seek skilled and semiskilled work and to start family retail businesses. In response, the territorial legislature passed a law in 1925 that banned the hiring of aliens and those ineligible for citizenship through naturalization, which included Japanese, in public works projects.[36] Thus in 1930, a plurality (36 percent) of employed Japanese American men were still laborers, with most of them on the plantations, while only 3.4 percent were professionals.[37]

To restrict labor organizing and strikes by Japanese Americans, after the 1920 strike the territorial legislature enacted several antilabor laws in the ensuing decade, which were intended to facilitate the prosecution of striking workers and their leaders and supporters. The anarchistic publications statute of 1921 limited what newspapers could print by broadly prohibiting the publication of materials "intended to create or have the effect of creating distrust or dissension between peoples of different races or between citizens and aliens."[38] This law was clearly directed against the Japanese newspapers that had supported the 1920 strike, such as the *Hawaii Hochi*, despite the Honolulu dailies regularly engaging in racist attacks against Japanese, Filipinos, and other racial minorities in Hawai'i. Two years later, another antilabor statute made it illegal to picket business establishments. The trespassing law of 1925 was repeatedly used to ban union organizers from entering the plantations. Fuchs emphasizes the retaliatory nature of these new laws: "After the [1920] strike, restrictive bills were sped through the legislature to punish the Japanese for their affronts"[39] in challenging Haole rule.

With regard to being culturally threatening, Japanese, including the Hawai'i-born second generation, were strongly criticized for continuing to follow many of their cultural traditions, beliefs, and values, especially their language and religion.[40] As a major cultural institution, the Japanese language schools were especially attacked for hindering the assimilation of Japanese American youth into American culture. They also were chastised for fostering nisei allegiance to Japan because their curriculum included Japanese culture, history, folklore, and moral values (*shushin*) besides language.[41] In 1920, 98 percent of Japanese American children, who totaled 17,541 students in 143 schools, including Fukunaga and his siblings, attended a language school, generally after the public school day ended.[42] With the birth of more children, the number of students and language schools expanded to their apex of 43,606 students in 190 schools in 1933.

In the first half of the 1920s the territorial legislature and the Department of Public Instruction established stricter controls over the Japanese language schools, which were intended to limit their operations, if not to close them. These new rules included revision of their textbooks, additional qualifications in English for their teachers, and elimination of kindergarten and the first and second grades, which greatly reduced the number of students and thus school revenues.[43] The Japanese American community was intensely divided in its response to these government restrictions. On one side was the resistance and advocacy position advanced by Fred Makino and his *Hawaii Hochi* newspaper, which was his platform for advocating for the rights of Japanese in Hawai'i, including Fukunaga. On the other side was the accommodationist and conciliatory approach taken by Yasutaro Soga, publisher of the rival *Nippu Jiji* newspaper, together with Rev. Takie Okumura, a conservative Christian minister.

To counter the territorial government initiatives against the Japanese-language schools, in 1922 Makino hired an attorney to submit a lawsuit in U.S. District Court that challenged their constitutionality.[44] The suit was filed on behalf of sixteen schools that organized themselves into the Society for Carrying-on the Test Case, which was eventually joined by eighty-eight of the 146 language schools.[45] On their part, Soga and Okumura urged parents and the other schools not to join the lawsuit, but in March 1926 the Ninth U.S. Circuit Court of Appeals ruled that the territory's foreign-language-school laws were unconstitutional. Unwilling to concede anything to the Japanese American community, the territorial government appealed the decision to the U.S. Supreme Court, which affirmed the lower-court ruling the following year.

The anti-Japanese movement was actively supported by the two leading daily newspapers in Hawai'i, the *Honolulu Advertiser* and the *Honolulu Star-Bulletin*, as is evident from their racial and political positions. The *Advertiser* was owned since 1899 by Lorrin A. Thurston, whose missionary grandparents arrived in Hawai'i in 1820. Despite being born in the kingdom, he led the overthrow of the Hawaiian monarchy. Thurston eventually became known for his "dyed-in-the-wool Republicanism" and once declared that "on principle the *Advertiser* is Republican,"[46] as if that were a mystery. His paper consistently advocated the political and economic interests of the dominant Haoles, including the territorial government, the sugar and pineapple plantations, and the fledgling tourist industry. In contrast, it was strongly opposed to labor organizing by Japanese and Filipino plantation workers in the 1920s and later decades and, according to former editor (1958–1986) George Chaplin, "shared the racist view of many planters that tough control" was the best means to deal with workers.[47]

As for the *Honolulu Star-Bulletin*, Wallace R. Farrington was its publisher while also serving as the Republican-appointed territorial governor between 1921 and 1929. As historian Helen Geracimos Chapin observes, "Farrington and the *Star-Bulletin* in these years perfectly illustrate the intimate relationship within the [Haole] establishment of business, newspapers, and government."[48] Like the *Advertiser*, the *Star-Bulletin* in its editorials and news coverage was pro-Haole, pro-Republican, pro-planter, and anti-Japanese, although the papers did not necessarily share the same position on all issues. In 1924, each newspaper had a circulation of about fifteen thousand, while the *Hawaii Hochi* and *Nippu Jiji* each had ten thousand, reflecting the huge Japanese American population.[49] But by that year, the anti-Japanese movement had obliterated Japanese labor unions by having their leaders sent to prison.

Racial Injustice against Japanese

Anti-Japanese racial injustice was especially directed against labor leaders for organizing plantation strikes and unions. In 1909, led by the Higher Wage Association, Japanese conducted the first multiplantation strike, which was joined by seven thousand laborers on six plantations on Oʻahu for four months.[50] The planters responded to this unprecedented threat to the sugar industry by having the four main union leaders—Fred Makino, Yasutaro Soga, Motoyuki Negoro, and Yokichi Tasaka—and others arrested on charges of "conspiracy and as dangerous persons" a month after the strike began. As labor historian Edward D. Beechert observes, a conspiracy statute, enacted in 1869, was frequently used during the 1909, 1920, and later strikes against labor organizers.[51] For the police and planters, he asserts, "labor actions were termed 'conspiracies.' Labor leaders did not meet; they 'conspired.'" Conspiracy to commit a particular crime carried a maximum penalty of ten years in prison, which could be considerably longer than for the crime in question.[52] All four leaders were convicted of conspiracy to obstruct the operations of the plantations and sentenced to ten months in prison and a

$300 fine each, although they were pardoned after serving four months in 1910. However, ten years later, government officials, the planters, and courts would be far less forgiving of Japanese labor leaders.

Japanese American plantation workers struck again in 1920 for five months, spurred on by the rising cost of consumer goods due to World War I and stagnant wages since the 1909 strike. Many of the repressive actions taken by the dominant Haoles against Japanese Americans during the 1920s can be understood as retaliation against them for leading and supporting the strike. As Fuchs comments, "When the strike failed, . . . the leaders of Hawaii sought to crush the spirit of the Japanese."[53] He continues, "Life on the plantations for the more rebellious of the Japanese workers became unbearable. Strike leaders were blacklisted; participants in the strike were kept from advancing to better plantation jobs; the Japanese generally were scorned by the others; and in Honolulu a concerted effort was made to destroy the Japanese-language press and schools and remnants of the Japanese labor movement."[54] All of the above were severe manifestations of the anti-Japanese movement, which escalated as a result of the strike.

The 1920 strike is unique in pre–World War II plantation labor history in its participation by Japanese and Filipino workers in contrast to the others that were all limited to a single group, such as Japanese in 1909 and Filipinos in 1924 and 1937. However, rather than "the first important interethnic working class struggle in Hawaii" as it has been mythologized,[55] the 1920 strike consisted of two unions on strike at the same time but not necessarily cooperating and coordinating their actions with one another.[56] The Japanese laborers were led by the Japanese Federation of Labor (JFL) and its secretary, Noboru Tsutsumi, while the Filipinos were represented by the Filipino Labor Union and its president, Pablo Manlapit. This separate organization of workers into two unions with their own set of leaders was a major factor in the relative lack of collaboration between them and to the eventual defeat of the strike. Nonetheless, the eighty-three hundred striking Japanese and Filipino laborers on six plantations on O'ahu, who together composed 77 percent of the work force, made the planters suffer $12 million in losses.[57]

That enormous financial setback and steadfast Japanese American challenge to the racial status quo demonstrated in the strike perhaps were the reasons why the dominant Haoles sought to eliminate the strike leaders by having them arrested and imprisoned, as they had in 1909. More than a year after the Hawaiian Sugar Planters' Association (HSPA) had declared the 1920 strike was over, in August 1921 twenty-one mostly former officials of the JFL, including the twenty-eight-year-old Tsutsumi, were indicted for criminal conspiracy.[58] A graduate of Kyoto Imperial University, Tsutsumi had arrived in Hawai'i in 1918 to become the principal of a Japanese language school. By fall 1919, he had established the Japanese Federation of Labor branch on Hawai'i island and later was appointed by the JFL directors representing its island branches to the federation secretariat.

Tsutsumi and the other JFL officials were charged with conspiracy to dynamite the plantation house of a Japanese interpreter, Juzaburo Sakamaki, in June 1920 at Ola'a Plantation on Hawai'i island. Viewed as a local incident, the dynamiting was given scant coverage in the next day's Honolulu and Japanese language newspapers and was not reported on by them again. Neither the Hilo police nor plantation officials mentioned that it was connected to the ongoing strike, which was limited to O'ahu plantations. Nonetheless, in February 1922 fifteen former JFL leaders were put on trial; three others had returned to Japan and were tried in absentia. The evidence against them was provided by two Japanese former plantation workers, who were among the twenty-one persons initially indicted for the crime.

At the trial, the two former laborers, Junji Matsumoto and I. Saito, offered highly dubious testimony against the defendants. Through "shameful plea bargaining," they were granted immunity by the city and county of Honolulu prosecuting attorney, William H. Heen, in exchange for their testimony.[59] Elected to his position in 1918 at age thirty-six, Heen would emerge six years after the trial as an important figure in the Fukunaga case but as an attorney in private practice. Matsumoto and Saito gave very similar accounts about their direct participation in the dynamiting of Sakamaki's house. They testified that they were separately told by JFL officers, including Tsutsumi, on May 22, 1920, at the Honolulu JFL office to travel that afternoon to Hilo, where they would be given further instructions by Hawai'i island JFL officials. They both also said the order to dynamite Sakamaki's home and to kill him was given to them by one of those Big Island leaders because Sakamaki was obstructing the strike, although Ola'a workers were not on strike. Matsumoto and Saito both testified they were told they would each receive $5,000 if they succeeded in killing Sakamaki, which they failed to do.

When cross-examined, both Matsumoto and Saito revealed that they were employed by Frank E. Thompson, the attorney for the HSPA, together with his law partner, who was serving as a special assistant prosecutor in the trial at HSPA expense.[60] That the planters' attorney had given jobs to the two key prosecution witnesses and his law firm partner was assisting the prosecution raise serious questions about the veracity of their testimony. Thus, Tsutsumi directly contradicted their claim that he was among the JFL leaders who told them on May 22 to go to Hilo. He testified that he and another JFL official, Yasuyuki Mizutari, returned that morning from Maui and spent the day at a restaurant in Waiau, which was confirmed by Mizutari and the restaurant manager in their testimony. Tsutsumi also provided a possible motive for why Matsumoto and Saito sought to frame him and the other JFL leaders for the bombing. Matsumoto had earlier testified about a fight he had with JFL officials, including several of the defendants, at a hotel in Honolulu in November 1920. He stated that he and Saito went there to ask the JFL officers about the $5,000 they had each been promised for the dynamiting. According to Matsumoto, while he was talking to Tsutsumi, someone said "kill him," and he struck Tsutsumi. He was then hit on the head with a bottle and later that evening filed an assault complaint with the police, during which he and Saito confessed to the bombing.

However, Tsutsumi testified that he met Matsumoto and Saito for the first time that evening at the hotel, but the former, "a big man," was intoxicated and speaking loudly, so he returned to his room. He said Matsumoto came in and hit him, so he kicked back and Matsumoto fell down, striking his head. Historian Masayo Umezawa Duus contends that this humiliation by a "pale intellectual" may have led Matsumoto to seek revenge against Tsutsumi and the other JFL officials by claiming they had directed him to kill Sakamaki.[61]

In his closing argument at the trial, defense attorney Francis M. Brooks virtually accused the prosecutor's office of colluding with the HSPA to destroy the JFL. He asserted that the prosecutor knew for months who dynamited Sakamaki's house but "dismissed the case against Matsumoto and Saito in order that private interests [HSPA] might break up the Japanese Federation of Labor."[62] Nonetheless, in March 1922 the jury returned guilty verdicts for all of the defendants, who were sentenced from four to ten years at hard labor at Oahu Prison. They were made victims of racial injustice because they had dared to challenge Haole settler colonialism in the territory. Duus observes, "No one . . . protested that the trial was intended to teach a lesson to those who opposed the HSPA."[63] This lesson was well learned because Japanese Americans stayed out of plantation labor organizing for longer than two decades afterward. When they completed their prison sentences, none of the JFL leaders resumed labor-union activity, which was the primary reason they were arrested and imprisoned. Their union had vanished before the 1924 Filipino strike, and Japanese were strike breakers against Filipinos.

Racial Injustice against Filipinos

As with Japanese Americans, racial injustice against Filipino Americans targeted their labor organizers, who similarly were imprisoned and later exiled. The leader of the Filipino Labor Union (FLU) during the 1920 strike was Pablo Manlapit, who had arrived in Hawai'i as a nineteen-year-old labor recruit in 1910.[64] After moving to Honolulu, he found employment as an interpreter and janitor for a downtown law firm. Probably with the support of his employer, he studied law during his spare time and was able to pass the bar exam in 1919, becoming, in his words, "the first Filipino lawyer to practice law in Hawai'i."[65] Earlier that year, Manlapit was elected president of the FLU at a mass meeting of a thousand Filipinos at A'ala Park in downtown Honolulu.[66] Even before the 1920 strike, the *Honolulu Advertiser* labeled Manlapit "the most dangerous person in Hawaii because he fomented class hatred and advocated sympathy strikes,"[67] indicative of how the press and planters would treat him.

In 1924 the Filipino Labor Union, renamed the High Wages Movement and still led by Manlapit, organized the first territory-wide strike that lasted six months, April through September. An estimated eighty-three hundred Filipinos joined the strike at different times as it proceeded in a "piecemeal" manner.[68] While Manlapit was able to avoid imprisonment during the 1920 strike, his turn for racial injustice came during the 1924 strike. Shortly after it began, on April 22, he was charged with libel against plantation manager E. W. Greene and Dr. R. J. Mermod of Oahu Sugar Company in a case involving the death of a three-month-old Filipino baby.[69] An article, "Dying Baby Forced Out from Waipahu Hospital," had appeared on April 12 in *Ang Bantay* (The Sentinel), the High Wages Movement newspaper. The story asserted that the baby's father, twenty-four-year-old Pantaleon Inayuda, was told by Mermod that he had to take his son from the plantation hospital since, as a striking worker, he was no longer a plantation employee. At the trial, Mermod denied the accusation and said he had instructed Inayuda to leave his sick baby at the hospital. The judge believed him rather than Inayuda and found Manlapit guilty of libel and fined him $100. Manlapit's legal problems had just started.

In June, Inayuda went to the Honolulu sheriff and admitted that he had lied at the libel trial when he testified that the doctor had ordered him to take his baby from the hospital.[70] He was accompanied by Juan Oxiles, a Filipino police detective, who worked closely with the HSPA to disrupt the strike. On the basis of Inayuda's assertions, later that month a grand jury indicted Manlapit and another High Wages Movement leader, Cecilio Basan, for conspiracy to commit subornation of perjury. They were charged with coaching Inayuda to testify that Mermod had ordered him to remove his baby at a meeting at Manlapit's union office.

Unfortunately for Manlapit and Basan, their trial began less than a week after the "Hanapēpē Massacre" on Kaua'i. On September 9, sixteen Filipino striking workers and four policemen were shot and killed in a five-minute burst of gunfire between strikers and the police.[71] The strikers maintained that the police opened fire first, only one striker fired back, and eleven of them were shot in the back because, as they ran away, the police continued shooting.[72] The police claimed that they fired on the strikers in self-defense, which became the "dominant discourse" about the massacre.[73] The *Star-Bulletin* hence referred to the deaths of the four police officers as "strike murders" and condemned "the criminal labor agitators."[74]

Thus, 130 Filipino strikers were arrested, including three Kaua'i strike leaders who were not even present when the violence occurred.[75] Racial injustice in the Hanapēpē Massacre is further evident in that no police officers were charged with any crimes in the killing of the sixteen Filipinos. Not provided with any attorneys or interpreters by the court, fifty-seven of the arrested strikers pled guilty to assault and battery, even though the primary evidence against most of them was that they had been present at the Hanapēpē strike camp.[76] A grand jury indicted seventy-six other Filipinos on rioting charges; the court appointed a single attorney for their defense. As for the prosecution, Governor Farrington had the territorial attorney general appoint two special deputy prosecutors, who were hired and paid for by the HSPA, as was previously the case in the JFL conspiracy trial. Hence in November 1924, fifty-eight of the accused were found guilty of rioting and received sentences of four years in prison, two strike leaders were given four years and eleven months in prison, while sixteen defendants were acquitted.[77] Many of those convicted, particularly the strike leaders, were later deported to the Philippines, as would eventually happen to Manlapit and Basan.

But before then, at their own conspiracy to suborn perjury trial in September 1924, Manlapit and Basan were both found guilty after the jury deliberated for only half an hour. Their attorney charged that his clients had been "railroaded into the penitentiary" based on perjured testimony in order to break the strike[78] and that they had been framed by detective Juan Oxiles.[79] Manlapit and Basan were both given sentences of two to ten years at hard labor at Oahu Prison. Very suspiciously, less than a month after the trial, Inayuda and other prosecution witnesses were returned to the Philippines by the HSPA.[80] One of those witnesses was Enrique Montecillo, who was Manlapit's "all-round helper" from April to June 1924 while also a police informer, and who Reinecke asserts gave "obviously perjured" testimony at the trial.[81]

Based on affidavits from some of the prosecution witnesses that they had lied at the trial, Manlapit's attorney filed an appeal with the Hawai'i Supreme Court. Basan chose not to appeal and, after serving a short prison sentence, was granted parole on the condition that he leave Hawai'i for the Philippines.[82] As for Manlapit, on May 25, 1925, the Supreme Court denied his appeal, ruling that it had been filed one day late, and he was sent to Oahu Prison that same day. Manlapit later wrote to the governor requesting that Farrington pardon him because he had an affidavit proving that he was the victim of a "frame up." The affidavit was from none other than Pantaleon Inayuda, his primary accuser at his trial, who signed it in July 1925.[83] He maintained that, in exchange for testifying against Manlapit, the HSPA paid him and five other witnesses, including police spy Enrique Montecillo, $10 each when the HSPA returned them to the Philippines and an additional $100 each upon their arrival. Reinecke therefore concludes that the 1924 strike "is remarkable for the range and severity of the legal, and sometimes extralegal, action taken against the strikers by the executive authorities and courts of Hawaii. As in the 1909 and 1920 strikes, prosecutors and police acted baldly and openly as agents of the planters, and the courts in general were hostile to the strikers," as well as the strike leaders.[84]

With Manlapit in prison and Basan exiled in the Philippines, by 1926 a labor movement among Filipinos (and Japanese) was nonexistent, and between mid-1925 and mid-1933 they did not conduct even a one-day labor disturbance on any plantation.[85] In July 1927, after serving seven months beyond his two-year minimum term, Manlapit was paroled, but on the condition that he leave Hawai'i, which he did—for California—leaving behind his wife and four children.

After completing his nearly five years on parole in California, Manlapit returned to Hawai'i in 1932 and was welcomed back like a returning hero by Filipinos.[86] He soon embarked on a speaking tour of plantations on the major islands arranged by the new Filipino Labor Union, whose president was Epifanio Taok. By 1934 Manlapit had become president of the Hawaii Labor Association, which was a multiracial but primarily Filipino union that sought to unite with Taok's union.[87] However, Taok was arrested in March 1934 and charged with gross cheat for collecting $5 membership dues to join his union from four Filipinos and promising that he could get them free return passage to the Philippines.[88] This effort to eliminate another Filipino labor leader was initially successful because Taok was found guilty and sentenced to nine months in the city and county jail. It was Manlapit's turn once again to suffer the wrath of the dominant Haoles. In July 1934, he was charged in the U.S. District Court in Honolulu with excessively charging a Filipino World War I veteran for assistance in obtaining a federal loan.[89] He was convicted and sentenced to one year in prison, but the judge commuted the sentence to five years on probation in the Philippines if he left immediately, which he did, a week later.[90] The authorities had succeeded once again in banishing Manlapit from organizing plantation laborers, this time permanently back to his homeland, as they had with Tsutsumi.[91] As Beechert emphasizes, "The technique of isolating the leadership with criminal charges had been used in each of the past major labor disputes" in 1909, 1920, and 1924 as a strategic means by the planters to break strikes and to break up unions.[92]

Racial injustice against Filipinos is also evident in their gross overrepresentation among those executed for murder in Hawai'i, whereas only one Haole was.[93] As I have written elsewhere, Filipinos made up 57 percent (24 of 42) of those hanged between 1900 and 1944, when the last civilian execution occurred, but a whopping 78 percent from 1911 when the first Filipino was executed.[94] During this period, Filipinos represented, at most, 17 percent of Hawaii's population (1930).[95] The other persons hanged for murder were seven Japanese, six Koreans, three Puerto Ricans, and one Native Hawaiian.[96] The extremely high proportion of Filipinos (all men) among those suffering the death penalty was not necessarily because they killed more often than persons from other groups but resulted from their racialized demonization as criminally inclined, prone to violence, and highly emotional.[97] This racialization may have contributed to the willingness of prosecutors to charge Filipinos with first-degree murder, which carried the death penalty, instead of second-degree murder or manslaughter, of juries to convict Filipinos of first-degree murder rather than lesser offenses, and of judges to sentence them to be hanged instead of life in prison.[98]

While Filipinos did not constitute a significant threat to kill Haoles (only one was murdered by a Filipino), they did contest Haole supremacy through their leadership and engagement in two major strikes in quick succession in the 1920s, which cost the planters millions of dollars in losses. Their very high percentage of those hanged demonstrated to Filipinos that they could expect no mercy or even justice from the police, prosecutors, and courts for the far lesser crimes than murder with which most of them were charged. Beyond racial injustice, anti-Filipino racism and discrimination were more than sufficient to keep Filipinos as the "bottom dog" in the racial hierarchy.[99] But the racism against Filipinos differed substantially from that directed toward Japanese in viewing and representing them as innately inferior, especially in terms of intelligence, planning capacity, and self-control.[100] In *Temperament and Race,* Porteus and Babcock described Filipinos, despite being adults, as "a fine example of a race in an adolescent stage of development," such that to make the educational system "too over-scholastic might be worse than no benefit at all."[101] Their supposedly biologically inherited "defects" were assumed to interfere greatly with "good judgment and a balanced and sane reaction to affairs in general." With their score of 33 on Porteus and Babcock's 100-point scale, Filipinos were dead last of the six groups in their study and well below Japanese. In short, they were very much perceived and treated as the extreme racial other by Haoles and other non-Filipinos. As a result, in 1930, 90 percent of employed Filipino men were still laborers, the great majority of them on the plantations.[102] During the Depression, the planters solved "the Filipino problem" of their being an unwanted and unemployed presence by deporting more than nine thousand of them to the Philippines.[103]

The Uneven Racial Divide

Writing about twenty to thirty years before the processes and events discussed in this chapter occurred, Du Bois in *The Souls of Black Folk* famously observed, "The problem of the twentieth century is the problem of the color line—the relation of the darker to the lighter races of men in Asia and Africa, in America, and the islands of the sea."[104] Hawai'i certainly was one of those islands in the Pacific where the color line prevailed most problematically in the highly unequal relation of darker non-Haoles to lighter Haoles. Like the color line dividing Blacks and Whites in the continental United States, that which reigned in Hawai'i similarly maintained the exclusion and subjugation of non-Haoles.

This chapter has sought to outline the oppressive racial setting of Hawai'i in the 1920s and how the Haole oligarchy punished those who defied their rule. They enacted their settler colonial dominance in economic, legal, and political arenas but somewhat disparately against different non-Haole groups. It was most harshly enforced against Japanese and Filipinos, the two groups that initiated the most threatening challenges to Haole supremacy by organizing costly multiplantation strikes, each of them twice before the end of the 1920s. Consequently, Japanese and Filipino labor leaders, like Tsutsumi, Manlapit, Basan, and Taok, were convicted and imprisoned for various conspiracy charges and, when released, were often banished from Hawai'i. Their convictions were often secured through likely perjured testimony, in many cases paid for by the HSPA, while the police recruited and paid agents to spy and testify against them.

While race economically subjugated Native Hawaiians, evident in their persisting aggrieved status, it was not as constraining in electoral politics insofar as they had far greater access to political power than the other non-Haole groups had. This racial anomaly can be attributed to the Haole need for Native Hawaiian votes, which led Haoles to establish a political alliance with them so that both groups could be elected to the territorial legislature and other government bodies and thereby maintain Republican rule. Thus, the racial boundary between Haoles and non-Haoles can be considered uneven in that it allowed for Native Hawaiian political representation but upheld economic oppression for them and the other groups.

From this discussion it should be quite evident that the killing by Myles Fukunaga of Gill Jamieson did not occur in a racial vacuum as an isolated incident on a sunny Tuesday morning in September 1928. It clearly had a much greater racial significance that went far beyond his personal guilt for first-degree murder. By brazenly killing a Haole child, Fukunaga, as a Japanese American, had grossly transgressed the racial boundary dividing Haoles and non-Haoles and thereby upset the racial order. To reassert their supremacy, Haoles wanted him convicted and executed as quickly as possible, despite substantial evidence of his possible legal insanity. While Fukunaga's unjust hanging for killing a White boy appears racially similar to the lynching of African Americans in the South for violating the color line, it differs insofar as Japanese Americans were viewed by Haoles as a far greater political, economic, and cultural threat than Blacks were by southern Whites. However, Japanese American men were not perceived as constituting a sexual threat to White women as African American men were, which may account for the more than four thousand of them being lynched. Fukunaga also was put on trial, albeit unfairly, while that was not the case for Blacks who were lynched.

As is evident in the imprisonment of Japanese and Filipino labor organizers on various conspiracy charges, a conspiracy also obtained among the HSPA, the police, the prosecutors, the judiciary, and the press to send Tsutsumi, Manlapit, Basan, Taok, and other union officials to prison. Most of the same parties would employ similar tactics to dispatch Fukunaga swiftly to death row. Furthermore, the significance of race manifested in the Fukunaga case invalidated the claims of colorblind justice and multicultural harmony asserted during that time. The subsequent chapters delineate the racial injustices inflicted upon Fukunaga, which followed those against Japanese and Filipino labor leaders and workers who had challenged the racial order. By the time of Fukunaga's trial, the dominant Haoles fully knew that they could subvert the criminal justice system to obtain their desired outcome because they had done so earlier with impunity.

2. Kidnapping, Killing, and Racial Profiling

The day after he killed Gill Jamieson, Myles Fukunaga tried to join the manhunt for himself and Gill as a special deputy at the police station.[1] This strange story was related by K. Y. Leong, his landlord at the downtown rooming house where he was staying, and is a clear example of his bizarre behavior. Fukunaga told Leong that he was rejected as a deputy because of his small size and youthful appearance. But because this incident was not known until the day after his capture and interrogation at the police station, he was not questioned about it, and his reasons for attempting to search for himself remain a mystery.

This and the next chapter provide a day-by-day review of the major activities in the Fukunaga case during its first eight days to highlight the speed with which he was raced to his eventual death. This chapter covers the first four days, beginning on Tuesday with the abduction and murder of Gill Jamieson, the finding of his body on Thursday, and a fateful visit that Fukunaga made on Friday to the plantation town where he excelled in school, which resulted in his arrest the next day. The massive publicity given to the crime by the Honolulu daily newspapers, both English and Japanese, began immediately during this period, as well as the roundup and interrogation of nisei young men, who were racially profiled as suspects in it.

Tuesday, September 18: Abduction and Ransom Collection

This morning probably began like most previous school days for young Gill after waking up at his home at 2751 Kahawai Street in Mānoa Valley. After breakfast with his parents, he likely bid his mother Lulu goodbye and climbed into his father's roadster to be dropped off at the exclusive Punahou Academy. His father then drove to downtown Honolulu to the Hawaiian Trust Co., where he was a vice president. But this Tuesday would be unlike all others for Gill because he would be brutally killed later that morning.

Gill was the maiden name of his forty-year-old mother, who was from Tulare, California, and went to Hawai'i as a teacher in 1912. Gill's father was born in Kirriemuir, Scotland, in 1888, the son of an "ironmonger," and worked for the Linen Bank in his hometown for four years before immigrating to Hawai'i in 1910.[2] "Fred," as he came to be known in Hawai'i, may have made the long journey with or after his older brothers David and William, who were both employed at Big Five companies. Fred first worked for Bishop Trust Co.; a year later he joined Hawaiian Trust and remained with the firm until he retired in 1946 as a vice president and director.[3]

September 18 was also an extremely significant day for Myles Fukunaga, who the previous night wrote about it as "this day no other." He awoke at about 5:30 that morning and lazed around his room until 8:00, when he left to have breakfast at a café but was too nervous so could not eat much.[4] Myles had recently quit his job as a kitchen worker at a Waikīkī hotel and was staying at the Serene Rooms, sharing a room with another young Japanese American. He found a telephone at a nearby Japanese cafeteria, which was empty except for an older Japanese woman at the back of the place, who would be unable to understand him speaking in English. Myles first called Gill's home and conversed with his mother and then the Hawaiian Trust Co. and spoke very briefly with his father, but he did not know either of them.

As the eldest of seven children born to immigrant parents from Yamaguchi prefecture, Japan, Myles had a much harder life than Gill's, which began for him on a sugar plantation on Kaua'i and continued on other plantations until his family moved to Honolulu in September 1925.[5] When not working, he spent most of his time reading magazines and books and said he preferred being alone with books than with people. Myles "planned and planned" what he would do that Tuesday, which he wrote on a sheet of paper and titled "Schedule of Undertaking Okay!" By his own admission four days later, he killed Gill that day after abducting him from Punahou. But Myles only learned of Gill's existence when he spoke that morning with his mother, who told him they had a young son who attended the school. Lulu Jamieson could hardly have known that such information, unsuspectingly given to Myles pretending to be from the Board of Health, would tragically lead to her son's murder. How could such a horrific event, soon referred to as "one of the most brutal crimes in the history of the territory," have happened in what already was being called the "Paradise of the Pacific?"

Gill became Fukunaga's intended victim after he learned that the boy was the son of Frederick Jamieson. He wanted a young boy related to an executive of the Hawaiian Trust Co. because of a contentious encounter he had with a rent collector from the company in early May 1928.[6] The Fukunaga family was renting a cottage in downtown Honolulu from Hawaiian Trust, which sent the collector to obtain $20 in overdue rent for the month. At that time, Fukunaga was unemployed and staying at home, so he heard the rental agent speaking harshly to his mother, who was brought to tears by the incident. He went to talk to him and later described their sharp exchange to the police: "He said he wanted money right away or he would chase us out of the house. I told him how can we pay when we haven't got the money."[7] Fukunaga said from that day he had a "hatred" for Hawaiian Trust, which would evolve into an irrational desire for revenge against the company, and thus Gill became his innocent victim.

It was crucial to Fukunaga that his victim be a young boy because in planning his crime he was copying the infamous Leopold and Loeb kidnapping and murder of fourteen-year-old Bobby Franks four years earlier in Chicago. Besides being lovers, nineteen-year-old Nathan Leopold and eighteen-year-old Richard Loeb were extremely wealthy and exceptionally bright University of Chicago students.[8] They plotted their misdeed for several months before abducting and killing Franks, a private-school student from one of Chicago's most established families. Fukunaga learned about their crime from a magazine at the downtown public library and was so intrigued by it that he cut out the article.[9] He duplicated details of it in his own crime, such as bludgeoning Gill with a chisel and then strangling him to death and demanding $10,000 in ransom. Fukunaga may well have decided to mimic their murder because he thought of himself as highly intelligent like Leopold and Loeb, and replicating their crime was a means for him to be viewed in the same way, despite his eighth-grade education. As he replied during his police interrogation about why he left a copy of a poem in Gill's hand, "I wanted to show that not a mere boy like me was doing this. I wanted to show . . . a college party who had college education was doing work like this."[10] Fukunaga also was copying the Hickman case in Los Angeles in 1928 in which twelve-year-old Marion Parker, the daughter of a prominent banker, was kidnapped and savagely murdered by nineteen-year-old Edward Hickman in what the *Los Angeles Times* called "the most horrible crime of the 1920s."[11] Posing as an employee of the bank where Marion's father worked, Hickman went to her school and told the registrar that her father had been injured in an accident and wanted to see her, which was very similar to the ruse that Fukunaga used to abduct Gill.[12]

Having learned where Gill attended school, Fukunaga telephoned Punahou at 10 A.M. and spoke with the principal, Mary P. Winne.[13] He told her that he was calling from Queen's Hospital and that they would be sending someone for Gill so he could be with his mother, who had been injured in a traffic accident and wanted to see him.[14] Dressed in a white coat and pants so that he looked like a hospital orderly, Fukunaga hired a taxi in downtown Honolulu and asked to be taken to the school. Principal Winne and her sister Jane Winne, a Punahou teacher who also saw Fukunaga, both described him to the police as Japanese.

After retrieving Gill, Fukunaga instructed the cab driver, Morizo Yoshioka, to take them to the Royal Hawaiian Hotel in Waikīkī.[15] A Japanese immigrant in his sixties, Yoshioka was questioned the next day by Arthur McDuffie, a private detective hired by the Jamiesons, through another Japanese detective who served as an interpreter. According to Yoshioka, when he reached the hotel grounds, Fukunaga told him to stop, paid the $1.50 fare and got out of his "machine" with Gill. He told McDuffie that Fukunaga spoke to him in Japanese, while the secretary of the Punahou Academy principal said the person who came for Gill spoke "perfect English." As a nisei, Fukunaga was fluent in both Japanese and English, although his speaking, writing, and reading abilities in English were very likely much better than those of most of his generational peers, especially males.

After alighting with Gill about 10:45 A.M., Fukunaga crossed Kalākaua Avenue and took him to the rear of the Seaside Hotel (now the site of the International Market Place).[16] He had been working there since mid-June and staying in a nearby cottage for hotel workers till the end of August. Fukunaga very likely did not tell the taxi driver to take him to the Seaside Hotel so that the police would not immediately track him there. Shortly after taking Gill to a nearby *kiawe* (algaroba) thicket where he liked to read, Fukunaga struck him hard on his head with a metal chisel several times. Screaming in pain, Gill fought back by kicking Fukunaga, so he hit him two more times with the chisel, choked him to death and, to be certain he was dead, tied a napkin tightly around his throat. The violent struggle left his white coat and pants soaked in blood, so Fukunaga stole a pair of trousers from one of the workers' rooms at the Seaside cottages and took his blood-stained pants with him. Keeping to his plan, at noon he boarded a trolley car at the Moana Hotel and got off at the downtown post office, where he bought a stamped envelope. He placed in it a ransom letter to Frederick Jamieson, which he had written the previous night, that informed him his son had been kidnapped and demanded $10,000 for his safe return. Fukunaga then walked to the Nuuanu YMCA and called the Territorial Messenger

Service to have his ransom note delivered to the Hawaiian Trust Co. in the Kauikeolani building on King Street; they sent Alfredo Reyes, a fifteen-year-old messenger.[17] As the young Filipino told the police the next day, he rode his bicycle to the YMCA, where a man, who he thought was Japanese, gave him an envelope addressed to "F. W. Jamieson" and thirty-five cents for the delivery fee.[18]

After receiving the ransom letter about 1:30 P.M., Frederick Jamieson initially thought it was a prank.[19] But he decided to call Punahou Academy and spoke with the principal, who asked how his wife was after her traffic accident. Ms. Winne also told him that Gill had been picked up that morning by a hospital attendant, who took their son to be with his mother. Jamieson recoiled in horror, but fortunately for him a friend of his, "Judge" William Heen, was at Hawaiian Trust at that time. Heen had been meeting with Jamieson and others in the directors' board room to discuss Heen estate financial matters handled by the company, which included the cottage rented by the Fukunaga family.[20] Of Chinese and Hawaiian ancestry and a leader of the struggling Democratic Party, Heen was appointed a judge of the first circuit court by President Woodrow Wilson in 1917 when Heen was just thirty-four-years old, the first non-Haole to hold that position.[21] He resigned after two years and subsequently alternated between private practice as a defense attorney and serving as a prosecutor, as he did in the Japanese Federation of Labor conspiracy trial in 1922.

Jamieson returned to the directors' room visibly agitated and said he had another meeting at 2 P.M. and requested Heen to speak with him in private.[22] He showed him the ransom note and asked what he should do. Heen advised that the police should be notified immediately, although the letter warned Jamieson not to contact them. Heen left for the second floor of the Kauikeolani building, where he and his partner, Norman Godbold, had their law firm office. He called chief of detectives John McIntosh, city and county sheriff Patrick Gleason, city and county attorney Charles S. Davis and his deputy, Francis M. Brooks, and private detective Arthur McDuffie and asked them to meet at his office, where Jamieson went shortly. The officials whom Heen called soon appeared and remained at his law office until 6 A.M. the next day.[23]

They commenced their deliberations by reviewing the two-page, handwritten ransom letter. It began: "The Fates have decided so we have been given this privilege in writing you on this important matter. We presume you will be alarmed at first. Nevertheless, we hope that you get over this surprise soon and listen to the writer's story. What is it all about? YOUR SON IS KIDNAPPED FOR RANSOM."[24] The note had very detailed instructions about the ransom demand and its delivery, including a breakdown of the old bills without any identification marks that should be used, including \$4,000 in \$5 and \$10 bills, \$4,000 in \$20 bills, and \$2,000 in \$50 bills. Jamieson was told to be at home at 9 P.M. when he would be informed by phone or letter where and when to go to deliver the ransom, which he should do alone in his car. These instructions revealed Fukunaga's familiarity with previous abductions or, as he wrote, "every kidnapping case we have studied," very likely referring to the Leopold and Loeb and Hickman cases. From them, he probably learned to demand that the ransom money be in unmarked bills of small denominations and that the note should be returned with the payment. As Fukunaga praised himself, "We are too cautious—even the 'telltale' typewriter is not used by us," he did not, however, retrieve the ransom note from Jamieson. Thus, its entire text was printed on the front page of the *Honolulu Star-Bulletin* late Tuesday night in an extra edition.

Fukunaga's letter also reflected his fondness for Shakespeare, which would be evident in his other writings related to the Jamieson murder. He wrote, quoting loosely from the Bard's *As You Like It*, "The world is a mere stage in which we humans are the humble actors or players.[25] We are about to play our part in our secret drama entitled 'THE THREE VANISHINK [*sic*] SHADOWS.' Note that we are but three poor walking shadows." The reference to the latter is from *Macbeth*—"Life's but a walking shadow"—but Fukunaga signed the letter "The Three Kings," and this accounts for his tripling the number of shadows.

Despite the references to Christianity in his ransom note, Fukunaga explained later that the idea of calling himself "The Three Kings" came from a package of cigarettes with that brand name he found at the Seaside Hotel.[26] It did result in the police initially looking for three persons responsible for the kidnapping of Gill and in the press referring to his "kidnappers" and "slayers." While Fukunaga claimed not to be religious, neither Christian nor Buddhist, on the second page of his letter was written, quoting Jesus as he was being crucified, "Oh Father forgive them they know not what they do."[27] The last line in the note is "We hope you will like our 'directorship,'" a term that very likely refers to another written text by Fukunaga found later in his room, which the press referred to as the "Scenario" because it seems like the outline of a film with actors and a director. The director is none other than Fukunaga, and his movie is about "The Father" making the ransom payment to "The Masked One" (also Fukunaga) for the return of "The son." Rather than a film, these events transpired Tuesday evening and hence indicate Fukunaga's planning of his crime.

After what probably seemed like an eternity for the Jamiesons, Fukunaga called them at 8:40 P.M.[28] He told Jamieson to drive to the rendezvous point,

Thomas Square, and to stop at the adjacent Academy of Arts on Beretania Street. Fukunaga was waiting for Jamieson under the banyan tree in the center of the square and walked over to his car with a handkerchief covering his face. He directed him to drive them to nearby McKinley High School and then told him to count the ransom payment into his hat. After counting $4,000 in $5 bills, Jamieson demanded to see his son before he would hand over the rest of the money. Seeing some men nearby, he got out of his car and shouted for help, but Fukunaga warned him to return or his son would be killed. Jamieson complied, and Fukunaga said he would come back shortly with Gill. Believing he had all of the $10,000, Fukunaga fled, running through backyards several blocks until he found a Japanese taxi stand and asked the driver to take him downtown but not directly to the Serene Rooms. Since he had no money of his own, he paid the fare with one of the $5 bills from the ransom, not realizing then that spending the money would lead to his eventual capture.

Two witnesses provided a detailed account of the encounter between Jamieson and Fukunaga near the McKinley High School baseball field.[29] Mainard Austin and William Choice were with a group of friends in a cottage opposite the road on which Jamieson parked after meeting up with Fukunaga. About 9:30 P.M. they heard shouts for help and ran toward them where they saw Jamieson standing next to his car. They also saw a "very short man" wearing a blue serge suit and necktie, who they believed was Japanese. Neither Jamieson nor the other man said anything for two or three minutes until Jamieson told them, "Go back, boys. I want to get my boy back." Unaware of what was going on, Austin and Choice went back to the cottage but decided to call the police, after which they returned to the car. As they approached, they saw the masked man disappear into nearby bushes. Jamieson told them, "He has gone off to count the money in the bushes. After counting it, he is going to bring my boy back to me." After waiting for fifteen long minutes, Jamieson finally gave up and drove toward downtown Honolulu, no doubt greatly disheartened he had not been reunited with his dear son, who he did not know was already dead. He probably went to the Heen & Godbold law office to report on his unsuccessful encounter with one of the kidnappers.

The first of the instructions in the ransom letter told Jamieson not to notify the police, which he did. City officials then decided that the public should be informed of the abduction so that the search for Gill and his kidnappers could begin immediately. They hence asked the *Honolulu Star-Bulletin* to report the news of the shocking crime, which appeared in an extra edition of the paper that was on the streets shortly after 11 P.M.[30] The banner headline in large block letters proclaimed "JAMIESON BOY KIDNAPPED; FATHER PAYS $4,000; ABDUCTOR SOUGHT." Also late Tuesday night, chief of detectives John McIntosh announced that ten members of the detective force had been assigned to the case and that they were looking for Gill in Palama, an area of Honolulu where many Japanese Americans lived. Instead of at the police station, decisions and discussions about the kidnapping by Sheriff Patrick Gleason and city attorney Charles Davis were already being made at the Heen & Godbold law firm. Heen stopped working on all legal business and with Godbold devoted all of his time to the case, thereby assuming an active role in it, despite being a private citizen.[31] His law office was the command center for the Jamieson investigation until Friday, when activities were transferred to police headquarters, which seems only appropriate for a criminal matter.

Wednesday, September 19: Manhunt and Suspects

Honolulu awoke on Wednesday morning to blaring newspaper headlines and radio broadcasts that Gill Jamieson had been abducted the previous day. The *Honolulu Advertiser* headline announced, "GILL, 10, KIDNAPED [*sic*]." City residents were provided with detailed accounts of how the boy was brazenly abducted from Punahou Academy and how his father made a futile ransom payment the night before.[32] They were also told that the kidnapping suspects were of "Oriental extraction, possibly Japanese."

The front page of the *Advertiser* also featured two recent photos of Gill and informed readers that when he left home for school the previous day he appeared much as he did in them—wearing a light-colored, long-sleeve shirt, bow tie, knee-length flannel breeches, and barefoot, like most young students in Hawai'i.[33] Gill was described as four feet, eight-and-a-half inches tall, weighing eighty-five pounds, and having light brown hair and blue eyes. The boy's innocent youthfulness, enhanced by his smiling face in the photos, could not help but generate heartfelt concern and sympathy for Gill and his parents. But the racial status of the Jamiesons as Haole and their class status as wealthy members of Honolulu's corporate elite undoubtedly were major factors in the tremendous news coverage given immediately of the abduction and in the massive search for Gill's kidnappers.[34] One cannot easily believe that the same vast resources and organized efforts by public and private parties would have been expended if the victim had not been Haole and from a privileged family

The elite Haole response to Gill's kidnapping quickly developed, which undeniably signified its racial significance. The board of directors of the

Honolulu Chamber of Commerce convened a special meeting at noon on Wednesday.[35] The board, consisting of Haole men, decided to request that Governor Wallace R. Farrington have the entire island of O'ahu placed under martial law.[36] This proposal to surrender their civil rights (and those of non-Haoles) reveals the absolute panic and fear that gripped the Haole community as a result of the abduction of one of their own. However, the governor rejected their request, stating emphatically, "This is a police problem, not a military problem."[37] So the board appointed a special executive committee, including J. K. Butler, secretary of the Hawaiian Sugar Planters' Association, Alan S. Davis, a vice-president of the Hawaiian Trust Co., Horace Johnson, a vice-president of C. Brewer & Co., and Riley Allen, editor of the *Star-Bulletin*, to work with Sheriff Patrick Gleason.[38] Butler maintained that the Jamieson kidnapping was the climax of a series of incidents demonstrating the prevalence of "evil conditions" in Honolulu that required immediate amelioration. He probably was referring to the increasing crime rate in the city, which would also be noted by the press and politicians as a likely factor in the abduction.

The Chamber of Commerce board also agreed to assist Sheriff Gleason with the swearing in of two hundred civilian special deputies for the search for Gill and his kidnappers.[39] Manifesting their mistrust of non-Haoles and not just Japanese Americans, the board declared that these deputies should be "Americans [Haoles] where possible." However, the sheriff advised them of his desire to have volunteers include "American citizens of Japanese ancestry" since they might obtain relevant information from Japanese Americans. The chamber assumed financial responsibility for providing food at the National Guard Armory for the deputies, who became part of what was already being described as "the greatest man-hunt in island history." Other resources of chamber members made available to the sheriff included fifty cars and as many drivers as needed from General Motors and Schuman Carriage Co.[40] Sheriff Gleason and city attorney Davis also accepted help from Honolulu automobile associations that had extensive ties with such Japanese organizations, which included most of the taxi and service-station operators on O'ahu.[41] It appeared as though all sectors of island society were joining the search for Gill.

The commander of the Hawai'i department of the army offered its assistance to Sheriff Gleason, including two intelligence operatives and twelve military police.[42] The territorial superintendent of public instruction sent a letter to all school principals on O'ahu with a picture of Gill requesting their cooperation in the manhunt.[43] It stated that Sheriff Gleason had asked for their help, so Gill's picture should be shown to all students, and they should be told to be on the lookout for him. Accordingly, public schools were dismissed early at noon on Wednesday so that twenty thousand students, clutching printed photos of Gill, could participate in the search.[44] In addition, the executive officers of both political parties organized precinct squads to visit every housing unit on O'ahu. If anyone refused to let them in, these squads were instructed to report the name of the person to the sheriff's office. They were joined by the National Guard and ROTC units from Punahou, McKinley, and Kamehameha High Schools and the University of Hawai'i, which patrolled strategic locations in Honolulu.[45] All roads leading into and out of the city were being monitored, and cars going to or from the city could be stopped and the occupants questioned if anything aroused the suspicion of the guards.[46]

The two hundred special deputies the Honolulu Chamber of Commerce, American Legion, and the National Guard had promised Sheriff Gleason were being recruited since Wednesday evening at the chamber offices, the Hawaiian Trust Co., and the police station.[47] At movie theaters, "lantern slides" were flashed on the screen asking for more volunteers, and the chamber offices remained open at night until the quota of deputies was met. Merchant Street near the police station was jammed with onlookers such that it could not be determined how many deputies were present, but their "glittering badges were thicker and brighter than stars in the sky." A huge and ever-growing crowd also emerged at the Hawaiian Trust Co., waiting to hear of the latest developments in the search for Gill and his abductors.

As part of the manhunt, all sampans, many of which were operated by Japanese American fishermen, leaving or entering the port of Honolulu had to provide information about their travels, crew, and any passengers. This cooperation with the authorities was arranged by Mr. T. Onodera, the Japanese Chamber of Commerce secretary, after a meeting with the directors of the Honolulu Chamber of Commerce.[48] On Wednesday morning officials of the Japanese chamber and other Japanese merchants met with David Jamieson, an uncle of Gill's and a cashier in the life insurance department of American Factors, and offered their help in the search for his nephew. Onodera made a similar offer of assistance to Sheriff Gleason, who requested that Japanese fishermen watch outgoing sampans to prevent the kidnappers from escaping.[49]

The headline of Wednesday's *Star-Bulletin*, "Ex-Chauffer Held in Kidnap Probe," announced that Harry Kaisan, a twenty-one-year-old nisei, was, at 9 A.M. that day, the first person to be taken into custody in connection with the kidnapping. Kaisan became the initial suspect after Peter Chu, manager of an employment agency, turned him over to the police as the former driver for the Jamiesons.[50] Chu told the press that Kaisan had been hired by the Jamiesons through his agency, and on Tuesday afternoon Mrs. Jamieson called and asked anxiously if he knew how to contact Kaisan, adding that it was very important they see him immediately. Chu said he left a message for Kaisan to contact him the next morning. "Bright and early Kaisan appeared," Chu remarked, noting that by then he had figured out why Mrs. Jamieson wanted to see him. He then took Kaisan, ostensibly with the prospect of a job, to the Hawaiian Trust Co. According to Chu, Kaisan "followed [him] willingly, apparently in the best of spirit. There was no trace of anxiety or fear in his manner. . . . If that boy had this conspiracy all that time on his mind, he is one in 10,000 for self-control." Perhaps Kaisan would have shown fear had he known how he would be abused over the next three days.

The police were waiting for Kaisan and took him promptly to the police station, where he was interrogated virtually nonstop until midnight in an effort to break him.[51] He was questioned for twelve straight hours by deputy city attorney Francis Brooks, city attorney Charles Davis, and Chester Doyle, who was described as obtaining "more confessions from criminals than any other man in Honolulu." However, Doyle failed to elicit an admission of guilt from Kaisan, who repeated his responses to the questions thrown at him—"I don't know the three kings. I don't know anything about the letter. I don't know anything about the kidnapping."[52] Even so, he would undergo three days of intensive questioning, including beating him in futile attempts to force him to confess. So convinced were the police of Kaisan's guilt that on Friday they took his sixteen-year-old brother into custody and interrogated him and later did the same to his eighteen-year-old sister. She was questioned about the possible existence of another Kaisan brother, who was supposed to be the third king.

During his interrogation, Kaisan was told to copy a portion of the ransom letter, and his handwritten version was printed alongside Fukunaga's original in the *Star-Bulletin*. According to Fred C. Bailey, an assistant cashier at the Bank of Hawaii whose testimony as a handwriting expert was recognized in territorial courts, Kaisan's handwriting and that on the ransom note were identical.[53] After earlier examining a copy of the letter, Bailey had contended that a person of "Oriental extraction, age undetermined, unquestionably" had written it, an example of the dominance of racial thinking at that time. When the ransom note was reproduced in a two-by-two feet section in Wednesday's *Star-Bulletin*, the newspaper reported that it was copied from a detective story or "represented meanderings of an unsound mind."[54] This observation was an early view of Fukunaga's insanity that was dropped after he was caught.

Kaisan later explained to the *Nippu Jiji* why his handwriting as printed in the *Star-Bulletin* appeared to be remarkably similar to that of Fukunaga's.[55] He disclosed that he was instructed by Bailey to write on two separate sheets of paper a portion of the ransom letter. Bailey first told him to write in his usual way as the letter was dictated to him, and Kaisan remarked that the two were not similar. Bailey then directed him to make an exact copy of the ransom note. That version, alongside the original letter, was the one printed in the newspaper, but this information was not mentioned by the *Star-Bulletin*, perhaps because it was withheld from the paper. Nonetheless, it does demonstrate an attempt by the police to manufacture bogus evidence against Kaisan, as they had against the Japanese Federation of Labor and Filipino Labor Union officials. Due to the dissemination of such false evidence about Kaisan, the press noted the "strong feeling against the former chauffeur, especially among the Japanese."[56]

As a result of the above and other incidents that occurred while Kaisan was being interrogated, the *Nippu Jiji* published in Japanese his account of his experiences while in police custody.[57] It then received numerous requests for an English version of Kaisan's narrative, so a *Nippu Jiji* translator was assigned to translate the Japanese version into English, which Kaisan read and approved for publication.[58] Kaisan's statement began, "I will begin my account from September 19 (Wednesday) at 9 A.M.[59] On that day I called at the employment office. I thought I was going to get a job, but . . . I was taken to the office of Judge Heen." Deputy city attorney Francis Brooks then informed him that Gill Jamieson had been kidnapped, and Kaisan wrote that it was the first time he had heard about it. He was then taken to the police station and confined in the city jail until about 2 P.M., when he was escorted to an office. Kaisan stated he saw "Dr. Porteus" there and was told to provide several handwriting samples with a fountain pen. He was later returned to the jail, where Boy Scout official Sam Robley questioned him, and he replied that he did not know anything about what he was being asked. Next Brooks tried to get him to admit his guilt: "He insisted that I confess, saying that he would exonerate me if I did. But I persisted that I did not know [anything]"—because he really did not.

Kaisan's account continued that late Wednesday afternoon he was returned to Heen's office where his father, Fred Makino, and others were, including a "Mr. Clark." He wrote that Clark told him he could go home with his father and, if he came back the next morning, Clark will give him $6,000. About midnight he was returned to the jail with the warning that it was his last chance to confess. At 2:30 in the morning Kaisan was awakened and interrogated further, about where he went to school and from whom he learned penmanship. Later that morning, he was escorted to the office of chief of detectives John McIntosh. Born in Ireland, he had served for twenty years in British colonial police forces in South Africa and New Zealand before immigrating to Hawai'i in 1921 and finding employment as a luna at Ewa Plantation. After two years, McIntosh was recruited by the Police Department and quickly rose through the ranks to his position, despite being criticized by his fellow officers for his harsh treatment of non-Haole suspects and subordinates and for his open animosity toward Native Hawaiians.[60] McIntosh once told an interviewer that he "was put there [as chief of the detectives bureau] by the business interests and the politicians."[61] No doubt it was to enforce their racial rule over non-Haoles.

Fulfilling his role for his Haole patrons, McIntosh told Kaisan, "Nishi [Paul, one of the suspects] has spilled the beans, so you've got no chance." According to Kaisan, "McIntosh then struck me on the cheek and near the mouth, then on each of my sides and another in my stomach. I felt wobbly and kind of hazy. A Hawaiian then came and said he saw me at Thomas Square on Tuesday night." Kaisan replied that he did not remember going there. He was returned to the jail, and a matron brought him breakfast, but McIntosh's punch to his stomach had left him in pain.

Kaisan's narrative continued that shortly he was taken to an office where he was shown a photograph of a boy (Gill) and asked if he recognized him, and he said no.[62] Dr. Faus, the city medical examiner, then asked if he could give Kaisan some injections, which was hyocine hydrobromide. Faus told him that the injections will make him sleep for twelve hours and that his mind will be clearer and he will be able to remember things he did. Faus said even if Kaisan refused, he would inject him anyway. After receiving an injection, Kaisan related that he was asked more questions and then began to feel sleepy. After a second injection, he wrote, "I was demanded to confess and my head was struck. I could not help it because I was sleepy. I heard a voice, 'Wake up.' I was then asked various questions. I felt as if I was crazy. Things were dim and I could not recall anything." Robley then told him that he had confessed to writing the ransom letter, which he denied. Kaisan continued, "Robley next struck me, throwing me back and my head struck the wall behind. After that I do not remember what I did."

According to Kaisan's statement, when he regained consciousness from the injections it was Friday morning; he was in Oahu Prison and was taken in handcuffs back to the police station. He saw Porteus and Bailey and was given some dictation to write, and then Bailey insisted that he had written an "f," which was similar to one in the ransom note. Robley then accused him of also writing the letter received by the *Star-Bulletin* the previous day that stated Gill was dead, but he denied it. Perhaps to make amends for hitting him, Robley bought Kaisan ham sandwiches, coffee, and tobacco, and gave him a dollar. Later that Friday afternoon, Robley told Kaisan that he had been cleared of the crime, but he was taken to Oahu Prison for his safety from possible mob violence should he return home. Kaisan concluded his account by stating that he was kept at the prison until being released on Sunday morning after Fukunaga's capture.

The *Nippu Jiji* provided chief of detectives McIntosh a copy of Kaisan's statement, and he responded by writing, in part: "On Thursday morning the 20th: I had Harry Kaisan in my office and questioned him as to what he knows of the kidnapping plot, he strenuously denied all knowledge of it. . . . He said that if he knew anything of the plot he would tell us. I absolutely refute all accusations that he was beaten, or in any way ill treated by me, or any of my men, at any time. If these rumors have been published by anyone with ulterior motives, and no doubt they have, all I have to say about it is they are cowardly and dastardly liars."[63] While McIntosh might charge the *Nippu Jiji* of having "ulterior motives" for publishing the accusations by Kaisan, what were Kaisan's motives in making them, especially with such detail? As prime examples of racial injustice, the attempt to create false evidence against Kaisan and his beatings by McIntosh and Robley, who was not a police detective, were a continuation of the illegal tactics used to obtain the convictions of Japanese and Filipino labor leaders earlier in the 1920s. As Kaisan told the press after his release, "I thought I was going to hang for something I didn't do. I seemed to be the fall guy in the case for a long time."[64] Kaisan might very well have been hanged if not for Fukunaga's capture.

The *Hawaii Hochi* was highly critical of the police attempt to frame Kaisan for the Jamieson killing. In an editorial, the paper remarked that people were so convinced of his guilt that preparations were made to lynch him, although it did not state who initiated them.[65] The editorial also asserted that, prior to Fukunaga's arrest, the city attorney's office was planning to have Kaisan arraigned for the murder of Gill the following Monday. These efforts by the police and prosecution to convict Kaisan, despite his innocence, make evident the larger racial significance of the Fukunaga case because three years later they would try to do the same to five local young men for raping a Haole woman, Thalia Massie. One of them, Joe Kahahawai, was shot to death after he, like Kaisan, refused to confess to a crime that he had not committed.

The "Dr. Porteus," whom Kaisan stated he saw at the police station, was University of Hawai'i clinical psychologist Stanley D. Porteus. Born in Australia in 1883, he began a long career at UH in 1922 after serving for several years as head of the Vineland Training School for the Feebleminded in

New Jersey. He had recently co-authored *Temperament and Race*, which claimed that temperamental differences among various non-Haole racial groups in Hawai'i "have an organic basis and are part of man's original endowment"—in short, biologically inherited.[66] Blatantly racist, Porteus's academic writings endorsed the hierarchical ranking of races on factors such as intelligence, which he tried to establish by measuring some ten thousand heads based on his belief in a direct correlation between head (and brain) size and intelligence level.[67] Historian David E. Stannard emphasizes that "Porteus' racial ideology was *not* consistent with scholarly opinion" concerning the significance of race when his book appeared (emphasis in original),[68] although it did reflect public opinion. In a detailed and lengthy analysis of Porteus's writings over the course of his academic career, Stannard concludes, "Porteus was a racist—and he was one throughout all of his professional life" and "a promoter, as well, of eugenicist ideas that were at times potentially genocidal."[69] Notably, the eugenics movement reached its peak in the 1920s.[70] It is not evident why Porteus became directly involved in the Jamieson case so early; possibly it was because he was a well-known UH clinical psychologist and the kidnappers were believed to be mentally disturbed. Porteus would continue to participate in the investigation and would interview Fukunaga and administer his "intelligence" tests to him following his apprehension.

By Wednesday afternoon, besides Kaisan, five young Japanese American men had been picked up in the kidnapping case.[71] Their names and ages were printed in the newspapers as Jack Kumamoto, age twenty-six; Charles Y. Miura, twenty-five; Saboro [*sic*] Nakasone, twenty-three; Paul F. Nishi, twenty-seven; and Hajime Ohta, twenty-two. They were detained after McIntosh ordered the police to take into custody all "suspicious characters," but they and others later can be considered victims of the racial profiling of young Japanese American men, perhaps the first racial injustice in the Fukunaga case. As Kumamoto related in an interview sixty years later, "They arrested me because . . . I didn't have a job, Japanese boy, walking down the street. I was frightened, shaking like a leaf. They had three or four police guard me, to protect me from the mob at the station. They wanted to mob me."[72]

Another primary suspect in the kidnapping was Samuel K. Nakamura, a "youthful Japanese ice worker."[73] He was picked up by the police on Wednesday as the person suspected of paying the messenger to deliver the ransom letter to Frederick Jamieson. In a packed room, including newspaper reporters, Nakamura was initially questioned by deputy city attorney Francis Brooks. He asked, "Nakamura, I'm interested in the kidnapping of a little boy. Do you know anything about kidnapping?" Nakamura replied that he had read about such cases in magazines and detective stories at the public library but had not read about the Jamieson abduction in the newspapers.

Nakamura was being interrogated by city attorney Charles Davis when William Heen pushed a "little messenger boy," Alfredo Reyes, through the crowd.[74] Nakamura raised his eyes toward Reyes without showing any sign of recognition, but Reyes shouted, "That's him! I know that's him. Look at him, same nose, same shirt, hair all bushy. I no make mistake, it's him!" Shaken and bewildered by the accusation, Nakamura protested, "I didn't do it. It's not right to suspect me. You say I got a flat nose?" "Yes sir, it you all right," Reyes yelled back, "Your nose is flat just like his was. The only difference is now you no wear khaki pants like on Tuesday." The questioning of Nakamura then intensified, but he continued to deny the accusations against him with such ignorance of their relevance that the police became pessimistic of his guilt. Nonetheless, the next day the *Advertiser* printed a photo of Nakamura captioned "Did He Give Ransom Note?" and noted his identification by Reyes as the person who gave him the ransom letter.[75]

Besides Kaisan and Nakamura, more than a dozen young Japanese American men were shortly taken into custody and interrogated by the police as suspects in the Jamieson abduction. In at least one case, the police "beat the hell out of him, damned near killed him" in an elevator between floors at the police station in a desperate attempt to force a confession, according to the secretary of the city attorney Charles Davis.[76] Three other young Japanese American men—O. Fujishiya, James Nakagawa, and M. Onyshi [*sic*]—all former waiters at the Moana Hotel in Waikīkī, were picked up and questioned.[77] The police gave no reason for why they were detained, but they had been living at the servants' quarters of the hotel, despite not working there anymore. Under intense interrogation by police detectives and private detective Arthur McDuffie, who had been hired by the Hawaiian Trust Co., they revealed the name of a fourth former Moana waiter named "Kobeyashi" [*sic*], who was thirty-year-old Henry Kobayashi. He was described as very intelligent and to have been somewhat of a leader among the waiters at the hotel, serving as their unofficial spokesperson during a recent strike. Perhaps that was the reason Kobayashi was taken into custody Thursday night because, after being questioned, he was released by the police. Nonetheless, that did not stop the *Advertiser* from falsely reporting that Harry Kaisan had implicated Kobayashi in the Jamieson murder after he was injected with a "truth serum" drug. This story is indicative of the unsubstantiated rumors, including not having the suspect's name spelled correctly, spreading wildly in Honolulu regarding the perpetrators of the crime.

The police appeared to have targeted Japanese American "hard-boiled, shifty-eyed and keen-witted youths" from "pool halls and questionable rooming houses" because they were viewed as products of "gangster conditions."[78] Transcripts of their questioning by detective McIntosh provided details of the "subterranean, murky world" they occupied in downtown Honolulu. One of them was asked how he made his living; he answered that it was by gambling. McIntosh then inquired if he was a "bunco man" (swindler), and the youth admitted he sometimes was. He also agreed that five other named suspects were all gamblers.

The questioning of another Japanese American youth revealed how they spent much of their daily lives in downtown Honolulu, which was said by the police to be typical of a good number of young men, including nisei.[79] Asked by McIntosh about his activities Tuesday night, the youth said another one of the suspects came to his house about 7 P.M., and they went to a pool hall in Chinatown. Later another of the suspects arrived, and they proceeded to the Rizal dance hall where they stayed for an hour, taxi dancing with local women. They then returned to the pool room, after which they went back to the dance hall and then went home. These activities of those interrogated were summarized by the press as consisting of "loafing, pool hall rendezvous, loafing, more pool hall, a dance hall, some gambling in between—idleness, shortage of money, susceptibility to off-color suggestions from this and that 'wise guy' and 'hard egg' so easy to meet in those dingy places where denizens of an actual underworld foregather." During his questioning, one of the suspects related how he learned of the Jamieson kidnapping late Tuesday night. At a corner store on Beretania and River Streets, he and his friend went in and he "got a Camel. From there we went up to his [friend's] room. About half an hour somebody shouted, 'Extra!' so [he] opened the window and called for the boy. We got a paper and heard about the kidnapping case."[80] So would most of Honolulu by the next day.

Also learning promptly about the abduction of Gill Jamieson were people in Tokyo through the *Asahi Shimbun* newspaper, whose Honolulu correspondent began sending daily reports about the case starting on Wednesday, probably because Japanese were suspected of being involved. Reflecting the keen interest in Japan about their fellow citizens in Hawai'i, the paper carried regular articles about the Fukunaga case for the next month.

As for Fukunaga, after a sleepless night due to recurring nightmares about killing Gill and hearing his screams, he awoke early on Wednesday, went out for breakfast, and purchased some new trousers for himself.[81] On the street, he saw the newspaper headlines and learned that what he did the day before was no longer a secret between him and the Jamiesons. As noted above, he bizarrely attempted later that day to volunteer for the search for himself. During this and the next day, Fukunaga stayed around town not doing much, since he had done more than enough, and went to an occasional motion picture show. But he was astounded to learn of the huge public commotion he had caused, which he had not anticipated at all when carefully planning his crime.

Thursday, September 20: Corpse and Letter

Sadly, Gill Jamieson's body was found two days after he was killed, lying on some old sacks under *kiawe* trees in Waikīkī. An autopsy performed that afternoon by the city medical examiner, Dr. Robert Faus, concluded that strangulation and a brain concussion caused Gill's death.[82] In his report, Faus wrote, "The body showed many discolored spots, black and blue marks about the face, arms and chest, the hands being torn and chafed in spots, apparent signs that after his abduction the boy had struggled with his captors and had attempted to regain his freedom. The concussion of the brain was the result of several blows on the head, apparently from some blunt instrument, probably a hammer. Five such blows were plainly visible." As a result of publication of such details from Faus's report, the newspapers soon began to refer to the Jamieson killing as "one of the most brutal murders in the history of the islands." By that afternoon, thousands of people were visiting the site where Gill's body was discovered a few hundred yards to the rear of the Seaside Hotel worker cottages.[83] All afternoon and continuing to Friday, the roads from Kalākaua Avenue heading "mauka [toward the mountains] were choked with automobiles and pedestrians."

Also indicative of the immense public interest in the crime, Gill's murder became the main topic of conversation throughout Honolulu, and chaos broke out in the city.[84] Thousands gathered around the police station on Merchant Street for the latest news in what had become a homicide case. The crowd, "raised to a high pitch of feeling by the fiendish murder," became so large that the police cordoned off the street to allow traffic to flow through and had to use force to maintain order.[85] The crowd shouted demands for action; the police, fearing mob violence might erupt, transferred the leading suspect, Harry Kaisan, to Oahu Prison.

The *Advertiser* reported that a "fiendishly written note hastily scribbled" on cardboard had been left covering Gill's face.[86] In his later interrogation by the police, Fukunaga related, "After I killed the boy, I laid beside him and wrote that 'tomorrow, tomorrow and tomorrow,'" quoting from *Macbeth*, of which the reporter was unaware.[87] He also revealed that, as he laid next to

Gill, he wept for half an hour for the just departed boy before writing his message.

> If you want to die, have you the right to kill others so that you in turn will be killed?
> It is for you to decide.
> Tomorrow, and tomorrow and tomorrow.
> Creps [Creeps] this petty pace from day to day and all our yesterdays—
> fools the way to dust death-out, and brief candle, life is just a mere shadow—
> a poor player that frets and struts his hours upon the stage and then is heard no more—
> It is a tale told by a [*sic*] idiot, flesh [full] of sound and fury signifying nothing.

The first line of the note is consistent with one of the principal motives that Fukunaga later gave for killing Gill—he wanted to die, as is evident from his two suicide attempts in early April.

Fukunaga covered Gill's body with an old newspaper, which he said he chose because it had an article about a murder, but he may have done so out of sympathy for his victim.[88] On top of the newspaper, he placed a cross made of tied-together twigs he found nearby. In Gill's left hand he left a copy of the poem "Immortality" by Spencer McGann, which Fukunaga had clipped from a magazine at the main public library. Nearby was a torn deuce of hearts playing card; on one half were written two lines from Walt Whitman's "O Captain! My Captain!" to which Fukunaga added a line of his own. More than a hundred feet from Gill's body were found a blood-soaked white coat, worn by Fukunaga when he went to Punahou Academy, and a bloody napkin.

The same day Gill's body was discovered, Fukunaga sent a letter, also signed "The Three Kings," to the *Star-Bulletin*, in which he claimed responsibility for the boy's death.[89] He included a $5 bill from the ransom money as proof of its authenticity. Fukunaga wrote:

> As a result of our recent exploits, we "Three Kings" find the community all agog and in a state of suspense and terror for the lost lad. To relieve it we have decided to clear just a part of the mystery.
>
> Mas. Gill Jamieson, poor innocent lad, has departed for the Unknown, a forlorn "Walking Shadow" in the Great Beyond, where we all go to when the time comes. . . .
>
> We will, as God's in Heaven, reveal ourselves to the light of justice. When? . . . The day shall be on the 25th exactly a week after the crime has been committed when we promise to mount on the scaffold of sin to plead guilty and the death penalty we are to receive.

> Meanwhile we hope that God will watch over us as he has done during our adventures in crime. We are bad, bad and we'll let him decide whether we shall be caught before hand. . . . The wrong cannot be righted now. We only regret that we have brought sorrows to the parents of the boy and to the community in general.

The reference to "the death penalty we are to receive" is in agreement with Fukunaga's death wish in committing his crime. That and other statements in the letter ("the crime has been committed") reveal that Fukunaga knew that killing Gill was wrong—an issue discussed in chapter 5 concerning his legal insanity.

Responding quickly to the finding of Gill's body, at a special meeting that same day the Honolulu Chamber of Commerce board of directors unanimously approved a resolution to establish a community reward fund.[90] It called upon chamber members and the community at large to contribute to the fund and offered a reward of $20,000 for evidence resulting in the arrest and conviction of those responsible for the kidnapping and murder of Gill. Almost half of the goal, about $9,400, was raised by the afternoon of the first day of the campaign, indicating the immense community concern about Gill's killing.[91] Also that evening, about one hundred business men held a meeting at Pier 2; attendance was so large that they moved it to the offices of John Balch in the Mutual Telephone Co. building.[92] Although the *Star-Bulletin* referred to them as "vigilantes," some of those present said the gathering was the first meeting of the "Vigilance Committee," while others related that they just wanted to assist the sheriff. They were described as ranging in age from about thirty years and older, "notably quiet, substantial, well-dressed" and including many well known in the business community. While race was not mentioned, one can assume that most of the men were Haole and none was Japanese American.

On its part, the Japanese American community joined the many others in the manhunt for Gill. At a Thursday morning meeting at the Japanese Consulate, representatives of Japanese associations in Honolulu voted to organize an immediate search in cooperation with the authorities. They issued the following statement: "The members of each and every Japanese organization in Honolulu are grevious [*sic*] for Mr. and Mrs. Frederick W. Jamieson in their misfortune. The representatives of these organizations pledge their co-operation in the search for Gill Jamieson, and urge every member, not only of the respective organizations, but of the whole Japanese community to make every effort to assist in locating the missing boy."[93] In a formal statement on Thursday, the Japanese Consulate also requested every Japanese to cooperate and assist in finding Gill.[94]

Before printing Kaisan's statement, the *Nippu Jiji* spread grossly false information about the Jamieson murder.[95] Reporting the discovery of Gill's body, the paper had a front-page article, partially titled "Kidnappers Cut Open Boy's Abdomen on Both Sides; Rip Open His Back and Strangle Him until Tongue Hangs Out." Without citing the source for its supposed facts about how Gill was killed, the newspaper claimed, "Gill Jamieson's body was terribly mangled and brutally cut open by the fiends . . . and to make sure of their work, the maniacs slit upon the boy's abdomen on his left and right sides, and then opened up a ghastly wound in his back," all of which was false, according to the official autopsy report. Since the article appeared in English, it can be assumed that it was written by Shinichi Maruyama, the English-language section editor of the *Nippu Jij*. Incredibly, he would serve on the jury that convicted Fukunaga of murder without being questioned by Fukunaga's attorneys during jury selection about this article, which might have resulted in his being challenged as a juror. The publisher and editor of the *Nippu Jiji* was fifty-five-year-old Yasutaro Soga, who had been an ally of Fred Makino as leaders of the Higher Wage Association in the 1909 strike. But during the next decade he and Makino became arch enemies, and Soga allied himself with the far more conservative Rev. Takie Okumura and served on the board of his New Americans Conference, which urged the nisei to remain on or return to the plantations.

In its editorial for Thursday, the *Nippu Jiji* observed, "One of the most revolting features of the crime is that the members of the kidnapping ring seem to be Japanese. The Punahou faculty say they identified the two persons who called at the school for the Jamieson boy as Japanese. . . . In case the kidnappers are definitely identified to be Japanese, it would mean a dirty stain on the escutcheon of the Japanese in the islands."[96] While noting at this time the racial impact of the Jamieson crime on the Japanese American community, after Fukunaga was convicted and sentenced to death, the *Nippu Jiji* would seek to minimize the racial injustices of both actions against him, following the colorblind lead of the *Star-Bulletin* and *Advertiser*.

The *Advertiser* editorial on Thursday, "All Eyes Out for the Boy," provided a sense of the widespread community concern about the Jamieson abduction.[97] It observed, "Honolulu is shocked to its center by the bold kidnaping [*sic*] of Gill Jamieson, aged ten. . . . There is not a home but is not grieving in sympathy with Mr. and Mrs. Frederick W. Jamieson. . . . It is the business of the entire territory to return Gill Jamieson to his home." Certainly, the massive effort to find Gill and his abductors did extend to all races and classes. The newspaper also remarked, "Public indignation [has been] roused to the highest pitch remembered in the history of the territory,"[98] which illustrated how Gill's kidnapping and murder were represented by the press as an unprecedented event in recent Hawai'i history.

As for Fukunaga, in an interview with two *Nippu Jiji* reporters following his arrest, he recounted his activities while the rest of Honolulu was looking for him.[99] The interview was arranged for the reporters by city attorney Davis, perhaps because he wanted Fukunaga's admission to killing Gill disseminated in the Japanese American community. Fukunaga related: "I stayed in town most of the time, walking in the streets and attending the movies. Usually I spent my time at the Central YMCA reading room. I spent my nights in my room in the Serene Apartments, although once in awhile I went out and talked with the boys and kept myself among the crowd." On Thursday night he visited a prostitution house and paid with one of the $5 bills from the ransom money, although it very likely cost him less than that.[100] Except for the latter, Fukunaga appeared to have been engaged pursuing his favorite leisure activities—reading and watching movies—seemingly oblivious to how his life would be changed forever in two days. He was alone as usual with no one he could tell that he had committed the horrific killing being reported in the newspapers and that everyone was talking about.

Friday, September 21: Last Visit

Three days after his crime, Fukunaga may have sensed that he would soon be caught, so he traveled to the plantation town of Waialua on the north shore of O'ahu because, as he said, he wanted to see his boyhood place. He probably realized that his visit was going to be his last to the site of much happier days in his life when he excelled as a student and enjoyed school. Indeed, his wandering in the town and spending some of the ransom payment led to his arrest the next day. Shortly after 9 A.M. Fukunaga went to a Japanese taxi stand in downtown Honolulu, paid the driver with a $5 bill from the ransom money, received his change, and settled in for the long ride.[101] Around 11:30 he appeared at the Sea View Inn in Waialua and ordered lunch from the waitress and paid with a dollar bill. While eating, he told her that he used to live in the town and had graduated from the grade school in 1925.

After finishing his lunch, Fukunaga left the café; about 12:30 he showed up at the OR&L (Oahu Railway and Land) train station and asked the station master, Robert Adams, when the next train to Honolulu would be departing.[102] After being told it would not be leaving until 2:59 P.M., he chatted with Adams for a short while, mentioning again that he had graduated from the local school, and inquired if his former teachers were still there. Fukunaga also asked Adams if he had heard anything new about the Jamieson murder and when the *Star-Bulletin* would be arriving. He then left for the school, hoping to see his teachers one last time.

Afterward, Fukunaga went to the Lunching Room of Yamada's Store and, after ordering pork chops and ice cream, conversed with Mrs. Yamada and her seventeen-year-old daughter. They noticed that he had a book about Herbert Hoover and a magazine with short stories in which he wrote with a fountain pen. Interviewed two days later about Fukunaga's visit to his store, Shigeki Yamada remarked, "Sure I remember this boy. He's stranger here—good looking boy. He talk about how Waialua has changed. . . . Tell us he used to go school here and ask us if we know Mrs. Churchill who used to be principal."[103] The Yamadas also recalled that while Fukunaga was having lunch, some Waialua youths came in and began talking about the Jamieson case. Fukunaga asked them, "What's the latest on the Jamieson murder?" and was told, "Nothing new." The teenagers then began discussing what they would do to the killer if they caught him, including tearing him limb from limb, a punishment with which Fukunaga was said to have agreed. He also asked the youths when the afternoon paper would be arriving, adding, "Why can't you get the newspapers out here quicker?"[104] Since he had been following the coverage of his crime in the papers, Fukunaga probably wanted to know if the police were closing in on him.

Fukunaga later returned to the train station, bought a first-class ticket for Honolulu, and left on the next train, reading a biography of Herbert Hoover on the long ride.[105] When the evening train arrived at Waialua with the *Star-Bulletin*, Adams, perhaps made suspicious by Fukunaga's questions, checked the serial number of the $5 bill with which he had paid for his ticket and found a match with one of the numbers listed in the paper (see below). Early the next morning, he went to the home of F. W. Carter, a special police officer, and informed him about Fukunaga being in Waialua and the matching $5 bill. They then called Sheriff Patrick Gleason in Honolulu, and the manhunt for Gill's killer became focused on Fukunaga.

After returning to Honolulu, that evening Fukunaga joined the other young men at the Serene Rooms, described in the press as a "modern, two-storey, balcony type tenement," in a card game for the first time.[106] One of them, Henry K. Sato, a nineteen-year-old Japanese American construction worker, commented about Fukunaga: "He was well dressed, quiet mannered, and I couldn't help but wonder what such a student was doing in a hotel like the Serene where mostly only working boys live. . . . We saw little of him. Once or twice during that time we heard him come in a little late at night."[107] Sato continued that the Serene residents usually played cards in the evening and that Friday night was the first time Fukunaga joined them. Fukunaga greeted him, "Hello, Sato," and he was surprised that Fukunaga, whom he described as a "pretty nice sort of boy," knew his name because Fukunaga had not spoken to him before. Sato related that he told Fukunaga how he thought the Jamieson crime had been committed and noted that Fukunaga replied merely "yes" or "no" without offering his own opinion. But when Sato remarked, "Gee, whoever did that must have had a lotta nerve, don't you think?" Fukunaga agreed, adding, "Whoever's behind this must have brains all right," perhaps complimenting himself on his letters to Frederick Jamieson and the *Star-Bulletin* in which he quoted Shakespeare.

The landlord at the Serene Rooms, K. Y. Leong, concurred with Sato's depiction of Fukunaga, who he said represented himself as a "school boy" and registered on September 14, four days before the killing.[108] Leong observed, "Fukunaga was a model guest. . . . He was quiet and unassuming and was always to be found with books, magazines or a newspaper under his arm. He read incessantly." Besides reading, Fukunaga also presented himself as a student by always dressing neatly in a shirt, tie, and trousers. Leong continued that Fukunaga occasionally joined their evening discussions of the Jamieson kidnapping and murder and heard all of them say what they would do to the perpetrator if they had the chance but rarely expressed his own view. Leong added that Fukunaga did not drink, smoke, or "seek the society of women;" in short, he was the typical Japanese good boy.

On Friday, Gill Jamieson's cremated remains were buried at Nuʻuanu Cemetery the day after his body was found.[109] In the services at the grave site, Rev. Philip Allen Swartz, pastor of Central Union Church, began by referring to Gill's short, innocent life: "We all thank Thee for this little life, for all its beauty and all the memories that are clustered about it." The newspapers described "the sorrowing forms of [Gill's] father and mother, quietly weeping. Massed in profusion about the burial place, thousands of flowers sent out their fragrance." Among those sending flowers to the Jamiesons was Fukunaga, together with a sympathy card, which he signed "The Three Kings."[110] In an interview soon after his capture, Fukunaga explained why he sent the flowers: "In doing this I took a risk; and I meant it. I sent the flowers because I knew from newspaper accounts how much the Jamieson family was suffering."[111] But he was also copying Leopold and Loeb, who sent flowers to their victim's family. Fukunaga may have signed the card with a fountain pen he purchased that morning with a $5 bill from the ransom payment since its serial number matched one of those from the ransom.[112] A female clerk at a downtown store where he bought the pen described him as "a young Japanese of the student type, slight of build and stature and rather good looking."

Besides floral offerings, the Jamiesons received radio messages of condolence from throughout the world, including New York, Boston, Washington, D.C., San Francisco, and many other cities, reflecting their prominence. Gill's death was even reported in his father's hometown in Kirriemuir, Scotland, which claimed him as a "Kirrie boy."[113] Another indication of the Jamiesons' stature in the community was that flags were flown at half-mast throughout Honolulu that day.[114] Businesses doing so included two of the Big Five companies, as well as Bishop Trust Co. and Hawaiian Trust Co., with the latter remaining closed.

Four more young Japanese American men were detained by the police on Friday: Charles Y. Miura, age twenty-six; Samuel K. Nakamura, nineteen; Paul F. Nishi, twenty-seven; and Hajime Ohta, twenty-two.[115] As a result of rumors about possible attempts to exact vigilante justice upon them and others in police custody, they were later taken to Oahu Prison, and two companies of the National Guard were on call should they be needed at the police station. Nine suspects previously picked up and interrogated by the police were discharged later in the day: M. Onyshi [*sic*], J. Nakagawa, Fukishi Fujishige, Masaru Shimota, Charles Nonaka, Saburo Nakasone, C. M. Yukumoto, Jack Kumamoto, and Candido Familada, the only non-Japanese.[116] None of the fifteen persons taken into custody by Friday was identified by principal Mary Winne or taxi driver Morizo Yoshioka as the person with whom they had interacted, so all were released late that day. After Harry Kaisan was detained, the police could have asked Winne and Yoshioka if they had seen him at Punahou, but the police were determined to have him convicted.

Concern about potential mob violence at the police station and the formation of the Vigilance Committee led the *Star-Bulletin* in one of its Friday editorials, "Let Us Have Law," to argue: "We are in the midst of a terrible tragedy—a calamity for this community, for the entire islands. The shock and bereavement in the Jamieson home is a shock and bereavement in every home. . . . No, citizens of Honolulu—this is no time to talk of violence. This is rather a time for every man and woman to line up squarely on the side of law and order."[117] While no vigilante violence occurred, one can question the extent to which the law was followed after Fukunaga's arrest the next day.

The *Star-Bulletin* published on its front page a twelve-by-fourteen-inch copy of the letter from "The Three Kings," which it had received the previous day.[118] Following disclosure of the letter claiming responsibility for Gill's murder, Haoles especially were terrified that they might be the next victim of "The Three Kings." Their fears were abetted by "sensational and spectacular rumors" spreading wildly about the receipt of letters and calls threatening prominent Haoles, including officials of the Mutual Telephone Co., where the Vigilance Committee had its first meeting, and John R. Galt, president of the Hawaiian Trust Co.[119] Galt was so concerned about the circulation of these false reports that he issued a public statement, which read in part: "New rumors are flying around the town on this subject every few minutes. I received a telephone call that . . . the telephone company had intercepted a call last night threatening that more lives were to be taken. . . . The people of Honolulu appear to be losing their heads, common sense, and good judgment in this situation." City attorney Charles Davis joined Galt in decrying the widespread dissemination of false stories, which he described "as prevalent now in Honolulu like an epidemic." These rumors reflected the tense racial climate and the heightened fear among many Haoles that they could be subject to anti-Haole violence.

Also on Friday, the *Star-Bulletin* printed a listing of the serial numbers of the eight hundred $5 bills that were paid as $4,000 in ransom by Frederick Jamieson.[120] The list of numbers was about two feet in length and nine inches, or eight columns, in width, and readers were asked to "Clip It Out! Watch It!" The caption stated, "Every merchant, operator of a service station or any other person who may receive any of the bills listed below is requested to check the serial number and to contact Judge Heen, Sheriff Gleason or *Star-Bulletin*."

Besides Heen, territorial senator Lawrence M. Judd, who would be appointed the governor of Hawai'i the following year, took a very active role in the Jamieson investigation.[121] The *Star-Bulletin* observed that Judd was seated at Sheriff Gleason's desk at the police station and that all inquiries and incoming information for the sheriff were being received by Judd or his assistants. An anonymous source was quoted in the article: "Lawrence Judd is handling it right now, or at least he's . . . receiving all callers, giving out any information about this kidnapping case that doesn't come out of Judge Heen's office, [while] denying that he issues any orders." Judd minimized his activities, contending, "We are here to give the sheriff and his staff assistance that they greatly need. . . . If a man tried to run this department and handle the crowd at the same time, he would go crazy in 24 hours."[122] As noted above, another private individual who had a major role in the investigation was Sam Robley, who was said by the *Star-Bulletin* to be in charge of the detective bureau while chief of detectives McIntosh was out of the office. Perhaps because of the perceived ineffectiveness of the police, the law office of Heen & Godbold continued as the command center for the investigation.

In the Japanese American community, the Japanese Chamber of Commerce expressed its sympathy to the Jamieson family and its willingness to assist in finding the persons who killed their son.[123] After the Honolulu Chamber of Commerce began its $20,000 community reward fund, it sent a letter to the "Oriental chambers," including the Japanese and Chinese chambers of commerce, requesting their assistance in soliciting contributions from their respective communities. The officers of the Japanese chamber met on Friday to discuss a contribution to the reward fund, while the Hawaiian Japanese Civic Association donated $200.[124] Motivated by a sincere sense of sympathy for the Jamieson family, Japanese Americans nevertheless also knew that if they acted otherwise, they would elicit scorn and criticism from other groups.

The *Star-Bulletin* began printing a daily list of contributors to the reward fund.[125] At the top of the list of donors were the Big Five companies, which each donated $1,000; other large contributors included Hawaiian Electric Co. ($500) and Oahu Railway & Land Co. ($500). Individuals gave as little as $1, and some had "A&B" (one of the Big Five companies) after their name. At $23,558, the fund had exceeded its initial goal of $20,000 about nine hours after Gill's body was found[126] and by Friday had grown to nearly $28,000, indicative of widespread concern about the killing.[127] The list of donors included many names of Japanese individuals, who made small contributions from $1 to $10, and of organizations, such as the Young Men's Buddhist Association, which gave $100.

As for the Japanese newspapers, in an editorial, "A Terrible Menace," the *Hawaii Hochi* made no reference to the suspects being Japanese and emphasized the growing crime rate in Honolulu, which the *Star-Bulletin* also did.[128] The editorial cited factors that directly affected the increase in crime, including "official laxity, community responsibility, economic causes, criminal literature, [and] degenerate movies. . . . These things we must take into consideration, and we must some day ask ourselves whether the society we have set up is not somewhat to blame for the abnormal conditions it produces," a position the paper would repeat at the end of the Fukunaga case in 1929. Like the Honolulu dailies and probably most city residents, the *Hochi* assumed that the Jamieson murder was committed by young criminals, given that "Honolulu is over-run with gansters [*sic*] and hoodlums and vicious degenerates." Thus, everyone in the city was absolutely shocked the next day when the confessed killer of Gill Jamieson was caught and turned out to be a mild-mannered and well-dressed teenager who could quote Shakespeare from memory.

3. Capture, Confession, and Court

After Myles Fukunaga was caught on Saturday, the police searched his room at the Serene hotel and found several torn sheets of paper with handwriting on them in a wastebasket. Pieced together, one of the sheets was titled "Schedule of Undertaking Okay!" and appears to be a detailed plan for the kidnapping of Gill Jamieson but not necessarily his killing.[1] In his "An Open Letter to Governor Wallace R. Farrington on Fukunaga's Insanity," University of Hawai'i professor Lockwood Myrick Jr. contended that Fukunaga wrote the schedule the night before he abducted Gill and immediately after he wrote the ransom letter to the boy's father because specific persons, dates, and places are mentioned.[2] Highly significant is that Fukunaga wrote on the back of the sheet, "No intent to kill." At his trial, his attorney Eugene Beebe would emphasize that it indicated that the killing, in contrast to the kidnapping, was not premeditated. However, Myrick argued that Fukunaga "subconsciously at least, . . . intended to kill from the beginning."[3]

This chapter discusses the next four days, from Saturday through Tuesday in the rapidly unfolding case, capturing the accelerated pace with which it proceeded through the criminal justice system after Fukunaga was apprehended. He immediately admitted to the police that he had kidnapped and killed Gill Jamieson, and his professions of guilt appeared several hours later in extra editions of both the *Star-Bulletin* and *Advertiser*, which referred to him as "the slayer" of Gill. Fukunaga was indicted and arraigned in court on Monday, and the next day his court-appointed attorneys proposed to the presiding judge that the trial begin the following Monday, which gave them less than a week to prepare their defense. For Fukunaga, justice delayed would not necessarily have meant justice denied. During those two days, the first racial references to the Fukunaga case (aside from how he and the initial suspects were identified as Japanese) appeared in the press, further demonstrating how Fukunaga was being raced to death, according to both meanings of race as used here.

Saturday, September 22: Arrest and Confession

"JAMIESON MURDERER CONFESSES: 'I Am Guilty!' Declares Youth in Confession" blared the bold headlines of the Saturday second extra edition of the *Honolulu Advertiser*. After being captured that afternoon, four days after his crime, Fukunaga freely admitted killing Gill during a police interrogation just hours before the *Advertiser* featured the confession. Fukunaga was apprehended by the police at the intersection of Beretania and Fort Streets in downtown Honolulu at about 4:30 P.M.[4] He was on his way to the nearby family home at 615 South Beretania Street, where he planned to confess to his mother and then turn himself in to the police. He spent the last free day of his life engaged in his favorite pursuits—reading at the Central YMCA and watching a movie at the Empire Theatre. He also went to a burlesque show in the afternoon and then dined at a cafe before heading home for the last time.[5]

Early that morning the police had begun to focus on Fukunaga as their primary suspect after receiving a telephone call from Waialua.[6] Chief of detectives John McIntosh sent detective John Troche, accompanied by Fred Makino, possibly as an interpreter, to Waialua, where some of Fukunaga's former schoolmates provided them with his name and address in Honolulu. With this information, Troche returned to the city and with McIntosh and another detective, Thomas St. John, went to the Fukunaga home; not finding him, they searched his room. They found more incriminating evidence of Fukunaga's involvement in the crime, including a map of the Punahou School campus.

St. John was instructed to wait at the house in case Fukunaga appeared. Private detective Ned Chillingworth of the Scharsch Detective Agency joined him there.[7] Due to the police and others showing up at the cottage, a crowd of curious onlookers gathered in front, and St. John realized that Fukunaga was unlikely to return once he saw so many people outside. So he asked Fukunaga's parents if one of them would accompany the police to look for their son, but they both declined. After some urging, the father, Jusuke, consented to one of their daughters going with them in a search of the city by car. The father initially hesitated because he was afraid that his daughter would be hurt if the mob in the streets attacked the police car should his son be captured.[8] Assured that the police would protect her, he instructed his twelve-year-old daughter Harue to go with St. John and Chillingworth and assist them in finding her brother. She directed their driver, Alfred Sing Luke, manager of the Scharsch Detective Agency,[9] to Fukunaga's favorite reading places—the public library, the Central YMCA, and the Nu'uanu YMCA—but she did not see him. Harue next suggested that they try the other venues frequented by her brother—movie theaters—so they drove by the Princess Theatre on Fort Street as the moviegoers were coming out, but he was not among them. Luke then turned onto Beretania Street, where the detectives spotted someone matching Fukunaga's description reading a newspaper. They asked Harue if that was her brother; she at first hesitated, then said "That's him." Fukunaga was standing on the corner, neatly dressed as usual in a shirt and necktie, waiting for a street car to take him home where he planned to tell his parents that he was the person responsible for the heinous murder everyone was talking about. But his plans were unexpectedly interrupted.

St. John and Chillingworth leaped from the car, took hold of Fukunaga and pushed him in, asking "Is your name Fukunaga? Do you know what we want you for?"[10] Fukunaga was reported to have replied, "Yes, I'll tell you the truth. I was on my way home to confess to my mother. I'm sorry. I'm a bad, bad boy."[11] Its horn blasting, the detectives' car sped away to the nearby police station and, as the car came to a screeching stop, the crowd surged forward, sensing that Gill's captured killer was inside. "Look out! The mob will get him," shouted St. John. Hearing the detective, Fukunaga allegedly said, "Let them get me. I don't care. I'm ready to pay the penalty." He was rushed into the police station and taken up to detective McIntosh's office as doors slammed shut behind them, and Fukunaga shortly began to give "one of the weirdest confessions ever made by a criminal." Soon afterward, a police officer, "white-faced and tight lipped," came out and announced to the small group of reporters who were able to enter the police station, "He's confessed to everything. It was a one man job," information they would soon write up for extra editions of Saturday's newspapers. Meanwhile, McIntosh left for Fukunaga's room at the Serene Rooms, where he found all but $90 of the ransom payment of $4,000 in a suitcase under his bed. After being questioned, Fukunaga was taken at 6:30 P.M. from the police station through the adjacent *Hawaii Hochi* building to avoid the immense crowd packing the streets and driven to Oahu Prison for his safety in case the mob sought to exact vigilante justice.[12]

Shortly after Fukunaga was taken to the police station, the word spread quickly that the killer of the Jamieson boy had been caught, and an estimated twenty thousand persons soon converged on the station.[13] Described as "milling, highly excited, and increasing minute by minute," the throng was held back by the police, including all available officers who were called to duty, three companies of the Hawaii National Guard armed with fixed bayonets, and ROTC units from several schools. In addition, Fire Chief W. W. Blaisdell sent two fire trucks, a hose wagon, and thirty men to the station to help maintain order. The firemen attached six water hoses and were ready to douse the crowd should they attempt to storm the police station and seize Fukunaga. Although few threats of violence were made, the excitability of the mob led city officials to fear violence might erupt. To keep the crowd back, police stretched ropes across Merchant Street and, as more police arrived, Sheriff Patrick Gleason ordered the crowd pushed farther back another block. As all the streets near the police station filled with people, city attorney Charles Davis and Sheriff Gleason came out and requested that they disperse and "let the law take its course." Davis's full statement to the crowd appeared on the front page of the Sunday *Advertiser* the next day.[14] It announced that "the guilty person is in custody. He has made a full and complete confession, covering every minute detail of his dastardly deed. He has admitted his sanity—that he knew fully that what he did was wrong. He alone was implicated in this crime—his own voluntary admission. Justice will be swift and speedy." Davis's brief statement is noteworthy in several respects. It pronounces Fukunaga guilty before he went on trial, invokes a legal definition of sanity in noting that Fukunaga said he knew "what he did was wrong," and promises "swift and speedy" justice.

Davis announced later that evening that the territorial grand jury had been called to convene on Monday at 1:30 P.M.[15] The Sunday *Advertiser* article reporting this development began, "As an earnest [*sic*] that there will be no delay in bringing to trial the man who *murdered* ten-year-old George Gill Jamieson" (emphasis in original), another indication that Fukunaga would be raced to a guilty verdict and death sentence. Yet another clear sign on Saturday evening of the intention to have Fukunaga quickly executed came from deputy city attorney Francis Brooks, who would prosecute the murder case with Davis.[16] After it was pointed out that in his confession Fukunaga gave his age as nineteen and so was a minor according to Hawai'i law, Brooks told the press that the circuit court had jurisdiction in any case in which the defendant is older than fourteen. He added, "In the case of a vicious crime as this is, . . . Fukunaga is not only subject to the death penalty but will in all probability receive it in short order." That was indeed the case, at least in terms of being sentenced to death.

The Sunday *Advertiser* carried an article by one of its reporters, Thornton Hardy, which claimed to be "the substance of Miles [*sic*] Yutaka Fukunaga's confession, as dictated from memory last night by Judge William H. Heen."[17] However, the article included several significant factual errors, which perhaps were due to Heen's faulty memory, Hardy's misunderstanding of Heen's statements, or Heen's unintentionally making incorrect remarks to him. The hasty publication of these false statements, without verifying their accuracy by speaking to others who were present during Fukunaga's questioning, contributed to the rush to put Fukunaga on trial toward his conviction and execution. According to Heen, as quoted by Hardy, Fukunaga said during his interrogation, "They [his parents] rented an apartment in Beretania street from the Heen estate. The Hawaiian Trust company was agent for the estate and collected the rents. My parents were poor. They could not meet the rent. . . . Early this year they were evicted." The latter statement is not true; the Fukunaga family was not evicted for not paying their rent for May, which they did in June when they paid the rent for that month at the same time. Furthermore, in the official transcript of Fukunaga's confession (see below), he does not state that his family was evicted.[18] The assertion, which Hardy attributed to Heen, that the Fukunagas were forced to vacate their home provides a seeming motive for Fukunaga to seek revenge against Hawaiian Trust by killing the young son of its vice president.

Accordingly, Fukunaga is then quoted as saying, "My thought was to avenge that shame [of being evicted]. . . . This idea of avenging my parents' shame I formed last March. Since then until this month I have been turning it over in my mind."[19] However, according to the transcript of his confession, Fukunaga said the rent collector came to their home after they did not pay rent for April and May.[20] As is evident above, Fukunaga's remarks were written in quotes as though they were his actual words rather than those of Heen based on what he could remember from the long questioning.

According to Heen as cited by Hardy, Fukunaga maintained that his primary motive for committing his crime was "revenge, impersonal revenge against the Hawaiian Trust company, and desire to send back my poor parents to Japan."[21] In the transcript of his confession, Fukunaga gave the latter reason as his principal motivation, although he also did mention developing a "hatred" for the Hawaiian Trust Co.[22] But imparting a primarily sinister motive to Fukunaga—revenge—as opposed to trying to help his parents return to Japan, contributed to portraying him as an especially depraved person who deserved the death penalty. Heen also asserted that it did not appear Fukunaga had been assisting his parents much with his earnings, perhaps to depict him as primarily driven by a desire to obtain money for himself. However, he gave all but $5 of his $40 in wages each month to his parents when he was working at Queen's Hospital.[23] Beyond the inaccuracy of Heen's and Hardy's reporting of what Fukunaga said during his interrogation is the racial injustice of publication of his alleged statements by the press well in advance of his trial. All of the members of the jury that convicted Fukunaga admitted during jury selection that they had read newspaper accounts of the case, including his admission of guilt. As such, they can hardly be said to have judged him with open and impartial minds.

Following his arrest, Fukunaga's parents were interviewed that same night through an interpreter at their home "near Henry Chang's store" by reporters from both of the Honolulu dailies.[24] The Fukunaga family was described as gathered at the dining table, the mother crying, the father "pale and aghast," their six children surrounding them, the entire family devastated by the news of Myles's confession to the Jamieson murder. Dressed in a frayed cotton kimono, his father Jusuke was dumbfounded by his son's alleged crime: "With such a mild nature, I can hardly believe that he could have done such a thing. Ordinarily he is so quiet, almost timid. He never did anything rough." He continued that Myles used to come home every weekend to pick up his clothes, which his mother washed for him, so they were expecting him that Saturday evening. Asked about his son's religion, the father responded that Myles did not belong to any church and that he could not recall him attending any church in Honolulu, adding "to him it seemed there was no Christianity or Buddhism." The question about Fukunaga's religion probably was prompted by his numerous religious references in his letters demanding the ransom and to the *Star-Bulletin*. Confirming Fukunaga's lonely life, his father remarked that he did not know of any close friends Myles had. His father did not mention that Myles was the *chonan*, or the eldest son in the family, and thus had the greatest obligation to assist his parents with the family expenses, which he fulfilled by giving them almost all of his monthly wages and foregoing his high school education.

Fukunaga's parents did not see their son until the following Friday in an emotional meeting at Oahu Prison.[25] As reported by the *Nippu Jiji*, when they visited him, Fukunaga was lying on a cot in his cell; he glanced at them, then tears welled up in his eyes and his head dropped. During their entire twenty-minute meeting, he never once looked up at his parents, who were also crying profusely. His father rebuked him for his actions: "I have been telling you all along not to do anything wrong. Why did you do this horrible thing?" His son replied, "I was wrong—wrong, and I regret from the bottom of my heart." No other words came from him, only crying. "You may have done it for reasons of filial piety, but your act did not serve your purpose," his father told him. He continued, "Ours is a family that produced a great criminal, but people are showing deep sympathy." The father ended, "I don't know how this thing is going to turn out. But in case you are sentenced to death, don't think any more about this world. Leave your body and soul entirely up to God and think in such a way that you can go to Him." Fukunaga did follow his father's advice by becoming a devout Catholic soon after receiving the death sentence.

After they learned that their fellow tenant at the Serene Rooms had confessed to the Jamieson murder, the residents cursed him that night, greatly upset about their lost opportunity to collect the reward money. "'Why, the triple distilled, five-starred umpty ump,' or words to that effect," was what one of them was reported to have said.[26] He added, "Here was I talking to him. And there was he with $20,000 on his head and $4,000 cash under his bed. Auwe!" The article continued, "You could hear that lament in Hawaiian, Japanese or Chinese style." The landlord, K. Y. Leong, wailed, "Look!" as he showed his special deputy's badge: "I'm a policeman and he's living right under the same roof with me. All the time he's living here, I'm hunting for him under bridges, in bushes, out Waikīkī, clear to Koko Head, at Waialua, night and day. We even talk about it. 'Too bad,' he [Fukunaga] say, 'they couldn't get that boy.' Well, they get him. But too bad, yes." It may have been too bad for Fukunaga, but it was far worse for Gill Jamieson.

As for the Saturday editorials in the newspapers, the *Star-Bulletin*'s "Honolulu's Peril," written before Fukunaga's apprehension, emphasized the pressing need "to halt the growth of crookdom" in the city, which bred the criminals responsible for Gill's murder.[27] The paper earnestly intoned, "Every citizen of Honolulu knows of the existence here of an underworld. . . . The stratum composed of liquor-runners, gambling 'kings,' fixers and politico-criminal go-betweens is more than a disquieting phenomenon; it represents a force that must be got under control before it wrecks us." The ineffectiveness of the Honolulu Police Department was continually raised as a critical problem as the kidnapping and homicide case developed.

In its editorial "Eradicate the Gangsters," the *Nippu Jiji* also referred to the involvement of criminals in the Jamieson killing: "The Japanese have been especially gloomy . . . because the claim that Japanese gangsters are involved in the crime has considerable foundation."[28] It observed that previously crime victims "have been mainly Orientals, especially Japanese, and consequently they have not attracted much attention. But this time the victim is the offspring of a wealthy resident of the so-called 'Silk Stocking' district [Mānoa]. And because of the boldness, brutality and mainland-like method with which the crime was committed, the entire community has been stirred up." No doubt, the tremendous community response to Gill's murder was because he was from a rich Haole, rather than a poor Japanese, family.

As noted above, an official version of Fukunaga's interrogation by the police was produced and submitted as evidence at his trial. I review it below because it absolutely sealed his fate.

The Confession

In a lengthy statement, apparently given voluntarily, Fukunaga admitted kidnapping and killing Gill, explained how the boy came to be his victim, and gave his reasons for his crime. He also explicitly addressed what was arguably the major issue at his trial—whether he was legally sane or insane when he committed his horrible misdeed. While key points from his statement indicating Fukunaga's culpability were printed by the *Star-Bulletin* the same night it was made, the "confession," as it was called by the press and prosecution, was published in its entirety on the first day of his trial. Written in question-and-answer format, most of the former were from city attorney Charles Davis and others later by city medical examiner Dr. Robert Faus.

The confession begins, "This is the statement of Yutaka Fukunaga taken at the police station at 5:14 P.M., September 22, 1928, in the presence of . . .," and goes on to list the names of nine persons.[29] They include Davis, first deputy city attorney Francis Brooks, detective John McIntosh, J. W. Brining (a court stenographer), attorney William Heen, his law partner Norman Godbold, city deputy attorney James Jarrett, someone named Kam Kwai, and Zena Mossman, who took shorthand notes of the interrogation and typed them up as its official transcription. Notably absent among those listed as present is Faus, who testified at Fukunaga's trial he arrived at 5:30 P.M. after the questioning had started.

The thirty-nine-year-old Davis, who grew up in Hawai'i and graduated from Punahou School and Stanford Law School, began the interrogation by asking Fukunaga for his full name. He replied it was "Yutaka Fukunaga," but "some boys call me Myles," although like many nisei, he probably chose his "American" name himself.[30] Davis continued with some general background questions regarding Fukunaga's birthdate, birthplace, education, and when he graduated from Waialua School. After responding "1925" to the last query, Fukunaga inexplicably added, "The money is under the bed in a valise." He was referring to the remaining ransom payment he had collected from Frederick Jamieson, which was in a suitcase in his room at the Serene Rooms. However, unlike Fukunaga, Davis was in no hurry to have him reveal other incriminating evidence of his responsibility for Gill's death, so he instead asked Fukunaga what he did after graduating from Waialua School. He said he worked with his father picking and planting pineapple near Wahiawa during the summer harvesting season. Fukunaga also related that his most recent employment was at the Seaside Hotel in Waikīkī and that his first job in Honolulu after his family moved there in 1925 was at Queen's Hospital, where he worked as an "elevator boy," "floor boy," and "office boy." Davis next asked how much rent they pay and to whom, and he answered ominously "the Hawaiian Trust Co."

At this point the interrogation shifted to the crime itself. Davis queried if Fukunaga knew Frederick Jamieson; after he said he did not, the city attorney continued, "You want to tell us about this, don't you?" and Fukunaga concurred, "Everything, yes, the truth."[31] So Davis gave Fukunaga the opportunity to reveal everything about his crime by encouraging him, "Just tell us how you planned this thing, and why you did it. It's a long story I know." Fukunaga willingly complied because, as he explained, he wanted to end his unhappy life.

Motives

Fukunaga began his damaging narrative about why and how he planned the abduction and killing of Gill by first discussing his failed suicide attempts in April. He revealed that his desire for death by execution was one of his primary motives for murdering the boy, since he had been unable to kill himself. He related, "Back in, I don't know exactly what month [March], I quit the hospital. The reason why I quit was . . . I wanted to die, commit suicide. I got the poison from the hospital. . . . One night I took the poison. Somehow it didn't work."[32] He continued that his parents found him the next morning in a closet with a rope tied around his neck because he tried to choke himself after the poison failed, and they called a doctor. Asked why he tried to kill himself, Fukunaga replied, "Because I hated life. Everywhere, especially in the hospital, I saw suffering about me. . . . I come from a poor family. My life is nothing but worries and sufferings and chagrin." Overcome with emotion talking about his unhappy life, he requested they question him because he could not continue. So Davis inquired about the financial problems his family had, and Fukunaga responded, "Yes, always we have. That's why we move from Kauai to Haleiwa. Then we came to town to see better place to live. We just barely got along."[33] In his opening statement at Fukunaga's trial, Davis would argue that he kidnapped and murdered Gill primarily to obtain money for himself because of the impoverished state of the Fukunaga family. But first he asked him about seeing the suffering at the hospital, and Fukunaga answered, "I didn't like the work, but I had to stick it out because my parents are poor, I have to help them. They could not send me to school. That was my biggest disappointment. I wanted to study."[34] Adding to his disappointment was his knowledge that he had been a bright student who had excelled in and enjoyed school. Living in downtown Honolulu, Fukunaga could have easily walked to McKinley High School or even taken the street car, but the poverty of his family meant that was not to be and he had to work instead.

Another principal reason that Fukunaga gave for his crime was he wanted to obtain money to give to his parents so they could return to Japan, which they wanted to do because of their financial struggles in Hawai'i. Questioned when did he first think about committing his crime, he said, "After my unsuccessful attempt to commit suicide. I thought, instead of killing myself, I wanted to leave some money for my mother."[35] Toward the end of the interrogation, Fukunaga returned to this topic: "The first thought was to give the money to my parents so that they would go to Japan. . . . We were so poor, we could not afford."[36] Asked if he believed that committing a crime would be an easy way to have himself killed, Fukunaga answered, "Yes, this matter will have a double purpose. I will die with false pretense." He related that his plans were, once he got the $10,000 ransom, to go to California, stay there a while, and then return to Honolulu and tell his parents he had made some money and send them to Japan.[37] Presumably, he would then confess to the killing and have himself executed.

The third and final reason Fukunaga gave for his crime was a desire for revenge against the Hawaiian Trust Co., which explains why Gill became his victim. Davis inquired how he happened to select Gill. Fukunaga's bitter response was, "We had so many troubles, and it came to a climax when the collector came and demanded money right away. . . . I don't blame him because it is his duty to get money. From that day I had a hatred for the Hawaiian Trust Co. A rich company like that could not wait for just a mere $20 sum."[38] Fukunaga had earlier described the encounter with the rent collector, who demanded payment from his mother, but she said "we haven't got the money. . . . My mother could not speak English. I spoke to the collector. He said he wanted money right away, or he would chase us out of the house. I told him how can we pay when we haven't got the money. Can't you wait? After he left, my mother broke down and cried because all those weeks we have not got enough money. We couldn't pay the doctor fees [for his suicide attempts]. I think it was all because of me, I gave trouble to my parents, making sick."[39] While near the end of the questioning Fukunaga referred to his hatred of the Hawaiian Trust Co. as "little," he also made it clear that his animosity was directed toward the company and not Frederick Jamieson or his son. As he related, "Personally, I have nothing against Mr. Jamieson." Asked why, then, did he have his hatred for Hawaiian Trust, he replied, "Because of the trouble about the rent money. It is hard when you are poor, you know."[40] Significantly, Fukunaga referred to the problem with the rent money and not the collector, so Gill became a proxy for his father's company. While Davis would argue at the trial that Fukunaga kidnapped and murdered Gill in order to extort money, this argument does not explain why the young son of a Hawaiian Trust Co. vice president was selected as his victim since any rich person could have served that purpose.

Sane or Insane

While Fukunaga admitted killing Gill, his confession did not automatically mean that he was guilty of murder because he still could have been found not guilty by reason of insanity. At his trial, the prosecution contended that Fukunaga was legally sane because he could distinguish between right and wrong when he abducted and murdered Gill. Fukunaga made the first mention of his sanity when he was questioned about a line from a poem. Fukunaga began, "I took my education seriously. I was handicapped. I wanted education so very much."[41] He then spontaneously uttered, "I hope you are getting this. I am not crazy. I am sane as ever." Later during his questioning, Fukunaga directly addressed the sanity issue again. After he stated, "Before I planned this, I was always a good boy," Faus inquired, "Did something happen in your head that made you bad?" Fukunaga answered, "If committing a crime is bad, then I was bad. I know what is right and wrong," without being asked if he knew the difference.[42] He probably had learned the legal definition of sanity from reading about the Hickman case. Faus later queried if Fukunaga was insane or sane, and he responded confidently, "I am sane." So Faus turned to the definition of sanity according to the law, inquiring if Fukunaga knew the difference between right and wrong. Fukunaga replied yes and also to the next question, whether he knew that he was doing right or wrong when he was planning his crime. Seeking evidence of intent, which was required for first-degree murder, Faus then asked if he deliberately did the killing, and Fukunaga obliged, answering he did. He also expressed remorse for killing Gill, which could be interpreted as demonstrating that he knew what he did was wrong. Asked how he felt about killing Gill, Fukunaga responded, "I feel sorry that I have done this thing" and added that he felt sorry for Gill's parents after reading in the newspapers about their sorrow.[43]

Fukunaga provided damning evidence that his crime was premeditated by asserting numerous times that he had planned it, foreclosing the possibility that he might be convicted of second-degree murder or manslaughter. As he related, "I went to the Seaside Hotel. I planned and planned. . . . I came upon this cave [clearing] in the bushes, and here's a good place where I could carry on my work, I thought. Then from that day on I planned to . . ."[44] He was interrupted, "What did you plan?" His answer was: "I planned to get money. I didn't think about the kidnapping case until I went to the Library of Hawaii. I saw about the Leopold and Loeb case. . . . That case I studied. The ransom letter was taken from that same letter as the boys. . . . My first plan was to get a rich man down the Hawaiian Trust Co." Frederick Jamieson became that rich man because Fukunaga claimed that he knew the president of Hawaiian Trust, John R. Galt, having met him when Fukunaga was working at Queen's Hospital.[45] "I thought for next, vice president, Mr. Jamieson," he explained; "You see the problem was hard. I didn't know whether he has a son or what." Fukunaga needed a young boy as his victim because Leopold and Loeb had kidnapped and murdered a fourteen-year-old.

Despite this and many other references to planning his crime, Fukunaga only learned that Frederick Jamieson had a young son a few hours before he abducted Gill, when he spoke to Lulu Jamieson. Asked about the letter sent to Jamieson informing him that his son had been kidnapped, Fukunaga revealed that he wrote it the night before.[46] When he spoke to Gill's mother, he pretended to be from the Board of Health, needing "to straighten out some statistics." Fukunaga continued: "I asked her how many children she had. She answered one. What's his name, please? George Gill Jamieson. How old was he? Ten. Is he going to school? Yes, he is going to Punahou School."[47] If they had a daughter or if Gill had been older, perhaps the Jamiesons would not have lost their only son hours later, and Fukunaga would have had to move on to the next Hawaiian Trust executive. His emotional reaction to Lulu Jamieson's information is indicative of his bizarre mentality: "I thanked her. I was so happy luck came to me. I was so excited. I almost go out of the cafeteria and run out into some action."[48] At least at this moment, Fukunaga did not seem to know the difference between right and wrong.

Fukunaga then phoned Punahou Academy and told the principal, Mary Winne, that he was calling from a hospital, and they would be sending an attendant to pick up the Jamieson boy to be with his injured mother.[49] The idea for this ruse to abduct Gill came to Fukunaga from reading newspaper accounts of the highly publicized Hickman kidnapping and murder case in Los Angeles earlier in the year. Dressed in a white coat so that he looked like a hospital orderly, Fukunaga next went to a taxi stand in downtown

Honolulu and asked to be driven to Punahou. Gill was waiting for him in the principal's office, clutching a book he had borrowed from the library that he planned to read to his mother. On the way to Waikīkī, Fukunaga said he "kept up conversation. I asked the boy all kinds of questions. Only he answered me yes and yes. Purposely I bought some candy and gave him. He didn't eat the candy. He seemed to be so afraid."[50] With very good reason, as it turned out.

Fukunaga claimed that his original plan was just to kidnap Gill but not to kill him, a point emphasized by one of his attorneys at his trial. However, when questioned if he planned to kill Gill from the beginning, Fukunaga admitted, "Well to tell you the truth, I intended to kill him because you see, in all kidnapping cases, it won't work."[51] He explained, "I worked alone in this case, and it was hard to do. . . . If I kill the boy, it would be easier to carry out the other plans. To send the kidnap letter, I have to go downtown."[52] So rather than tie up Gill and leave him as a hostage, he wasted no time in killing him.

During Fukunaga's trial, his attorneys raised a significant issue concerning his confession, whether Fukunaga had given it voluntarily and without coercion or inducement. At one point during the interrogation, by which time Fukunaga had admitted killing Gill, Davis asked, "Are you telling this willingly, voluntarily and not against your wishes," and Fukunaga replied, "Yes, I know it's all up, that's why."[53] Conceding his guilt was very consistent with Fukunaga's death wish in killing Gill, so it is hardly surprising that he would speak openly about his crime. The confession also indicates that he planned to turn himself in to the police on the same day of his capture after first going home to tell his mother what he had done.[54]

Poetry Recital

Fukunaga's confession reveals much about his intellect and his view of his intellect. When Davis requested that Fukunaga recite poems and Shakespeare, which were part of the written evidence against him, he did so from memory, something he did while working at Queen's Hospital, according to his former co-workers. Asked what he wrote on a playing card left at the crime scene, Fukunaga responded that he wrote a poem by Walt Whitman, adding that he "used to be studious, and [he] used to remember [his] poems."[55] Requested to recite it, Fukunaga willingly obliged, "Oh heart!/Oh the bleeding drops of red/Herein lies the body of an innocent lad/So cold and dead," although the third line, which obviously was a reference to Gill, was his own. Asked to narrate the poem on another card, Fukunaga began,

"If you can tell me the first word, something about forgive us," but then he remembered: "The fates shall decide when we shall pay for this/But oh God, forgive us." By reciting these poems, Fukunaga confirmed that he was the person who had written them on the playing cards found at the crime scene.

Since the ransom letter included lines from *Macbeth*, Davis queried if Fukunaga had ever read the play at school. He said he had not but got a copy from a magazine at the public library.[56] He was then asked about some writing on a piece of cardboard covering Gill's face: "How about that 'tomorrow and tomorrow,' do you know that?" "That's from Shakespeare I suppose," he responded; "Yes, I can recite that," which he then repeated from memory. Davis next turned to another poem that was left in Gill's hand, "Immortality," which Fukunaga said he clipped from another magazine at the library. Requested to deliver it, he first said, "I used to sing that to the tune of 'There's a Silver Lining through the Dark Clouds Shining.' The tune fits that verse, you know."[57] Fukunaga then proceeded as with his previous recitations, displaying his impressive memory: "There is no death . . ." The poem was obviously intended for the just-departed Gill.

The confession also reveals Fukunaga's view of his intellectual ability, for which he had a high regard. About the poem "Immortality," he commented that he wanted to show that a college student was responsible for the crime rather than a teenager like himself.[58] In committing his misdeed, Fukunaga wanted people to think that he was educated beyond his eighth grade schooling—not to deceive them but to impress them. Asked later where he got the idea of "forlorn walking shadows in the great beyond," which appeared in his letter to the *Star-Bulletin*, Fukunaga explained that he read all kinds of books, and that is from where the idea came.[59] Questioned if those phrases meant anything to him, he remarked, "Those sentences look rather smart" because they made him look rather smart. Thus, a possible reason why he copied Leopold and Loeb in his own crime was because they were brilliant students, and Fukunaga wanted to be viewed in the same way.

The confession ends very strangely with Fukunaga being asked if he knew a "Jimmy Ohta," who probably was Hajime Ohta, one of the first suspects picked up by the police. Fukunaga's transcribed response was: "I have few friends in Honolulu. I am a lonesome boy. Books are my only friends. I never can make friends easily. . . . I addressed that envelop [*sic*] to The Star-Bulletin any old way. I took up penmanship. I know how to write. I went to the Serene hotel September 1."[60] This very disjointed statement at the end of the lengthy interrogation is very likely based on what the stenographer could remember of what Fukunaga said at different times while being questioned rather than what he actually stated at the end. In objecting to the admission of the transcript of the interrogation as evidence at Fukunaga's trial, one of his attorneys emphasized this difference in the content of the confession, between what was transcribed and what Fukunaga said.

Sunday, September 23: Another Admission

As though his confession admitting his kidnapping and killing of Gill Jamieson was not sufficient for the prosecution, Fukunaga was questioned again the next day at Oahu Prison. Those present included Francis Brooks, William Heen, both of whom were at the interrogation the previous evening, two newspaper reporters, and a stenographer.[61] A graduate of Harvard Law School, the sixty-two-year-old Brooks, who had practiced law in Shanghai and Bangkok from 1904 to 1920, was one of the defense attorneys for the Japanese Federation of Labor officials in their conspiracy trial in 1922.[62] The two reporters were Thornton Hardy of the *Advertiser* and E. P. White of the *Star-Bulletin*, who both wrote articles about the interview that appeared the next day in their respective papers. The interview was printed in the *Advertiser* in question-and-answer format, presumably as it was recorded by the stenographer, and is much shorter than Fukunaga's confession.[63] The *Advertiser* article begins, "Myles Fukunaga, who murdered 10-year-old Gill Jamieson a week ago tomorrow . . .," even before he had been arraigned in court.[64] Like his confession, the interview includes highly damaging statements wherein Fukunaga professes his guilt a week before jury selection would begin for his trial, which prospective jurors easily could have read or learned about. The questions Fukunaga received came primarily from Brooks and Heen. Many of them had been asked the previous evening, especially about the planning of the crime, but Fukunaga provided new information about his motives for it. However, the prosecution did not submit this second interrogation as evidence at his trial, perhaps because they believed that they did not need it.

Brooks began the interview by inquiring, "Did you sleep well last night, Myles?" and he replied, "Not so good."[65] Later during the questioning, Fukunaga revealed why he had trouble sleeping: "He [Gill] screamed. They have haunted me every night since. That is what makes me nervous." Brooks then asked why Fukunaga decided to commit his crime, and his response was, "To get money, that's all. Did not know how. Tried different kinds of ways to get money."[66] But Fukunaga made it clear that just getting money was not his primary motive when Brooks asked if anyone with money was acceptable. He answered that it had to be someone connected to the Hawaiian Trust Co. Questioned why Hawaiian Trust, he said: "Because we had hard time paying rent to Hawaiian Trust. Had many troubles. I had hard feelings against company, and I knew that rich men were with Hawaiian Trust. Did not think of Jamieson. It was just a freak that I picked the Jamieson family." Queried if he had thought about other people, he responded, "Yes, in my plans I think about all officials of Hawaiian Trust. Then I thought, suppose Mr. Jamieson hasn't any son. . . . Well, I succeeded in getting the information I wanted. Everything was easy for me." Things were easy for him because the very first Hawaiian Trust executive he contacted had a young son, which is what he wanted as his victim, like Leopold and Loeb's.

William Heen then asked if Fukunaga had compiled a list with names besides that of Jamieson, and Fukunaga agreed. Heen continued that a piece of paper found in his room had names on it, "Stanley McKenzie, Mr. Russell, others." Fukunaga explained that there were other names on the list because he did not know about Frederick Jamieson. Later in the interview, Fukunaga was asked if he had stood outside the Hawaiian Trust Co. and wrote down the license plate numbers of cars of people who looked like they were wealthy. He admitted that he had and said he could tell them where he got the names of the car owners but was not asked about it.

Heen then turned to the dispute about the overdue rent, and his concern may have been because his family owned the house the Fukunaga family was renting. He inquired about when Fukunaga's family had the problem with the rent, and Fukunaga answered incorrectly, saying it was in February or March; it was in May. Heen then asked if it was after he started thinking about the crime, perhaps because he wanted to establish that the Heen family's ownership of the cottage was unrelated to Gill's homicide. However, Fukunaga corrected him that it was before and from then on he started to plan his crime. Brooks then inquired if Fukunaga thought his parents were badly treated, and Fukunaga concurred, "I suppose so because I remember my mother crying. . . . We begged them to wait. . . . Had very hard time. My father was ashamed." His father's shame and his mother's tears over the confrontation with the rent collector were crucial factors in Fukunaga's desire for revenge against the Hawaiian Trust Co.

Returning to the issue of Fukunaga's motive, Brooks questioned, "You wanted money, that's all? It was not vengeance?" Fukunaga then revealed that revenge against Hawaiian Trust was another significant reason for him, "Something like that. Vengeance against company and those connected with it."[67] To be certain, Brooks queried if Fukunaga's intended victim must be connected with Hawaiian Trust, and he agreed. Perhaps still skeptical, Brooks repeated if he merely wanted to get money and not vengeance, but Fukunaga maintained that he wanted both. The *Star-Bulletin* reporter present during the interview apparently did not believe Fukunaga when he asserted that revenge was a principal motive for his crime because the journalist wrote, "The vindication of a fancied personal grudge against the Hawaiian Trust Co. was incidental in the crime."[68] The *Advertiser* reporter at the interview would also write that "love of money" was Fukunaga's primary reason for killing Gill, which the prosecution would argue at his trial.[69]

Later in the interview, Brooks again tried to establish that obtaining money was Fukunaga's main reason for kidnapping Gill after Brooks learned that Fukunaga had six younger siblings. He asked if Fukunaga wanted money to help them, but Fukunaga repeated what he had said the previous day: "My idea was to help my parents. They always long to go Japan. We always had hardships." Brooks then questioned if Fukunaga had intended to leave Hawai'i after his crime, and he responded: "I wanted to sacrifice myself so I could bring happiness to my parents. If I have money right away and give my parents, they scared. I think about leaving after getting money and giving them some excuse to go San Francisco and stay there for some time." He thought he would return later to Honolulu and tell his parents he had made a fortune and send them back to Japan. Fukunaga continued he would then give himself up to the police because "crime never pays. I read too many stories. You can't fight against it." Asked if he thought turning himself in would bring happiness to his parents, his reply was, "My plans were all wrong. I didn't look ahead. I did not know this trouble would be so much to this community." One can agree that, after collecting the ransom money, Fukunaga's plans completely fell apart.

As in his confession, Fukunaga expressed deep remorse for killing Gill, saying, "I feel very ashamed and very sorry." He added, "Now I realize terrible mistake. That's why I am telling every truth." Asked if he felt unkindness toward Gill, Fukunaga said, "No, I feel sorry for him. It was terrible trying to kill him." Questioned about whether he was sincere when he sent flowers to the Jamiesons, he responded, "I meant it. I felt grief. I thought how the Jamiesons suffered." The interview then includes a notation, "Here Fukunaga broke down, laid his head on his arms and wept." His uncontrolled display of his feelings is in marked contrast to the testimony at his trial by the psychiatrists who examined him several days later and testified that he showed "absolutely no emotion."

Toward the end of the interview, Brooks inquired if Fukunaga was going to plead guilty, and he answered that he would have to because there was no other option. Brooks then asked if he looked forward to spending the rest of his life in prison, but Fukunaga replied, "I rather expect the death penalty." The *Star-Bulletin* reporter asked if he was going to plead insanity and described Fukunaga's reaction: "Myles Fukunaga may be nothing now but a pulverized, seething mass of nerves but his indignation is yet penetrable. For an answer to that, he stiffened in his seat, raised his head to an accusing angle and setting his jaw, said, 'I am not insane. I am perfectly sane,'" as he had declared the previous day.[70] Responding to a question about knowing right from wrong, Fukunaga asserted, "Yes, I know what is right and what is wrong. I know I did wrong." He thus claimed to be legally sane, although it was after he had killed Gill.

The interview provides additional personal information about Fukunaga not revealed in his confession. Brooks inquired whether, when Fukunaga was in school, he ever dreamed about what he would like to be when he became a man. Fukunaga replied, "Sure, I have both thought and dreamed. I wanted to be a great man." Asked what kind of great man he desired to be, he elaborated, "The one thing I wanted was to write books. I love books." He added that he wished he could write biographies and about "adventure. I love adventure and romance [books]." After determining that Fukunaga had been following the Jamieson abduction and murder in the newspapers, he was asked, when planning his crime, whether he had a desire to see his name in the papers. He strongly denied that was the case: "No, I hate publicity. In school I used to be very bright pupil, but I hate publicity. I don't want anybody to praise me." Perhaps Fukunaga was referring to stories in school newspapers about his achievements. But he need not have been concerned that anyone was about to praise him for what he did, although he did attract more publicity for himself than he could have ever imagined.

Monday, September 24: Indictment and Apology

The pace of the Fukunaga case increased dramatically over the next two days. On Monday morning at the police station Fukunaga was formally charged with first-degree murder for killing Gill Jamieson.[71] In the afternoon before Judge Alva E. Steadman he was indicted for the same crime by the territorial grand jury at 2:08 P.M.[72] City and county attorney Charles Davis called only three witnesses to present his case: William Jamieson, a brother of Frederick Jamieson and treasurer of C. Brewer & Co., who testified to the identity of Gill; Francis Brooks, who was questioned about Fukunaga's confession on Saturday; and Dr. Robert Faus, who described the condition of Gill's body when it was found. The three witnesses took about twenty-three minutes for their testimony, and the grand jury deliberated less than ten minutes, so the entire proceedings took just thirty-three minutes from the time the jurors assembled in the courtroom at 1:35 P.M. to the filing of the indictment.[73] Similar to the jury that would convict Fukunaga the following week, the grand jury included only one Japanese American. The names of the sixteen other jurors included three that were Hawaiian, although some with English names could have been of Hawaiian ancestry.

Promptly after Judge Steadman received the indictment, he, along with Davis and Brooks, held a conference to determine the hour when Fukunaga would be arraigned, which they decided would be later in the afternoon.[74] Less than an hour and a half after being indicted, Fukunaga was returned to the same packed courtroom to be arraigned—or when, as the press commented, "the ink on the signatures . . . had scarcely dried on the legal document."[75] Led in by Sheriff Patrick Gleason, Fukunaga was handcuffed to private detective Arthur McDuffie and accompanied by four police officers, probably for his safety. Judge Steadman asked, "Is your name Myles Yutaka Fukunaga?" and he replied "Yes, sir" in a barely audible voice. Fukunaga was described as "on the verge of tears" and exhibiting "every sign of a complete breakdown and nervous collapse. . . . The stoicism of his race was entirely absent." At five feet and two inches, which was said to be about the same height as a Haole in his early teens, Fukunaga rested his head on the arm of the much taller McDuffie until he put it around the youth's waist to support him.

After handing a copy of the indictment to the "accused boy," Davis read the indictment charging him with the first-degree murder of the "little Jamieson boy."[76] Judge Steadman then inquired if he spoke English, and Fukunaga assented, as he did to the next question about whether he understood the indictment against him. The judge then asked if he was guilty or not guilty, and Fukunaga responded, "I am guilty." Steadman stated that, according to Hawai'i law in cases calling for the death penalty, a guilty plea cannot be entered, and he directed that a not-guilty plea be made for Fukunaga. This refusal to accept his guilty plea would be the basis of subsequent appeals of Fukunaga's conviction. Questioned if he had a lawyer, Fukunaga answered firmly that he did not want one. However, Steadman declared the issue would be addressed again the next day at 9 A.M. and, if Fukunaga still did not have an attorney, he would appoint one or two for him. At that point, the brief court proceedings were over.

Later that afternoon a clerk in Judge Steadman's court and a police detective called on Fukunaga's parents to assure them that their son would receive a fair trial and that two attorneys would be appointed and paid by the territory for his defense.[77] The parents said they had no money or intention to hire lawyers to defend their son and expressed their appreciation for the efforts to provide him a fair trial. On the same day, they issued a public apology for their son's actions through Nobuhiko Fukunaga, Myles's uncle, who delivered it to the *Star-Bulletin*.[78] The statement read: "Mr. and Mrs.

Jusuke Fukunaga, parents of Myles Fukunaga, want to express their profound regret for the terrible thing that has happened, and their deepest sorrow for the trouble and anxiety their son has caused the entire community. To Mr. and Mrs. Frederick Jamieson, they offer their deepest sympathy in this, their hour of bereavement."[79] The uncle, "with tears running down his cheeks and his countenance showing plainly his profound sorrow and despair," told the newspaper that his nephew had always been a quiet and "good boy." He related, "Our minds cannot grasp the tragedy that has occurred. There are not words for us to express our sorrow and regret. The boy's father cannot work, as he has not recovered from the shock. His mother is heartbroken, and she sits in her home and mourns for her oldest son and the sorrow he has caused. . . . His oldest sister, who is seventeen years old and who has been working to support the family, is unable to work." He added that many people had come to the Fukunagas' home to offer sympathy, but many others were just curious.

Also on Monday, a more explicit apology from Fukunaga's parents for their son's wrongdoing was published in the *Nippu Jiji*.[80] Admitting his guilt, the statement read: "Our son, Yutaka, has committed a terrible crime, not only killing Master Gill of the Jamieson family but also disturbing the public and causing uneasiness to the people. We are extremely ashamed of ourselves that our son committed such a crime and furthermore stained the reputation and honor of the Japanese race. Inadequate family education on our part has caused this, and we are very sorry. We wish to express our deep sympathy to Mr. and Mrs. Jamieson over the loss of their son and to apologize to the general public." Their reference to their son's crime having "stained the reputation and honor of the Japanese race" shows that Fukunaga's parents were aware that he had not brought shame just to their family but to the Japanese American community.

Davis announced that the entire transcript of Fukunaga's interrogation by the police would not be made available to the public until his trial began.[81] He declared that, as city and county attorney, it was his duty not only to prosecute Fukunaga but also to ensure that he received a "fair and impartial trial." Davis pronounced that, if the full text of Fukunaga's "confession" was made public, he was certain that the accused "could not and would not" get a fair trial. Given this argument, Fukunaga's statement to the police should not have been released at all. However, incriminating parts of it had already been published in the newspapers more than a week in advance of jury selection, which made a fair trial almost impossible in Honolulu, if not O'ahu.

The press was already noting the speed of the judicial proceedings, predicting that Fukunaga's trial probably would begin before the end of the week.[82]

The *Advertiser* reported that it was intimated Fukunaga might be tried before a jury starting on Thursday—in which case, a verdict might be possible by the end of the week, less than a week after his arrest. Fully confident of victory, deputy city attorney Francis Brooks asserted that the prosecution would be ready for an immediate trial. Noting that defense attorneys still had to be appointed by the court, the press maintained that a reasonable amount of time would be allowed for them to prepare their case, which would have been two days if the trial began during that week. This speculation about the prompt start of Fukunaga's trial was probably because the press and public expected a speedy guilty verdict.

Adding its voice for a quick trial and execution of Fukunaga was the Citizens' Vigilance Corps, which was organized Thursday night following the discovery of Gill's body.[83] The group issued a "Statement to the Public of Hawaii," signed by its executive committee, which read in part: "One of the purposes which this organization has for its object is the speedy trial of the self confessed murderer of Gill Jamieson. It respectfully requests the district attorney of the city and county of Honolulu and our trial courts to proceed immediately with the necessary legal procedure in the conviction and execution of Myles Fukunaga, the cold-blooded murderer." The statement continued that the "terrible examples of dilatory action of legal procedure" in the Leopold and Loeb case in Chicago and the Hickman case in Los Angeles should not be allowed in Hawai'i. The organization expressed its opposition to spending "tax-payers' money in employing alienists [psychiatrists]" for the Fukunaga trial and requested that it and his execution be completed within the minimum time required by law. As is evident, a week before Fukunaga's trial would begin, for the Vigilance Corps, the Honolulu dailies, and very likely most Hawai'i residents, Fukunaga's conviction and hanging were foregone conclusions. The opposition to the court hiring any psychiatrists to examine Fukunaga was because it might delay his prompt execution, as in the Leopold and Loeb and Hickman cases.

Also on Monday, the *Star-Bulletin* published a letter to the editor signed "LM, J" and dated September 22 (Saturday).[84] It was sent by UH professor Lockwood Myrick Jr. before he learned of Fukunaga's capture. He would later write a much longer "Open Letter to Governor Wallace R. Farrington on Fukunaga's Insanity" in which he analyzed his mental status (see chapter 5). Myrick wrote to the editor: "Sir: One cannot but regret to see this kidnapping and murder case stir up racial ill-feeling. This is . . . so far as I know, the first in which Orientals have been involved. Why should this case lead us to hate all Orientals any more than our other kidnapping cases should lead us to hate all Anglo-Saxons? . . . Let us show the human feeling which everyone with a spark of humanity in him cannot but feel; but let us keep from bringing in the totally irrelevant matter of race." Myrick was probably one of a very limited number of Haoles and other non-Japanese who were sincerely opposed to race being a significant factor in the Fukunaga case. When he referred to race as a "totally irrelevant matter," he was arguing that, while the suspects in Gill's killing had been identified as "Oriental," it should not result in "hate [for] all Orientals." Myrick was deploring that the murder had become highly racialized because the suspects were Japanese American, whereas if they were Haole, that would have been less the case. The "racial ill-feeling" toward "all Orientals" or, more specifically, the racial blame pinning of Japanese Americans for Gill's killing, as opposed to the individual responsible for it, starkly revealed the primacy of race in Hawai'i.

Perhaps in response, Myrick's letter was followed the very next day by a *Star-Bulletin* editorial, "Not a Racial Crime," but it suggested a very different understanding of the significance of race in the Fukunaga case and in Hawai'i more generally.[85] The editorial began with valid assertions that being of Japanese descent was not a causal factor in Fukunaga's wrongdoing: "The crime of Myles Yutaka Fukunaga was not a crime of a racial character. Whatever the complex currents that led to this tragic episode, the fault cannot be laid to the fact that he was of Japanese ancestry. For other countries and other races have produced similar crimes, and though the shadow of his deed falls particularly athwart the Japanese community, it is not the Japanese community which is to blame." Similar to Myrick's letter, the editorial argued that the Japanese American community should not be faulted for Fukunaga's crime, and it recognized how, nonetheless, "the shadow of his deed" had resulted in its racial scapegoating.

However, the rest of the *Star-Bulletin* editorial digressed into racializing Fukunaga's crime, if not criminal behavior in general, instead of viewing it as the act of an individual, as Myrick argued.[86] The editorial related that a physician in Hawai'i, an expert who specialized in psychiatry, was certain that the killing was done by an "Anglo-Saxon—or, at least, a Caucasian." According to the newspaper, he based his conclusion on all of the published evidence, including the reported events of the crime, the letters sent, and the kidnapper's actions after the ransom was collected. The physician concluded, the crime "has not the attributes of Oriental criminality." Despite claiming to have considered all of the evidence, this expert perhaps did not read the numerous articles in the daily newspapers, which reported the eye-witness accounts of cab driver Morizo Yoshioka, Punahou principal Mary Winne, messenger Alfredo Reyes, and Mainard Austin and William Choice, who responded to Frederick Jamieson's calls for help. All of them identified the person they either interacted with or saw participating in significant aspects of Gill's kidnapping as Japanese, and Yoshioka added that his passenger spoke to him in Japanese. Nonetheless, one can fully agree with the expert that Fukunaga's crime lacked the "attributes of Oriental criminality," whatever those might be. But it also lacked any attributes of Caucasian or any other racial criminality because race, widely misunderstood as biologically based in the 1920s, was not a determinant of Fukunaga's criminal behavior. The physician's opinion reveals the dominance of racist thinking at this time in which race was generally accepted as a direct causal factor in crime, intelligence, personality, morality, and many other social attributes and behaviors. Thus at his trial the following week, the prosecution would racialize Fukunaga and seek to account for his actions because he was of the "Japanese race."

Agreeing with the *Star-Bulletin* editorial, the Honolulu Inter-Church Federation passed a resolution that declared race was not a factor in the kidnapping and murder of Gill Jamieson.[87] It read in part, "This Council, assured that it fully represents the spirit of the Christian community of Oahu, wishes to assure the Japanese community that it considers this crime entirely as a personal and in no way a racial matter, and is convinced that no feeling of racial antipathy has been aroused thereby." While the federation members understood that Fukunaga's crime was an individual and not a racial matter, their Christian goodwill may have prevented them from noticing the heightened racial hostility directed against Japanese Americans as a result of Fukunaga's personal actions.

Tuesday, September 25: Attorneys

Only a week had passed since the kidnapping and killing; Fukunaga had been caught, had confessed and been arraigned. All that remained before his trial could start was the appointment of lawyers to defend him. After lengthy meetings with attorneys in his chambers, Judge Alva Steadman appointed Eugene H. Beebe of the Thompson, Cathcart, Beebe & Winn law firm and Seba C. Huber of Huber, Kemp & Stainback as Fukunaga's attorneys on Tuesday morning.[88] Beebe arrived in Hawai'i in 1921 from Seattle to practice law with the Thompson, Cathcart & Lewis firm.[89] The fifty-six-year-old Huber had recently served as the U.S. district attorney in Hawai'i for six and a half years. After the announcement of their appointment, the judge and the two defense counsel left immediately for Oahu Prison to confer with Fukunaga. Later that afternoon, Huber and Beebe met again with Judge Steadman and proposed that the trial begin with jury selection the following Monday, which gave them six days to prepare their defense.[90]

A *Nippu Jiji* editorial that day offered commentary about the Fukunaga case.[91] It began by noting that the case showed that the Honolulu Police Department was "almost hopelessly inefficient" in apprehending criminals. The editorial then turned to the racial dimensions of the case, particularly for Japanese Americans, by remarking that an "atrocious crime creates a tremendous effect on the racial feelings of the community. The murderous acts of simply one youth, maniacal and still in his minority, have brought about a curse and damage to the Japanese community to an enormous extent." While the *Nippu Jiji* initially acknowledged how Fukunaga's wrongdoing had impacted the "racial feelings of the community," it eventually would adopt a colorblind view of the case and deny that race played any role in his conviction and death sentence. The paper would also later contend that Fukunaga was perfectly sane, rather than "maniacal," when he committed his crime.

Two days later in another editorial, "Embarrassment to Japanese," the *Nippu Jiji* commented on the "unpleasant feeling which the American [Haole] community" began to hold toward Japanese since the Jamieson murder.[92] It observed that many Japanese Americans who had been employed in Haole homes as trusted domestic workers for many years had been fired and that a similar number of such employees had left their jobs because of the embarrassing position in which they found themselves as a result of Fukunaga's misdeed. The editorial emphasized that "there was no racial consideration involved in the crime. It was simply a crime involving a private individual. If any racial feeling has been stirred up on account of it, everyone should be prepared by this time to blot it out." As an indication of the extent of anti-Japanese animosity generated by the Jamieson killing, the S. M. Damon Estate, one of the largest private landowners in Hawai'i, published a front-page announcement in the newspapers, which denied persistent rumors that it was going to discharge all of its Japanese workers.[93]

Three days after Fukunaga was arrested, the first claims for a portion of the community reward fund, totaling about $28,000, were submitted to the Honolulu Chamber of Commerce.[94] A person described as a "well known local resident of Japanese ancestry" was quoted that he doubted Japanese Americans would seek any of the reward money.[95] A movement led by the Japanese Chamber of Commerce emerged to discourage any Japanese persons from applying for or accepting any amount from the reward fund.[96] This effort by the chamber was initiated because its leaders were very aware of the magnitude of anti-Japanese sentiment, which had escalated with Fukunaga's confession. To accept reward money might appear as though Japanese Americans were profiting from a crime that one of them had committed.

The opposition to receiving any reward funds underscored how Japanese American community leaders understood that not just Fukunaga was held responsible for Gill's murder because racial blame pinning had implicated the entire community in his crime.

In the aftermath of the Jamieson homicide, the press and government leaders called for a modernized and more efficient police department, the deficiencies of which were made glaringly evident during the manhunt for Gill's killer. A *Star-Bulletin* editorial on September 25, "Looking to the Future," argued that during the search the Police Department was handicapped by a lack of men and cars.[97] On the same day, the city and county board of supervisors convened a special session with Sheriff Gleason to discuss ways to increase immediately the effectiveness of the Police Department.[98] The next evening, the board approved all of his recommendations, including expenditures of $10,695 for two cars, eleven motorcycles, and an intelligence bureau consisting of two investigators and a fingerprint expert.[99]

Since elections were scheduled for October 6, it is not surprising that the issue of police inefficiency and ineffectiveness made apparent would be politicized. On one side were city attorney Davis and Sheriff Gleason, both running for reelection as Republicans, the party in power in Hawai'i, and on the other was supervisor Manuel C. Pacheco, Democratic leader of the police committee of the board of supervisors.[100] Davis emphasized that he and Gleason had already told the board that Honolulu needed a motorized police department so that a net can be instantly thrown about the city in emergencies such as that of the previous week. Supervisor Pacheco prefaced his call for a complete reorganization of the Police Department by arguing that one of the main reasons it was so ineffective last week was because it lacked full administrative authority.[101] Pacheco claimed that Sheriff Gleason "practically abdicated his office to civilian administration . . . by a dozen other ambitious influences." Pacheco's criticisms very likely referred to Lawrence Judd's taking control of the sheriff's office and to how the Heen & Godbold law office served as the command center for the manhunt. The acknowledged ineffectiveness of the Police Department may have led Judd and Heen to intervene in the case.

Following its initial meeting the previous week, the Citizens' Vigilance Corps (CVC) announced its preliminary goals.[102] They included: reelection of Davis as city and county attorney and Gleason as sheriff; increasing the penalties for kidnapping and rape; and instituting hard labor for inmates of Oahu Prison. John A. Balch, chair of the CVC executive committee, also disclosed that, with the approval of the Jamieson family, the CVC was being dedicated to the memory of their son.

Responding to the CVC announcement, the *Nippu Jiji* editorialized, "The Republican Citizens Vigilance Corps of Hawaii is not in shape to do business."[103] The paper remarked that it had added "Republican" to the CVC's name because the organization had endorsed Gleason and Davis for reelection, thereby branding itself a partisan group. The editorial observed that the CVC resulted from the hysteria created by the murder of Gill Jamieson. It continued that other crimes had been just as deplorable, but none had produced in the CVC members the required "amount of hysteria which would translate inertia into action."[104] While the editorial did not mention race, it may have been alluding to Gill's being Haole as the factor that generated the sufficient level of fear and panic among CVC members for them to take action. The same could be said of the Honolulu Board of Supervisors, which appropriated additional funds to the Police Department after Gill's killing but not previously when non-Haoles were murdered. Perhaps in response to criticism from the *Hawaii Hochi* and the *Nippu Jiji*, the CVC felt compelled to issue a statement, which revealed its perception in Hawai'i as a White supremacist organization: "The Citizens' Vigilance Corps has no connection or affiliation with the Ku Klux Klan or any political party. On the contrary, it is a body of citizens open to all residents of the Territory irrespective of race, creed or political affiliation."[105] Nonetheless, the emphasis on citizenship was a proxy for race that eliminated tens of thousands of non-Haoles, including Japanese, as potential members, although it is extremely unlikely they would have joined.

Criticism of the CVC extended beyond Japanese Americans. Referring to them as the "vigilantes," a *Star-Bulletin* article observed that the organization was the butt of most of the jokes during the noon-hour gathering on October 2 at the "Bethel St. soapbox," which served as an open forum for speakers in downtown Honolulu.[106] After hearing the previous speakers, a CVC executive committee member climbed up on the box to denounce as lies the statements the speakers had made. He declared, "You have referred to the 'vigilantes' as the Mānoa Republican Club . . . and so far as I know there is no connection between the two organizations." The connection between them was that both groups consisted predominantly of Haoles of higher class status and probably included some common members.

Seven eyewitnesses to events described in Fukunaga's confession were taken to Oahu Prison on Tuesday, and they all positively identified him as the person they saw at places and times noted therein.[107] Davis hence pronounced that the case against Fukunaga was "nearly perfect." He continued, "We have a complete chain of exterior evidence, both direct and circumstantial; and the internal evidence—by which I mean the personal and psychological consistency between what the accused did and what he says—is without a flaw of self-contradiction. For everything the accused says he did, there is a witness to swear that he did it." Since he wanted to be convicted and be put to death, Fukunaga contributed greatly to the almost perfect case against him through his confession. Thus ended the first week of the case, setting the stage for Fukunaga's short trial the following week.

4. Racial Bias and Injustice in Jury Selection and Trial

After a break of five days, legal proceedings in the Fukunaga case resumed on October 1 with the voir dire examination of prospective jurors in Judge Alva E. Steadman's courtroom in the Ali'iolani Hale judiciary building. Representing the prosecution were Charles S. Davis, city and county of Honolulu attorney, and Francis S. Brooks, first deputy city and county attorney, while Fukunaga's court-appointed attorneys were Seba C. Huber and Eugene H. Beebe. As for the judge, the thirty-four-year-old Steadman was known to express openly his racist views that Haoles were "natural leaders" and hence should always be given superior positions over non-Haoles.[1] After arriving in Hawai'i with his Harvard Law School degree, he soon married into the elite Cooke family of missionary descendants, who had co-founded the mercantile company Castle & Cooke, one of the Big Five corporations.[2] By 7:30 A.M. the large courtroom was packed to capacity with 150 persons, while many others waited outside in the corridors for a chance to witness the trial of "the most horrific crime in the history of Hawaii." Those in attendance consisted of more women than men, more Native Hawaiians and "part-Hawaiians" than Haoles, and almost no Japanese Americans.[3] Given the immense public interest in the trial, extraordinary measures were taken to maintain order and safeguard Fukunaga, as is evident from the eighteen police officers posted at the courtroom and around the building by 6:30 A.M.[4]

Escorted by two plainclothes officers, Fukunaga entered the courtroom shortly after 9 o'clock wearing an oversized coat and tie to begin the judicial process that would determine the rest of his life and how long it would be.[5] After those present had the opportunity to see him, the general sentiment in the courtroom was "how could such a delicate but refined young man have committed such a heinous crime."[6] Already on the first day of jury selection, the *Honolulu Advertiser* predicted that the verdict was likely by the end of the week with one or two night sessions being held toward the close of the trial to reach a quick decision.[7] This chapter reviews the process by which the twelve men who would decide Fukunaga's fate were selected, which took only two days. It evaluates the examination of the potential jurors, particularly those who were seated on the jury, because their responses to questions from both the prosecution and defense make one wonder how it was possible for them to have been accepted by the latter. The chapter also discusses Fukunaga's swift trial and its injustices, especially by his own attorneys, which thoroughly show how he was raced to death as a Japanese American.

Monday, October 1: "I was satisfied they caught the boy that murdered the Jamieson boy"

Starting with Otto Meyer, a Bank of Hawaii employee, the court clerk called twelve men to the jury box and swore them in.[8] Prosecuting attorney Davis began with several questions that he would ask the other prospective jurors, or "talesmen," as the press referred to them, including if any had heard or read about the crime, and whether they had any opinion about the guilt or innocence of the defendant.[9] Since it was not permitted, Davis did not inquire *what* a prospective juror's opinion was, and this procedure was followed by both the prosecution and defense attorneys with the other jury candidates. Most of them did say that they had formed an opinion about Fukunaga's guilt or innocence, so Davis would then ask if they could "set aside" their opinion, and most of those who became jurors claimed that they could ("I believe I can and I will try") or already had.

In his examination of the potential jurors, Davis posed a series of standard questions to each of them in what appears from the trial transcript to be in somewhat rapid-fire manner. These questions included if they had any scruples against imposing the death penalty, if they knew of any reason why they could not give Fukunaga a fair and impartial trial, and if they knew the defense counsel. Perhaps to save time, Davis often would begin by inquiring whether they had heard his questions of the previous jury candidate, and if they would answer them in the same way. Compared to the defense counsel, he did not probe very deeply into the opinion of the prospective jurors about the case and asked them far fewer questions, probably because he assumed that the great majority of them, like most people in Hawai'i, believed that Fukunaga was guilty.

Seven of the final jurors were selected on the first day of jury selection. During the examination of George Swift, a Hawaiian Electric Co. meter reader of Haole and Hawaiian ancestry, defense attorney Eugene Beebe asked a very significant question, which he would repeat to some of the others: "After seeing his [Fukunaga's] picture, did you wonder what prompted him [to kill Gill]?"[10] Swift replied that he did, which clearly demonstrated his belief that Fukunaga killed Gill, but Beebe did not challenge him for cause to have him dismissed from the jury for his obvious bias against Fukunaga. Four other jurors gave similar responses but were not challenged either for cause or peremptorily by the defense. A peremptory challenge did not require the defense or prosecution to state a reason why they wanted someone excused from the jury. The defense was given twelve such peremptory challenges, while the prosecution had six. A prospective juror could also be challenged for cause, which required a valid reason that needed to be approved by the judge.

Another juror who stated he believed that Fukunaga was responsible for killing Gill was Robert L. K. Fuller, an engraver of Haole and Hawaiian descent in his own jewelry firm. He replied affirmatively to Davis's questions that he had read the newspapers about the crime and talked about it with others but claimed that his mind was not made up.[11] However, in response to Beebe, Fuller related that his opinion about the case was not very fixed until Fukunaga was captured and, from then on, he "was satisfied that they caught the boy that murdered the Jamieson boy." This was an explicit statement by a jury candidate that he believed Fukunaga killed Gill, and thus he should have been challenged by the defense, whether for cause or peremptorily. Instead, Beebe asked if Fuller thought he would like to be on the jury in the Fukunaga trial. He remarked, "I felt that I could be one of those who could give the boy a square deal." Could Fukunaga really expect that from someone who just a few minutes earlier had stated under oath that he thought Fukunaga murdered Gill?

Victor Hurd, a salesperson of Haole ancestry with the Big Five firm Theo H. Davies & Co., also asserted his belief that Fukunaga killed Gill. He told Davis that he had an opinion about the case and, when questioned if he could remove it, uttered, "I feel I can do it."[12] But when Beebe inquired about his opinion, Hurd claimed not to have it anymore. So Beebe asked when was his opinion dissipated, but Hurd's answer was, "When this man was arrested. I may say I had conceived an image of a different type of man doing it." Beebe then repeated the query he gave to Swift and others: when Hurd saw Fukunaga's picture in the newspapers, did the question arise concerning what made him do it? Hurd agreed, "That's it," which indicated his belief in Fukunaga's culpability in Gill's killing, but he was not challenged by the defense.

The other men approved for the jury on the first day included Wallace E. Saffery, a bookkeeper at Palama Settlement of Haole and Hawaiian descent; Nelson R. N. Robinson, a clerk at Hawaiian Electric Co. also of Haole and Hawaiian ancestry; Hamilton P. Agee, director of the Hawaiian Sugar Planters' Association experimental station; and Harry A. K. Burgess, a consulting engineer with a construction company and a graduate of Kamehameha Schools. Of the seven jurors selected on the first day, two were Haole and five were "hapa Haole," or of White and Hawaiian descent, and four of the latter held middle-class occupations.

As for those on the first day who did not become jurors, four of them, all non-Haole, were excused for cause because they lacked sufficient knowledge of English to serve on the jury. However, this deficiency initially was not considered a valid reason for dismissal by the prosecution and the judge. I review the examination of the first of the possible jurors to be so exempted because it demonstrates how the prosecution and judge strongly resisted not having them on the jury but not necessarily in the interest of racial justice. James Y. Wong, a twenty-year-old Chinese American, said he had a fourth-grade education and worked as a carpenter for $7 a day.[13] When Davis asked if he had heard the questions posed to the others, Wong replied, "Yes, I did, but some of those words are too deep for me. My education doesn't meet it." Davis then inquired if he knew the meaning of "doubt" and "reasonable doubt," and when Wong answered yes, Davis continued with his usual questions before accepting him for the jury.

Under examination by Huber, Wong related that he had not been reading the newspapers about the crime and had not come to an opinion about Fukunaga's guilt or innocence but then added, "I would like to get off [the jury] if I could." Ignoring his remark, Huber queried if Wong believed that because a grand jury indicts someone, that alone is partial evidence of his guilt, and Wong agreed. Huber then asked if he understood words such as "premeditated," "malice aforethought," and "reasonable doubt" and, after Wong admitted he did not, Huber challenged him for cause because he lacked an adequate understanding of English. Opposing the challenge, Davis argued that jurors are not expected to know the meaning of legal terms which many lawyers do not.

So Judge Steadman began questioning Wong about his work as a carpenter, if he read books ("only when I was in school"), and if he knew the meaning of certain words, such as "unreasonable." After Wong answered "not fair" for the last word, it became apparent that the judge also wanted to have him on the jury when he asked, "What would you say if someone told you this courtroom was absolutely dark at this minute? Would that be a reasonable or an unreasonable statement?" When Wong replied "unreasonable," Steadman pronounced that his responses appear to "the Court to reflect his having a thoroughly intelligent mind. . . . I think it is far from decisive that he cannot define these words" and denied the challenge. Huber made an exception to the ruling and requested to discuss the issue further, but the judge declared a recess for lunch until 1:30 P.M. Before their break, Steadman instructed the accepted jurors and those waiting to be examined not to discuss the case and not to read any newspapers because "they can serve no useful purpose except to distort your minds and block your ability to be good jurors. . . . Trial by law does not mean trial by newspapers." Steadman was at least acknowledging how the extensive press coverage of the case had already seriously jeopardized trial by law.

When court resumed, Huber immediately began questioning Wong whether he knew the meaning of numerous legal terms, including "feloniously," "inadequate provocation," and "bias." Taking no chances that Steadman might allow Wong on the jury, Huber asked him if he understood the meaning of nearly forty legal words and expressions, the overwhelming majority of which Wong said he did not. Huber then renewed his challenge, and this time Davis did not oppose it, and Steadman excused Wong. The prosecution and perhaps the judge wanted to include on the jury persons without sufficient knowledge of English because they could more easily be persuaded by the more articulate jurors (primarily Haoles) to vote for a guilty verdict.

Learning from their experience with Wong, the defense attorneys afterward used the same tactic of asking for the definition of legal terms to have other jury candidates with limited English ability, who were Chinese American and Native Hawaiian, dismissed. Both the prosecution and the judge were subsequently far less resistant to defense challenges of their seating. While the elimination of those working-class non-Haoles from the jury by the defense counsel may appear to be a race-and-class assault on justice, that was not necessarily the case. Certainly, compared to the situation in the continental United States, particularly the Deep South, the defense wanting to exclude non-Haoles from the jury in a trial involving a non-Haole defendant might seem racially illogical. The same could be said about the prosecution seeking to include working-class non-Haoles on the jury, who might be sympathetic to Fukunaga because he shared their racial and class status. However, the prosecution very likely wanted to have those less educated Chinese Americans and Native Hawaiians on the jury so that the Haole jurors could then dominate the jury deliberations toward a guilty verdict. Thus, the defense strategy to have those non-Haoles not seated probably was in Fukunaga's best interest. But Beebe and Huber could have also made similar efforts to exclude obviously biased Haoles from the jury, such as those who stated they believed that Fukunaga had killed Gill.

Another reason the court could use to excuse potential jurors was if they admitted they had an opinion about Fukunaga's guilt or innocence, usually because they had read about the case or had discussed it and could not remove their viewpoint. On the first day of jury examination five men were challenged for such cause successfully by the prosecution. Given the enormous pretrial publicity and ongoing conversations about the case, one wonders how the other jury candidates could so easily rid themselves of their opinions about it. The honesty of those five men in stating they had come to a decision about Fukunaga's guilt or innocence, which could not be changed, brings into question the many more prospective jurors, who maintained under oath that they held such an opinion but could remove it or already had.

On the first day of jury selection, Fukunaga was described by the press as more assured than during his previous court appearance a week ago and as smiling occasionally when humorous remarks were made in testimony. As the *Star-Bulletin* reported, "Chin cupped in his hands, the youth studied each juror as the examination progressed, and once or twice, his drooping mouth lifted in a faint smile."[14] Fukunaga's parents, dressed in black, went to the courthouse in the afternoon and, unable to find seats in the courtroom, sat sadly in the lobby until the end of the session without seeing their son, his mother occasionally wiping away a tear.

Tuesday, October 2: "I know you all"

Jury selection resumed the next day at 9:20 A.M. with eleven jurors having been accepted the previous day. Not all of them served on the jury because four of them were later challenged peremptorily either by the prosecution or defense. Of the five jurors selected on the second day, the questioning of several of them is especially salient in terms of injustice. Shinichi Maruyama, a nisei graduate of McKinley High School, was the only Japanese American called to serve on the jury because not many of them were adult citizens.[15] He related that for the past ten years he had been the English-language section editor of the *Nippu Jiji*. Maruyama responded to Davis that he had "talked about the case but never formed any definite opinion." He also told him that he knew of no reason why he could not give Fukunaga a fair trial.

Huber promptly questioned Maruyama about a possible reason, asking if he had written anything about the case for the *Nippu Jiji*. Maruyama replied that he "wrote the facts as they developed" about the kidnapping and murder of Gill and the arrest of Fukunaga. As noted above, among the facts that Maruyama wrote about the case was that when Gill's body was found, it was "terribly mangled and brutally cut open," his "abdomen [was slit] on his left and right sides, and . . . a ghastly wound [was] in his back," none of which was true.[16] Maruyama also wrote a lengthy summary of Fukunaga's statement to the police that he titled "Confession of Myles Y. Fukunaga."[17] Nonetheless, he responded to Huber that he knew absolutely nothing about the case that could bias him one way or the other, despite having written and not just read that Fukunaga was the "slayer" of Gill. Without even being challenged for cause for having written that about Fukunaga and thus publicly declared his bias against him, Maruyama became a juror. Beebe and Huber also failed to challenge him peremptorily to have him dismissed from the jury. After the trial, according to a *Star-Bulletin* translation of a *Hawaii Hochi* article, the *Hochi* questioned, "Why must Shinji Maruyama . . . ask Mr. Yasutaro Soga, 'Is it all right to serve on the jury?' and be told by Soga, 'Go ahead and do your duty.'"[18] Mr. S. Furukawa, acting business manager of the *Nippu Jiji*, is said to have related this story to the *Hochi*. After being directed by Soga to serve as a juror, Maruyama very likely knew how Soga wanted him to vote on Fukunaga's guilt or innocence.

Another juror whose selection was highly questionable was Arthur F. Wall, who was co-owner of a jewelry firm, Wall & Dougherty, and became the jury foreman.[19] Davis began, "Of course, you know Judge Huber and Mr. Beebe?" and Wall agreed. The prosecutor continued, asking if Wall's acquaintance with them might influence him in the trial, and Wall revealingly remarked, "Not any more than with you and Mr. Brooks. I know you all." He also admitted that he knew Frederick Jamieson quite well, and to defense questions he said that, during the manhunt for Gill, he had offered his services and his car and driver to Davis.[20] Despite this obvious partiality toward the prosecution, Wall joined the jury after being briefly examined by both the prosecuting and defense attorneys because as an elite Haole he knew them all, and they knew him.

Like Wall, the three other men (besides Maruyama) who became jurors on Tuesday were all Haoles of middle-class status: LeForrest N. MacComiskey, a cost accountant at Castle & Cooke; George E. Jurgensen, a clerk at another Big Five corporation, C. Brewer & Co.; and Albert E. Coxhead, a contractor.

As for those who were not selected for the jury on the second day, the lengthy and aggressive questioning by the defense of Thomas A. Mossman demonstrates the extent they occasionally went to have a juror removed, unlike their far shorter examination of Haoles of status. Mossman, a purchasing agent for a fertilizer company, may have been of Hawaiian ancestry because his family name was and continues to be indicative of such. Asked by Davis if he had any opinion about the case, Mossman replied that he did but it was not fixed.[21] Davis seemed surprised when Mossman answered affirmatively to his next question, whether it would require evidence to remove his opinion, because Davis blurted, "It would?" Mossman concurred and also to Davis's next query, if he would carry his opinion into the jury room. But Mossman then contradicted himself by agreeing with Davis that he could put his viewpoint aside and so was added to the jury. Davis very likely concluded that Mossman thought Fukunaga was guilty, as he probably did of others whom he quickly approved as jurors.

Beebe returned to Mossman's response to Davis that he had formed an opinion regarding the case, and Mossman conceded he still had that opinion. So Beebe asked if he still had his opinion, how was he going to disregard it? Mossman's answer was, "If there is enough evidence to show he is not guilty," which obviously indicated that he thought Fukunaga was guilty. After posing several questions to be sure that he understood Mossman's position, Beebe declared, "Right now looking at the boy, you don't believe him innocent, do you?" and Mossman concurred. Beebe then challenged him for cause, but Davis, apparently oblivious to what Mossman had just said, opposed it. So Beebe requested that Davis's further examination of Mossman not include asking "leading questions," which had been his practice, and Judge Steadman agreed. But in further questioning Mossman, Davis did not request clarification of his assertion that he did not believe Fukunaga was innocent. Instead, he offered more general queries such as, "If the court instructs you that this defendant on trial is presumed by the law to be innocent . . ., will you follow that instruction?" After such leading questions and appropriate answers, Davis grandly pronounced, "I submit the juror is qualified as well as any juror who ever sat in a criminal case."

Beebe then tried another tactic to have Mossman dismissed by testing his knowledge of English, perhaps because he was Native Hawaiian. He asked Mossman for the meaning of "premeditated," which he answered correctly, but Mossman could not define "extenuation," "extenuating circumstances" or "reasonable doubt." Beebe's next question, which had been directed to others, was if Mossman were to change places with Fukunaga and be charged with murder, did he think that if a juror like himself sat on his case, would he receive a fair trial? Mossman agreed, but Judge Steadman seemed not to believe him because he inquired, "You would not want him [Fukunaga] on the jury if he had the same opinion as you have if you were charged as he is charged?" When Mossman said no, the judge demanded to know what he meant by that, and Mossman asserted, "Without the evidence produced, I would not have a fair trial," contradicting his previous statement to Beebe. The latter then asked, "Right now, Myles is not innocent with your opinion in your mind?" Mossman responded that it was doubtful. Beebe, in exasperation, declared, "I don't know how to go forward. I will renew my challenge," and Davis finally relented. Such intensive questioning by the defense attorneys of other jurors regarding their opinion of Fukunaga's guilt or innocence probably would have resulted in removing several of them from the jury. But Huber and Beebe were not going to subject Haoles to such a rigorous and possibly embarrassing interrogation, especially requesting them to define legal terms as though they did not understand English.

Asked early in the afternoon by Judge Steadman for the territory's sixth and last peremptory challenge, Davis pronounced, "The jury is satisfactory." Huber stated the same for the defense after they had a brief conference with Fukunaga, and the jurors were sworn in. As the courtroom began to empty, one of Fukunaga's prison guards whispered something to him, and he broke into a smile. Asked what he had said to him, the guard replied, "Ah, just kidding, something about girls."[22] Perhaps he was referring to the "line of young girls of Japanese extraction" seated at the back of the courtroom, their "faces tinted and their heads marcelled [and] dressed in the current fashion."[23] They may have attended the trial to have a look at Fukunaga, who was reported to be "good looking" in the newspapers.

Race and Class on the Jury

The twelve men who would decide Fukunaga's fate included six Haoles, five who were described by the press as "part-Hawaiian," and one Japanese American.[24] As is apparent from their last names, all of the Native Hawaiian jurors were hapa Haole or of White ancestry also. Like the Haoles on the jury, they all held middle-class occupations, including engineer, clerk, and owner of a jewelry firm.[25] The overwhelming predominance of Haoles and Native Hawaiians on the jury is not surprising since the former (37 percent) and the latter (27 percent) were the two largest groups of adult citizens in Hawai'i in 1930.[26] Between 1927 and 1931, among all jurors in Honolulu courts, an overly high two-thirds were Haole, and more than half of the jurors were employed in executive or professional positions.[27] Although Japanese Americans were by far the most numerous group at about 38 percent in 1930, and by 1924 a majority of them were American citizens by birth, most of the latter were not adults and hence could not sit on juries. As members of a longer resident immigrant group, six Chinese Americans were questioned for the jury, but none was selected to serve, especially because of their limited English ability.

One of the most disturbing aspects of the jury selection process was that a majority of the thirty-seven men examined admitted that they had formed an opinion about Fukunaga's guilt or innocence but claimed they could set it aside or previously did. Eleven of the prospective jurors were challenged for cause by the prosecution or defense and excused because they stated they could not change their opinion. Huber observed that, in comparison to the murder trials he had prosecuted as the U.S. district attorney for Hawai'i, he considered the number of jury candidates with such fixed views in the Fukunaga trial as unusually small.[28] In other words, many, if not most, of the potential jurors probably lied under oath when they maintained that their opinion about the case was not fixed. Since ten of the jurors asserted that they held an opinion about the case but could remove it, they probably thought that Fukunaga was guilty before the trial began, especially because all twelve jurors said they had read about the crime, including Fukunaga's confession, in the newspapers.

Although before the jury was finalized it very likely consisted of biased jurors, they could easily have been eliminated by Fukunaga's attorneys with their peremptory challenges. They did use eight of them to have some suspect jurors removed, but when they informed the judge that the jury was acceptable, the defense still had four remaining peremptory challenges, which they could have used to dismiss the most obviously prejudiced jurors.[29] They included those who expressed their belief that Fukunaga killed Gill Jamieson, who claimed they had an opinion about the case but could set it aside, or who were personal friends of Frederick Jamieson or the prosecuting attorneys.

Among those friends were the six Haole jurors whom Beebe and Huber may have been unwilling to challenge, in contrast to Chinese Americans with inadequate understanding of English and working-class Native Hawaiians. To challenge them might appear as though the defense attorneys were questioning their personal character and honesty, particularly since they all were part of the same circle of privileged Haoles. Of the six Haoles on the jury, five of them related that they knew Frederick Jamieson personally, while the other said he worked with his brother. In addition, three of the Haole jurors were employed by Big Five companies, one was an administrator with the Big Five-associated HSPA, and two had their own businesses. All six stated that they had read newspaper accounts of the case and came to an opinion about Fukunaga's guilt or innocence but could remove it. Hence, for the defense counsel to interrogate them further if they really could or had cast their opinion away would be to imply that they were lying under oath. Thus, the racial bias, and therefore the racial injustice in the jury selection process, was the inclusion of such Haoles by the defense attorneys rather than the exclusion of non-Haoles, with the notable exception of hapa Haoles of middle-class status. Beebe and Huber did challenge and have removed other Haoles from the jury, but they were clearly disqualified, such as those who had been deputized for the search for Gill and his killer. Furthermore, the jury-selection process exposed the fiction of colorblind justice in Hawaiʻi, particularly the right of non-Haole defendants to be tried by an impartial jury, let alone one of their peers. With the jury stacked so heavily against him, could Fukunaga really expect justice and a fair trial when it began promptly the next day, or was a guilty verdict a foregone conclusion?

The Trial

That Myles Fukunaga was rushed to his death sentence is readily evident in the extremely brief defense of nineteen minutes provided by his attorneys, who called no witnesses on his behalf. While they initially were very aggressive in their defense of their client, especially Eugene Beebe, by the afternoon of the first day of the two-day trial, they had become quite conciliatory toward the prosecution, which hastened the pace of the proceedings. The issues discussed in this section demonstrate how Fukunaga was unjustly raced to his death, according to both meanings of race as used in this book. During the trial, he was racialized as Japanese by the prosecution and some of their key witnesses in accordance with widespread stereotypes of them in Hawaiʻi instead of being tried as an individual without reference to race. In addition, the trial moved quickly along due to the cooperation of Fukunaga's attorneys, particularly their inexcusable stipulation that he killed Gill Jamieson.

Wednesday, October 3: The Prosecution

As with jury selection, the trial began in a jammed courtroom, including many women and a large number of Japanese Americans, with a crowd of spectators standing outside in the corridors, hoping for a seat should anyone leave.[30] After reading the indictment against Fukunaga, which charged him with first-degree murder, prosecuting attorney Charles Davis argued that Fukunaga "deliberately planned to kidnap and to kill and murder this boy George Gill Jamieson for the purpose of obtaining money from his father."[31] Davis went on to describe in detail how Fukunaga abducted and killed Gill, how he obtained the ransom payment from his father, and how he had "confessed" to the murder and pled guilty at his arraignment. He directly addressed the issue of Fukunaga's legal sanity by declaring, "We will show you he knew the difference between right and wrong, and knew what he was doing and deliberately planned to kill the boy from the beginning, and carried out his plan."[32] Defense attorney Seba Huber informed Judge Steadman that they would reserve their opening statement for later, but they never gave one.

The key prosecution witnesses were the three psychiatrists—Dr. Robert Faus, Dr. A. B. Eckerdt, and Dr. Mon Fah Chung—who together conducted a mental evaluation of Fukunaga for about an hour and a half on September 25 at Oahu Prison.[33] In their report, they maintained that Fukunaga was of "sane mind" when they examined him, although they differed in their opinions about his legal sanity when they each took the stand. In their testimony, Faus and Eckerdt, together with Davis through his questions, can be seen as racializing Fukunaga as Japanese and as invoking race to account for his behavior, instead of viewing him as an individual with his own psychological problems and life experiences. Chung in his testimony and Beebe in his questions followed the latter approach. I discuss these issues concerning the evaluation of Fukunaga as legally sane and his racialization by the prosecution to underscore the racial injustices perpetrated against him during his trial.

When they took the stand, both Faus and Eckerdt stated that Fukunaga was legally sane not just on the day they examined him but also on the day he killed Gill and on the day they testified, even though they had not spoken to him since their evaluation. In his questions to the psychiatrists, Davis employed the primary legal definition of sanity in Hawai'i—the capacity to distinguish between right and wrong. Davis asked separately if Fukunaga, when he was examined, knew the difference between right and wrong, whether he now knows that difference, and if on the day of the killing he knew that difference. Both Faus and Eckerdt responded affirmatively to each question.[34] In contrast, when Davis inquired about Fukunaga's knowledge of right and wrong on the day he killed Gill, Chung testified that he could not give an opinion.[35] He gave the same response when asked about Fukunaga's knowledge of right and wrong "today," explaining that it was because he had not questioned him that day. Beyond the differences in opinion of the psychiatrists, by focusing on legal sanity as the ability to distinguish between right and wrong, Davis (and Judge Steadman) ignored another principal factor in the definition of insanity according to Hawai'i law—being compelled by a force that one could not withstand. This criterion would be emphasized by Lockwood Myrick Jr. in his analysis of Fukunaga's insanity (see chapter 5). Another critical problem with Faus and Eckerdt's conclusion that Fukunaga was legally sane was that their examination of him was much too short and should have been conducted over a ten-day period. Faus admitted to the brevity of their evaluation when Davis asked if he found any complex in Fukunaga; Faus replied that he had not because he could not locate it in that short time frame.[36]

Faus's testimony as an expert witness on Fukunaga's legal sanity was especially dubious and raises major questions about his professional honesty in the pursuit to have Fukunaga executed.[37] In his cross-examination of Faus, Huber sought to demonstrate that Faus might have serious doubts about Fukunaga's sanity by referring to a *Honolulu Star-Bulletin* article from the previous afternoon in which Faus made observations about Fukunaga's mental status that differed markedly from his testimony.[38] Huber noted that the article quoted Faus as saying that if Fukunaga had been placed in an institution for observation last spring when he had attempted suicide, Gill's death might have been averted, and he asked Faus whether he had been accurately quoted. He claimed to have been misquoted and was not referring specifically to Fukunaga. However, according to the paper, Faus contended that if Fukunaga had been hospitalized, "a study of the boy, his mentality and the reason for his attempt on his own life might have been made, and the atrocity [killing of Gill] might never have happened. We might have reached the depth of the boy's difficulty and effected a cure."[39] If Fukunaga was mentally normal as Faus testified, why would he need to be hospitalized, and what was the cure for?

Offering a possible explanation for Fukunaga's homicidal behavior, Faus stated to the *Star-Bulletin*: "Fukunaga's act was perhaps the accumulation of suppression from which he was never released in his secluded and sublimated existence.[40] . . . The case does not present a racial aspect. It is the problem of an individual. . . . It could have been nearly any individual subject to the same influences and of the same suppressed or sublimated nature."[41] Emphasizing the magnitude of Fukunaga's mental problems, Faus claimed, "This, indeed, would be a case for Sigmund Freud or any well known or reputed psychiatrist." Nonetheless, the day after making those statements to the press, when Faus testified in court that Fukunaga was legally sane, he made no mention of Freud or any other psychiatrist who might have a different opinion. He also referenced Fukunaga's Japanese "race" in his testimony, despite asserting to the *Star-Bulletin* that the youth's "case does not present a racial aspect" and is "the problem of an individual."

While Faus denied to the press that race was a relevant factor in Fukunaga's murderous actions, at the trial he, Eckerdt, and Davis racialized Fukunaga by invoking his being Japanese to account for his behavior. Responding to a series of questions from Huber about Fukunaga's emotions while being examined, Faus said, "He was nondemonstrative. The emotion seemed there; that is, he didn't express his emotion as you and I would."[42] Faus's answer to Huber's next question ("Is that a normal condition?") makes it clear that he was referring to racial difference in his previous statement: "I think it is perhaps characteristic of his race," in contrast to that of himself and Huber as Haoles. Faus added later, "As patients in the [mental] hospital they [Japanese] are very stoical individuals . . . ; they do not show . . . undue expression of pain or suffering. I attribute his emotional state to that." Faus was racializing Fukunaga based on prevalent stereotypes of Japanese in Hawai'i as stoic, instead of evaluating him as an individual with his own way of expressing his emotions, including his quiet and reserved personality. A little more than a week before when he was arraigned in court, Fukunaga was described by the press as "displaying every sign of a complete breakdown and nervous collapse. . . . The stoicism of his race was entirely absent."[43] In short, he was showing "expression of pain or suffering," which was highly appropriate for someone being arraigned for first-degree murder.

In questioning Eckerdt, Davis also raised the issue of racial differences between Japanese and "Anglo-Saxons" by inquiring if "suicidal tendencies vary in races," as a way to normalize Fukunaga's suicide attempts. Eckerdt obliged by asserting that he thought they were more prevalent in Japanese.[44] So Davis asked if the suicidal tendency "is not so abnormal with the Japanese as possibly with other races?" but Eckerdt replied he did not think so. Davis next questioned if Japanese control of their emotions differs from the "Anglo-Saxon races or other races?" Eckerdt agreed and also concurred with Davis's contention that "they [Japanese] don't react . . . the same way that other races do," rather than providing an explanation for Fukunaga's display of his emotions specific to himself instead of his race.

In his examination of Chung, Davis again tried to relate Fukunaga's suicide attempts to his being Japanese, first inquiring if suicidal tendencies differ among races.[45] However, in contrast to Faus and Eckerdt, Chung disagreed, so Davis asked if Japanese are more inclined to commit suicide than other races. Chung responded, perhaps referring to issei, that older Japanese are, but Davis would not relent and remarked, "May that not be transmitted?" Chung said he did not know, and we do not know if Davis was referring to a cultural or genetic transmission of suicidal tendencies. But in the 1920s, biological notions of race prevailed, particularly the genetic inheritance of attributes, such as intelligence, temperament, and perhaps suicidal inclinations. It is clearly evident that Davis viewed Fukunaga primarily as a representative of his "Japanese race," which for him accounted for his suicide attempts, rather than as an individual with his own depressed personality and depressing life circumstances, which led to Fukunaga's trying to kill himself.

In marked contrast to Davis and the two other psychiatrists, Chung in his testimony focused on Fukunaga as a person with his specific psychological makeup and without reference to his being Japanese. Asked by Beebe if Fukunaga's "showing lack of emotion was evidence of normality or abnormality," Chung replied, "It all depends on the individual man. I presume he has control of the emotions." He responded to another question regarding Fukunaga's minimal assertion of emotions by stating that it "depend[s] on what his [Fukunaga's] experience has been," again emphasizing him as an individual rather than simply Japanese.

Differing conspicuously from Davis, Beebe in his questions sought to diminish the significance of race in Fukunaga's expression of emotions and behavior in general. He asked Chung, "You mean we have a boy [Fukunaga], neither Japanese nor haole, in a susceptible state of life, working around hospitals, which tends to harden the emotions?"[46] By referring to Fukunaga as neither Japanese nor haole, Beebe was arguing that race was far less relevant to account for Fukunaga's mental condition than his personal experiences and "susceptible state of life" with no friends and no prospects for the future.[47] But Beebe and Huber did not provide any evidence that Fukunaga was legally insane when he killed Gill. They were only able to have Chung concede that Fukunaga had an "abnormal state of mind."

While Chung in his testimony and Beebe in his questions to the psychiatrists asserted that Fukunaga's suicide attempts and seeming lack of emotion were specific to himself as a mentally abnormal person, Davis and his expert witnesses Faus and Eckerdt maintained that they were more characteristic of the "Japanese race." They thus racially othered Japanese Americans compared to "Anglo-Saxons," who believed themselves to represent the psychological, social, and cultural norm. In short, rather than being prosecuted as an individual with his own mental problems and life experiences, Fukunaga could not escape being viewed and treated as Japanese, manifesting the dominance of race over colorblind justice in Hawai'i. But his racialization was shared by other non-Haoles, who also found themselves restricted in their life chances as a result.

Another prosecution witness on the first day was Zena Mossman, who, as a clerical worker in Davis's office, took shorthand notes of the interrogation of Fukunaga in question-and-answer format and transcribed them that same evening.[48] Her testimony is significant in showing how the defense counsel initially were very zealous in defending Fukunaga, but that would no longer be the case by the afternoon. When Davis sought to offer into evidence Mossman's transcript, which included Fukunaga's admission to killing Gill, Beebe objected and requested the opportunity to cross-examine her. He posed numerous questions to challenge the accuracy of Mossman's transcription, such as if she had recorded everything that was said, before objecting to its admission into evidence. He also argued that they did not know what had transpired prior to the time she entered the interrogation room. Davis countered with an extended argument that the prosecution had "*prima facie* shown a case of voluntary confession," which placed the burden on the defense to demonstrate its "involuntariness."[49] Beebe retorted with a taunt, "This is not time for oratory.... Cannot my brother Davis bring the people here who had Myles Fukunaga first and tell what took place? Is he afraid of that?" That kind of harsh exchange between the defense and prosecution also would not be evident in the afternoon and would be replaced by collegial cooperation between them, which moved the trial along without having to discuss any objections from either side.

But before then, Judge Steadman agreed with Beebe, pronouncing that evidence should be provided about the circumstances in the interrogation room just before Mossman entered. So she temporarily left the witness box and was replaced by deputy city attorney Francis Brooks, who was present when Fukunaga was brought in. His questioning by Beebe brought up the issue whether Fukunaga should have been advised that he need not answer any questions from the police. The U.S. Supreme Court "Miranda" ruling that arrested persons need to be informed that they have the right to remain silent and that anything they say can and will be used against them in court was not in force until 1967. Nonetheless, Beebe asked Brooks a question related to the Miranda warning: "Did you tell him he need not make any statement?" and Brooks answered no.[50] Beebe followed by asking if Brooks told Fukunaga that any statement he made could be used against him in court, and the deputy attorney again said no. Beebe then renewed his objection, but Judge Steadman ruled that in the territory an arrested person need not be specifically warned that whatever they say could be used against them and later ruled the transcript would be received in evidence. But since all of the jurors had already read Fukunaga's profession of guilt in the newspapers, even if the transcript was not admitted as evidence, it probably would not have made any difference in their voting for a guilty verdict.

The issue of whether Fukunaga should have been advised that he did not have to speak to the police arose earlier in the trial when Huber was cross-examining Faus. He asked if, while Faus was in the interrogation room, Fukunaga was told that he need not answer any questions put to him.[51] Davis immediately responded, "Objected to as incompetent, irrelevant and immaterial," which is indicative of the adversarial relation between the prosecution and defense in the morning of the first day. Huber replied, "It certainly has been the practice in this Territory."[52] However, that practice was not extended to Fukunaga, and so his confession was accepted into evidence against him.

In the afternoon session the courtroom was again filled to capacity, including many women, "mostly Oriental and young girls."[53] Davis read the confession transcript into evidence, a twenty-page document that required an hour and a half as he droned on, and it was almost 3 P.M. when he finished. He next offered and read the ransom letter into evidence.[54] The defense did not object, and this marked the beginning of their far more cooperative stance toward the prosecution for the rest of the trial. Perhaps aware of this change, Davis requested that the letter the *Star-Bulletin* received, revealing that Gill was dead, be admitted into evidence without having to be read, and again the defense had no objection.

Davis then called Charles T. Littlejohn Jr., an assistant cashier at the Bank of Hawaii, to the witness stand.[55] He testified that on the evening of September 18, $10,000 from the bank was turned over to Frederick Jamieson. Littlejohn was not asked and did not testify whether the $10,000 was from an account that Jamieson had at the bank, which may be an indication that it assisted him, given his standing in the community, to come up with the ransom payment. He continued that he and two other bank officials recorded the serial numbers of the bills and that he had the lists of the $5 bills and thought that the lists of $10 and $50 bills had been destroyed. Littlejohn then confirmed that $4,000 in $5 bills was delivered to Jamieson and that $6,000 was returned to the bank but not the other $4,000 in $5 bills. Davis next offered into evidence four lists of serial numbers of the $5 bills, and Huber said they did not object and also waived cross-examination.

The next three prosecution witnesses each testified about seeing Fukunaga engaged in significant acts related to the abduction of Gill Jamieson on the day it occurred, and two of them stated they saw him with Gill. The witnesses were Morizo Yoshioka, the taxi driver who drove Fukunaga and Gill to Waikīkī; Mary P. Winne, the principal of Punahou Academy who handed the boy over to Fukunaga; and Alfredo Reyes, the messenger who received the ransom letter from him.[56] They all provided damaging testimony against Fukunaga by identifying him in the courtroom as the person with whom they had interacted on the day Gill was kidnapped. Also, they were all not cross-examined by the defense. As one of the trial reporters wrote about the witnesses, "It's a procession. And no cross-examination. Yes, a procession and a debacle."[57] It certainly was for the defense and Fukunaga, but worse was about to come for him.

The prosecution's next witness was chief of detectives John McIntosh. He confirmed that he entered Fukunaga's room at the Serene Rooms on the day of his capture and found a suitcase, which he identified as the one in the courtroom. Davis then offered the suitcase and its contents, except for the remaining ransom money, into evidence.[58] As the prosecutor began removing the contents, Beebe requested that the jury be excused while he made an objection, and they left the courtroom. He began by noting that the suitcase contained a pair of bloody trousers and argued: "We admit . . . that Myles Fukunaga killed the Jamieson boy. The sole purpose of the admission of these trousers . . . would be to inflame the minds of the jurors. . . . I have read authorities [rulings] and know that there are authorities that under the circumstances that exist in this case, where the *corpus delicti* is admitted, and where the killing is admitted, it is prejudicial error to admit blood-stained garments."[59] Did Beebe really believe that a pair of bloody pants would prejudice the jury against Fukunaga to a greater extent than a stipulation that he killed Gill? While Beebe may have read relevant case law regarding Fukunaga's case, it was his first murder trial, and his inexperience was made hugely evident, much to his client's disadvantage.

Judge Steadman asked to see the trousers and remarked that the objection was "well taken, in view of the . . . admissions of [defense] counsel."[60] Davis replied that if the judge thought it might prejudice Fukunaga's case, he would withdraw his offer. He hardly needed the suitcase and blood-stained pants as evidence anymore after Beebe admitted that Fukunaga killed Gill, which the prosecution had been seeking to establish up to that point. But the stipulation, if it was a defense strategy, was not followed, as would have been expected, with evidence demonstrating that Fukunaga was legally insane when he killed Gill. This horrendous blunder of admitting that Fukunaga killed Gill was considered by his new attorneys so harmful to him that they included a separate section on "Effect of Stipulating that Defendant Did the Killing" in their appeal brief to the Ninth U.S. Circuit Court of Appeals (see chapter 6).

During Beebe's cross-examination of McIntosh, he testified that he conducted a search of Fukunaga's room at the Serene. Beebe asked if he found in the room sheets of paper with writing on them, which were the "Schedule of Undertaking Okay!" and the "Scenario." But before McIntosh could respond, Davis interjected that the prosecution was perfectly willing to have them introduced as evidence because he knew that they indicated Fukunaga's planning of the crime.[61] For the remainder of the trial, both the defense and prosecuting attorneys would continue to make such significant concessions for the benefit of their ostensible opponents, which accelerated the pace of the proceedings. The trial also moved faster because both sides, especially Beebe, made far fewer objections than one might expect in such a trial. Any objections that afternoon also lacked the harshness of those during the morning session, such as when Davis objected to a question as "incompetent, irrelevant and immaterial," almost as though he was challenging the legal competence of the defense attorneys. In addition, the trial proceedings were hastened by the defense waiving cross-examination of five consecutive prosecution witnesses and the last two of them.

Carl Vickery was the prosecution's next witness, who testified that he went to the area where Gill's body was found with "Mr. Holt and the two Matsumoto boys."[62] Vickery discovered the body during his second trip to the crime scene, so Davis began by inquiring, "The first time you went out there did you find anything?" The twenty-two-year-old Vickery responded that he found a candy box and some string. Davis repeated his question, and Vickery replied, "In the den." Sensing Davis's frustration, Beebe returned the favor recently made by his "brother" Davis by offering, "We will admit he discovered the body." Davis next handed Vickery a deuce of hearts card torn in half, which was what Davis had wanted him to say he found, and inquired if Vickery had seen it before. The defense again passed on cross-examination.

Fully aware by now of his more collegial relationship with the defense counsel, Davis asked if they would stipulate that a note of sympathy was sent by Fukunaga together with flowers to the Jamieson home on the day of Gill's funeral, or would he have to call the florist to testify such.[63] Huber said they would so stipulate. Davis next requested the defense to stipulate that a letter and a $5 bill were received by the *Star-Bulletin*, or they would call Wallace Farrington, the newspaper's publisher and the governor of Hawai'i, to so testify, and Huber agreed again. Davis then brought up the earlier defense stipulation for the benefit of the jury, and Beebe complied, "We have agreed to stipulate and do stipulate that the defendant killed George Gill Jamieson."[64] It was almost as if a tacit agreement had been made between the defense and prosecuting attorneys to have the trial end as quickly as possible with a guilty verdict for Fukunaga. In particular, the defense making objections and cross-examining witnesses during the morning court session appears to have been a public performance to show that they at least tried to defend Fukunaga.

Shortly before 5 P.M., after the last of the fourteen prosecution witnesses had taken the stand in an avalanche of damaging evidence against Fukunaga, Davis brought their case to a close by simply stating, "We rest." After a recess, Davis requested that it be stipulated between the prosecution and the defense that all written exhibits submitted into evidence would be considered as having been read to the jury, and Huber agreed for the defense. Before adjourning court, to be certain that the jury understood the meaning of stipulation, Judge Steadman informed them that they "mean admissions, and they are the same as if given from the witness stand" and are part of the evidence to be considered by the jury.[65] Of course, the most crucial stipulation in the trial was the defense admission that Fukunaga killed Gill, "the same as if given from the witness stand" by Fukunaga himself.

Thursday, October 4: The Defense

Before court began, Fukunaga's mother Hide met with him for ten minutes in the judge's chambers and then had a brief conversation with his attorneys.[66] A journalist who observed a portion of her meeting with her son described her as a "spare, work worn little woman, who appeared in a cheap but spotlessly clean wash dress with her hair done up behind in a tight knot," a description that would have applied to thousands of issei middle-aged or older women. Mrs. Fukunaga was said to have "bowed dutifully to everybody from the judge who showed her into his chambers to the men in uniform standing guard—bowed when she went in, bowed again when she came out." But this time she and her son parted with no tears in their eyes, and it would be the only appearance of Fukunaga's parents at his trial.

The trial resumed before 8:50 A.M. with Beebe recalling Dr. Faus for further cross-examination. Although no testimony had been presented on the subject and nothing said about it by Fukunaga in his confession, Beebe inquired if Faus found a "history of a hatred of Japanese women." Faus replied, "Not of Japanese women. He said he had been educated in American schools and learned to dislike everything Japanese, that is, referring to old Japan."[67] Fukunaga's public-school education probably reflected the ongoing anti-Japanese movement, which had made its way into the school curriculum.

Beebe then addressed the court, bringing up yet another agreement between the prosecution and defense. He began by saying that they considered calling "Yutaka's mother" as a witness, but not for sympathy; however, Fukunaga did not want her to testify. Beebe related that "the prosecuting attorney has kindly consented to stipulate the fact that Myles is now . . . under twenty years of age," which made him legally a minor.[68] He continued with what his mother would have testified: "That prior to the occasion in question he had always been a good boy; that while he worked at the Queen's Hospital he contributed the sum of . . . thirty-five dollars of the forty he made [a month] to his parents . . . ; that he was kind to the children and kind to animals." Beebe added that Fukunaga's mother would also have testified that, at the time of his suicide attempt, she did not know it was such, but he was "worried and down-hearted."

Beebe next said he wished to draw the jury's attention to some statements in the sheets of paper retrieved from Fukunaga's room—the "Schedule of Undertaking Okay!" and the "Scenario" handwritten texts. He noted that the first sheet was a plan that was mentioned in Fukunaga's confession.[69] Beebe then read the Schedule into evidence and pointed out the statement, "With no intent to kill," on the back of the sheet to emphasize that Fukunaga's killing of Gill was not premeditated. At 9:05 A.M., after presenting their case for a total of nineteen minutes, the defense rested without making an opening statement or calling any witnesses on Fukunaga's behalf.[70] Beebe and Huber very likely decided not to have Fukunaga testify because, under cross-examination by Davis, who had already questioned him, he probably would have repeated the incriminating statements made in his confession, which indicated his deliberation and premeditation of the killing. Fulfilling his reciprocal role, Davis responded to the defense, "No rebuttal." Beebe next requested that they have the same stipulation concerning their sole exhibit of the nine sheets of paper as having been read into evidence as the prosecution had with their written exhibits, and the judge agreed.

Judge Steadman then told the jurors to proceed to the "*makai* side" (toward the sea) of the courthouse until they were called back for closing arguments. Deputy city attorney Brooks spoke first for the prosecution. He pronounced, "The killing has been admitted and that the defendant is the man who did it. . . . Gill Jamieson was the victim of a deliberate plan by the defendant to murder. The little boy had done no wrong. He was of those of whom Our Saviour spoke when He said, 'Suffer little children to come unto me for theirs is the Kingdom of Heaven.' He was like a lamb led to slaughter."[71]

Beebe then spoke for the defense, relating that it was his first murder trial and he hoped his last. He continued: "How could such a person as this defendant do a crime of such magnitude? That is the question I have been asking myself—why?[72] . . . When I look at him, when I read his history, when I saw his mother, when I talked to the people at the hospital, the thought constantly recurred to me, why? You must answer that question, why? The prosecution says that it was premeditated, deliberate and with malice aforethought, but look what he did before anything was done. Can you imagine a sane man doing what the defendant did? He starts out with a 'Schedule of Undertaking Okay!' and on the second page, writes in his own handwriting, 'No intent to kill.'"[73] Beebe argued there was evidence that the kidnapping was premeditated but not the murder. He ended, "They call him cool, calculating, cunning. Can you imagine a rational human doing the things he did? If you can, then do the popular thing and hang him."[74] While Beebe asked the jurors to ask themselves *why* Fukunaga killed Gill Jamieson, the more significant question, which he also posed to them, was *how* could Fukunaga have committed such a brutal murder that was totally at odds with his mild-mannered, quiet, and responsible character. He implied that it was because Fukunaga was not a "sane man" or a "rational human," but that hardly established he was legally insane—that he could not differentiate between right and wrong when he killed Gill. Beebe weakly argued that Fukunaga lacked this ability because he had no religious education.

In his closing argument for the prosecution, Davis asserted in part: "We may engage in mental gymnastics, psychology or anything you wish, but what I shall give you is the facts in the case from the evidence. Did this boy know the difference between right and wrong? If he did, he is guilty of murder in the first degree. If not, he is insane. He was just as fortunate as you and I. He was born under the American flag. He had more education than many of those who sit on the jury have testified that they enjoyed. . . . I say this boy had all the opportunities afforded any American citizen." Davis continued that Fukunaga had revealed himself through his actions and confession to be "cowardly, egocentric, . . . actuated by greed and a petty cause of revenge. What he really wanted was money, lots of money, and to get it easy. No sane or intelligent mind can for a moment say that this boy does not know the difference between right and wrong."[75]

At this close of the trial, Davis dropped his previous references to Fukunaga belonging to the "Japanese race" and wrapped him in the American flag. He maintained in colorblind mode that Fukunaga "had all the opportunities afforded any American citizen" and was "just as fortunate as you and I," conclusions which required Davis to engage in mental gymnastics of his own. He also referenced what has been termed "constitutional colorblindness" in arguing that Fukunaga had been given a fair and impartial trial by the court, which is provided by the Fifth and Fourteenth Amendments to the Constitution, particularly rights to due process and equal protection under the law. Both Davis and the defense attorneys invoked the legal definition of insanity based on the inability to distinguish between right and wrong and ignored the issue of compelling force.

Thursday, October 4: Jury Instructions and Verdict

Judge Steadman had told the jury earlier that the trial would finish before the end of the week so that it would not interfere with their voting in the primary election on Saturday.[76] True to his word, he gave his instructions to them on Thursday afternoon. They were lengthy, detailed, and specific and took more time to deliver than the defense did with their case. Steadman began by reading the definition of murder according to Hawaiʻi law: "Murder is the killing of any human being with malice aforethought, without authority, justification or extenuation by law, and is of two degrees, the first and second, which shall be found by the jury."[77] He explained that "malice aforethought signifies the intent from which flows an unlawful and injurious act" and that an act committed with it shows "general malevolence or unkindness of heart." Steadman then differentiated between first-degree murder, which involves "deliberate, premeditated malice aforethought," and second-degree murder, in which, while malice aforethought is evident, deliberation and premeditation are not. He also instructed the jurors that, "when the act of killing another is proved, malice aforethought shall be presumed, and the burden shall rest upon the party who committed the killing to show that it did not exist or a legal justification or extenuation" did.[78] The stipulation that Fukunaga killed Gill Jamieson thus placed upon him the burden to demonstrate that the killing was not done with malice aforethought or that it was justified legally or by extenuating circumstances.

The judge then turned to the legal definition of being considered sane or insane. He informed the jury that if one has sufficient understanding to know right from wrong concerning a certain act and is able to comprehend the consequences of such an act, the law considers one sane. He continued, if they find that Fukunaga "was so mentally deranged or insane that he could not discern the nature and criminality of the act done by him," they should find him not guilty by reason of insanity.[79] However, Steadman failed to instruct the jurors about another section in the territorial insanity act, which provided that a person could be found legally insane, and hence not guilty, if it was established that she or he was compelled to act by a force which could not be resisted.

Last, Judge Steadman told the jury that they could find Fukunaga guilty as charged; not guilty as charged but guilty of second-degree murder; or not guilty by reason of insanity.[80] The option of finding Fukunaga not guilty of both first- and second-degree murder was not included for the jury after a discussion among the prosecution and defense attorneys and the judge and resulted from the stipulation that Fukunaga killed Gill.

The jurors left the courtroom for their deliberation at 2:45 P.M. and returned with their verdict about an hour and forty-five minutes later.[81] It was read by the court clerk: "In the Circuit Court of the First Circuit, . . . The Territory of Hawaii vs. Yutaka Fukunaga, also known as Myles Yutaka Fukunaga, also known as Myles Fukunaga, Defendant, . . . we the jury in the above-entitled case, find the defendant guilty as charged."[82] Beebe declared pro forma, "We except to the verdict as being contrary to the evidence . . .

and give notice of motion for a new trial," but they never submitted it. Judge Steadman then addressed Fukunaga, informing him that he had been given the "benefit of every safeguard which the wisdom and experience of seven centuries have developed for the protection of persons charged with crime."[83] Unfortunately for Fukunaga, the Miranda warning was not established in law for another forty years, but, even if warned, he probably still would have admitted killing Gill.

Before adjourning the court, Judge Steadman delivered fulsome words of praise for the defense counsel, emphasizing that he had chosen them because of their "ability as lawyers," "integrity as men," and "standing in this community." He continued that he wanted Fukunaga to have a trial consistent with the very best traditions of American law, which he said Fukunaga did have, and that his defense by Beebe and Huber was "in all respects clean and competent and fine."[84] Whatever Steadman meant by clean, Huber and Beebe can scarcely be said to have provided Fukunaga with a competent defense, not if it took less than twenty minutes, which was one of the more flagrant racial injustices in his trial. Another certainly was the mutual cooperation between the defense and prosecuting attorneys, which culminated with the stipulation that Fukunaga killed Gill.

Fukunaga was then taken by two prison guards to a small court anteroom, where he sat dejectedly as people passed by to have a look at him.[85] Three young women, two Japanese Americans and a Native Hawaiian, entered the room, all of them nurses at Queen's Hospital where they had known Myles. Upon seeing them, he stood up, and one of the Japanese women took his hand and began crying quietly and was joined shortly by the two others. Overcome with emotion, Myles began crying himself but quickly turned away so they would not see his tears, which he wiped away with the back of his hand. After he turned to face them with an attempted smile, the women whispered quiet words of sympathy to him, and each in turn lightly took his hand and said good-bye. One of them placed her arm around his back in a momentary embrace, and he bowed to her as she left the room. Two guards then escorted Fukunaga through a corridor lined with onlookers to a waiting car. Once inside, his head fell forward and his body collapsed in the seat as the weight of his conviction overwhelmed him.[86]

Monday, October 8: Death Sentence

According to Hawai'i law, forty-eight hours must pass between conviction and sentencing in first-degree murder trials and, because two days later it was Saturday when court was not in session, Fukunaga was sentenced on

Monday. In contrast to when his guilty verdict was announced, no Japanese Americans were present. The law provided only one sentence for first-degree murder, and so Fukunaga received the death penalty before another packed courtroom. Given the opportunity before his sentencing to address the court, he spoke in a barely audible voice full of emotion: "I wish to say that I have been given a fair trial and that I will accept the punishment my penalty gives to me, and only in the fulfillment of this punishment I will be forgiven in the eyes of God; and, if possible, I wish to be forgiven by my family. I thank all the people and all the jurymen and the court officials who have done everything for me. And to my lawyers standing beside me I give all my thanks. That is all."[87] Since Fukunaga spoke so softly, the court stenographer did not hear all of his statement and so asked him to repeat it. It then became apparent that he had memorized his speech because he repeated it verbatim, although he appeared emotionally to have difficulty saying it again.

Judge Steadman then issued his sentence: "Myles Yutaka Fukunaga, it is the sentence of the court that you be taken to Oahu prison . . . and that upon a date and place designated by the Governor of the Territory of Hawaii you shall suffer the punishment of death; that you be hanged by the neck until you are dead, dead, dead."[88] Fukunaga thus received the death penalty less than three weeks after committing his crime because Haoles wanted immediate revenge for his murdering one of their own. Already the newspapers predicted that his execution would likely take place in about three weeks. While that was not the case, Fukunaga's death sentence was still racially significant as a prompt assertion of Haole power to enforce the racial boundary between themselves and non-Haoles.

In only one other murder case in territorial Hawai'i can the convicted person be said to have been raced to death as quickly as Fukunaga.[89] On October 26, 1904, Jose Miranda, a twenty-four-year-old Puerto Rican immigrant, was hanged for stabbing to death a well-known Haole banker, Samuel "Eddie" Damon of Bishop and Co., on September 27 just outside of Honolulu.[90] Miranda and two other Puerto Ricans had been stopped by Damon for taking a lantern that had been placed along a road. The three individuals, described by the press as "all dissolute Porto Rican thieves and vagrants," were arrested by the police later that night.[91] Miranda had immigrated to Hawai'i four years previously as a plantation labor recruit and had been released from prison ten days earlier after serving a two-year sentence.[92]

The day after the killing the grand jury indicted Miranda for first-degree murder. Despite difficulty finding attorneys to defend him, two were appointed by the court on September 29.[93] Four days later, jury selection began on October 3 and was completed the next day, so the trial commenced with witness testimony on October 5 and was over the following day. On that same day, the jury was given the case and, since the "feeling of horror and justice was prompt," it returned a guilty verdict after deliberating briefly.[94] On October 11, Miranda was sentenced to be hanged, just two weeks after he killed Damon. With no appeal of his conviction by his attorneys, Miranda was hanged less than a month after his crime. Besides the speed of his execution, other racial features of the case were that Puerto Ricans were arguably the most despised group in Hawai'i at that time and that Miranda had murdered a Haole of prominent status. In stark contrast, only one Haole was hanged during the territorial period because they were often charged with lesser crimes than first-degree murder, particularly when they killed an Asian (see chapter 6).

Another indication that the judicial proceedings in the Fukunaga case differed significantly from that in other homicide cases is evident from a *Hawaii Hochi* interview with Dr. Harry Arnold, president of the local medical association, about a week after Fukunaga's sentencing. He denied a rumor prevalent in Honolulu that the association members had agreed to boycott the defense and decline to testify about Fukunaga's possible insanity.[95] Arnold said he did not know of any such agreement and cited the case of a Japanese man in Wahiawa who had killed his wife and whose sanity was questioned. He related that the court ordered the accused kept under observation for several weeks and appointed three doctors—himself and Drs. Chung and Eckerdt—to examine the Japanese man. Together they conducted observations for three to four hours daily for several days until they were convinced that he was legally insane and reported their finding to the court. As a result, he was not tried for murder but instead was committed to a mental institution. Arnold remarked that this same procedure of an extended examination should have been followed in Fukunaga's case and added that it was perhaps appropriate. However, it was not pursued because it would have delayed putting Fukunaga on trial, and a lengthier evaluation might have uncovered evidence of his legal insanity.

While waiting for his sentencing and possibly earlier during his imprisonment, Fukunaga began reading the Bible, which someone had given him.[96] According to a prison guard, "He reads that and magazines and a couple of books he has. Oh, he's all right. He eats and he sleeps. Nobody has been to see him." But one of Fukunaga's visitors after he was found guilty was Rev. Tokuji Komuro, pastor of Harris Memorial Methodist Church, who met with him the next day for twenty minutes. Two days later Fukunaga telephoned the reverend, who went to the prison and spoke with him about Christianity and life after death for about an hour and fifteen minutes.[97] Komuro related that

Fukunaga was calm and composed in his prison cell, showed repentance for his wrongdoing, and told him that he was prepared to be hanged. Fukunaga would shortly be baptized a Catholic, probably because the prison chaplain was a Catholic priest, whom Fukunaga requested to meet with a week after he was sentenced to death.

Eighty Years Hence

In 2009, criminal defense and civil rights attorney Clayton Ikei of Honolulu was requested by the *Hawai'i Herald*, the English-language counterpart of the *Hawaii Hochi*, to review the judicial record of the Fukunaga case and to provide his legal opinion of the quality of justice therein. In his written evaluation published in the *Herald*, Ikei asserted, "The record of this case clearly discloses that Fukunaga's court-appointed counsel failed to accord their client a minimal degree of competent representation essential [for] a person charged with such a heinous crime."[98] He listed several significant defense issues. First, Fukunaga's attorneys, Beebe and Huber, should have requested a change of venue for the trial from O'ahu, where public passions had especially arisen, and should have moved for a continuance so they could have sufficient time for developing their defense.

Second, Ikei pointed out that Judge Steadman allowed on the jury two jurors who both had participated in the search for Gill Jamieson, knew his father Frederick, and had formed opinions about the case. He observed that this claimed error of permitting biased jurors to decide the case was denied by the territorial Supreme Court on the grounds that the defense could have used its peremptory challenges to have them removed from the jury. Third, Ikei emphasized that Fukunaga's attorneys stipulated that he killed Gill but did not advance an insanity defense and did not have him testify "to expose his obvious derangement to the jury." Ikei concluded, "Hawaii's court system proved not only incapable of providing Fukunaga with the competent and vigorous defense he deserved, but became the community's accomplice in hastening the process to his ultimate execution." While certainly valid from a legal perspective, which is what he was asked to provide, Ikei's review does not discuss the racial injustices of the Fukunaga case, which became increasingly apparent following his death sentence, beginning with the issue of his possible insanity.

5. The Insanity Question

Two days after he killed Gill Jamieson, Myles Fukunaga sent a letter signed "The Three Kings" to the *Honolulu Star-Bulletin*, which revealed that the boy was dead. The paper described the letter as "written in ink in a fine hand that suggested a criminal of more than the usual intellect and education, or a crazy religious lunatic whose garbled brain conceived a crime."[1] Such references by the press about Fukunaga being mentally disturbed would soon end after he was arrested two days later; otherwise, he might escape being hanged. But the day Fukunaga was sentenced to death, the *Hawaii Hochi* brought up the issue of his possible insanity. Also following the trial closely were UH professor Lockwood Myrick Jr. and U.S. Navy doctor Joseph Thompson, who would state in writing that Fukunaga was legally and mentally insane, respectively. Based primarily on Myrick's more substantial analysis, this chapter addresses, to the extent possible, whether Fukunaga was sane, mentally insane, or legally insane, according to the territorial Insanity Act of 1925.

"An Open Letter"

In the preface to his "An Open Letter to Governor Wallace R. Farrington on Fukunaga's Insanity," sent on November 5, 1928, the thirty-five-year-old Myrick explained why he decided to research and write it.[2] He had been at UH Mānoa as the sole faculty member of the Department of Philosophy since 1926, having earned both a bachelor's degree in 1915 and a master's degree two years later from Harvard University.[3] Joining the chorus of voices that claimed the killing of Gill Jamieson was unprecedented in the annals of crime in Hawai'i, he asserted that "nothing like it has ever occurred before, nothing like it is likely ever to occur again." As for Gill's slayer, Myrick observed, "I was interested in Fukunaga, . . . not as an intriguing psychological specimen, but as a human being. I had expected the murderer to be as brutal as the crime he had committed; instead he proved to be finer-grained than three-quarters of our population. Here was a discrepancy which tantalized my mind and would give me no rest."[4] So Myrick devoted more than three weeks with little rest to working on his study.

Before he began the research for his report, Myrick believed that Fukunaga was legally sane and should be hanged for his crime.[5] However, by Friday, September 28, before the trial began the following Monday, Myrick's interest in Fukunaga as a "human problem" had escalated, so he asked Sheriff Patrick Gleason if he could interview Fukunaga and was told he could once the trial was over. Thus, on the day Fukunaga was sentenced to death (October 8), Myrick informed Attorney General Harry Hewitt about his desire to interview Fukunaga, and Hewitt was sufficiently interested that he told him to contact Governor Farrington. The governor said he had no objection and advised that Hewitt and a stenographer should be present with Myrick during the interview. Hewitt at once called his stenographer, and the three of them went to Oahu Prison to speak with Fukunaga, who agreed to be questioned. Hewitt then asked Myrick to call him the next morning to schedule the interview, but when he did, Hewitt informed Myrick that it was not going to happen. Hewitt said he just had a meeting with the governor and Prof. Stanley Porteus, and Hewitt and Farrington concluded that further questioning of Fukunaga would not yield anything important. Given the governor's initial consent to Fukunaga's being interviewed, the rescinding of his permission just two days later can be understood as part of the larger cover-up by government authorities and the press of any evidence indicating Fukunaga's insanity or even abnormality. It is especially significant that Farrington reached his decision after meeting with Porteus, who had examined Fukunaga before the trial and thus was aware of what he might say to Myrick, which might demonstrate that he was at least mentally insane.

Before writing his "Open Letter," Myrick was involved in the Fukunaga case in other ways. In an October 8 letter to the editor in response to a *Star-Bulletin* editorial about the case published that day, Myrick wrote in part, "Instead of saying that anyone fortunate enough to be born under the American flag has only himself to blame if he fails to rise to eminence, would it not be . . . a little more American, a little more Christian, to see that every American child really does have a fair chance?" However, Myrick's letter was not printed in the *Star-Bulletin*, so he sent it to the *Hawaii Hochi*, which did publish it.[6]

Two days later, Myrick wrote a second letter to the *Star-Bulletin*, which appeared in the street edition of the paper but not in its main edition sent to subscribers, criticizing another of its editorials (October 9) about the Fukunaga case. So he again requested the *Hochi* to print his letter, and the paper agreed.[7] Myrick began by pointing out several errors in the *Star-Bulletin* editorial, which also could be said of some of its news articles concerning the incident. He noted that Fukunaga did not leave Queen's Hospital on March 13 as part of a plan "to commit a terrible crime," as the *Star-Bulletin* claimed, because it was not until "after May 7 [when the rent collector came] did he ever think of doing any wrong." Myrick then raised the issue of racial equality for Fukunaga, denying that he had been given a fair chance in life: "He had just enough schooling to whet his desire for more, which we refused to grant him. To say that he could have gone on with his education had he been determined enough is to talk nonsense. Out of the 168 hours of each week he was working 80." Emphasizing the issue of societal responsibility for Fukunaga's wrongdoing, advanced also by the *Hochi*, Myrick asserted, "Everyone knows that to a very large extent he was the victim of circumstances. If his death leads us to study these circumstances . . . and to do what we can to correct them, his life will not have been wasted." Myrick concluded that he hoped he could recognize that Fukunaga's tragic life revealed the "painfully difficult situation of our American-born children of Oriental descent" and that he had sufficient appreciation of "American fair play to realize our own share of responsibility" for his crime. Besides these poignant letters to the *Star-Bulletin*, at about the same time, Myrick signed the petition initiated by Japanese American community leaders to Governor Farrington, which requested that Farrington allow Dr. Thompson to perform a complete psychiatric examination of Fukunaga.

Before turning to a review of Myrick's study, it is useful to note the observations about Fukunaga by his former teachers, employers, and co-workers that appeared in the press shortly after his arrest. These personal comments are overwhelmingly positive, and many include the remark that they found it very difficult to comprehend he had committed such a brutal murder. Those who knew Fukunaga when he was a student consistently described him as very bright and quiet and not the sort of person they would even think might kill someone. George Raymond, the principal of the school on Kaua'i that Myles attended for four years, related, "It is inconceivable that the boy Yutaka Fukunaga that I knew as a student in the Kapaa School could be capable of the crime with which he is charged."[8] Raymond said he recalled Myles very well and explained that when a student graduates, the principal remembers them as "bad, naughty, average or exceptional," and Fukunaga was the latter. The Kapaa School Bulletin included "Yutaka Fukunaga" on its editorial staff for several years. A brief note in the December 9, 1924, issue stated, "Yutaka Fukunaga of grade eight left for Oahu last week. He was a great worker, and we all will miss him."[9]

After his family moved to O'ahu, they lived in Waialua, and Fukunaga's father worked for the Waialua Pineapple Company. Myles attended the eighth grade at Waialua School, where he was said to be very popular among his classmates. His teachers considered him "one of the brightest scholars of his class," and his grades were so high at the end of the school year that he was excused from taking all of his exams.[10] He was also given the honor of delivering the opening address at the commencement ceremony for his eighth-grade class in June 1925, of which he was quite proud.[11] Continuing to demonstrate his writing skills, Myles was the editor of the Waialua School paper for several issues, and his class compositions were held up for his classmates as "models of excellency" by his teachers.[12]

In September 1925 Fukunaga's family moved to Honolulu, and he soon found employment at Queen's Hospital, where he remained for about two-and-a-half years. His former fellow workers described him as "polished, courteous and industrious" and able to recite "yards of Macbeth" with no difficulty.[13] The superintendent of Queen's told Myrick that Fukunaga "had not only been courteous and reliable, but he had an unusually pleasant manner with the patients." At the Seaside Hotel, the head waiter informed Myrick that "he had never known a boy quite like Myles. . . . Besides being trustworthy, Myles was smiling, clean and never 'saucy.' He was thoughtful and reserved; he brooded over things, was nervous, and was a constant reader. He had no bad habits."[14] These uniformly positive descriptions of Fukunaga are consistent with the comments of those who knew him best—his parents and other close relatives—that they could not believe he had carried out such a heinous murder because it was totally at odds with his personal character.

Turning to Myrick's study, after several weeks of intensive research, he completed it on November 5 and sent it to Governor Farrington. Myrick also provided copies to the *Star-Bulletin* and *Advertiser*, both of which chose to ignore it, not even mentioning it having been written, which also can be seen as part of a concerted effort to conceal any information that might bring into question Fukunaga's conviction and death sentence. As for why he did not finalize his analysis until a month after Fukunaga's trial was over, Myrick explained that he could not finish it earlier because it required more than three weeks of "the hardest kind of mental work."[15] He implicitly argued for a new trial for Fukunaga by quoting from a *Star-Bulletin* editorial of October 22, which stated that if evidence proving Fukunaga was insane developed after his trial that "due diligence" could not have uncovered before, then "every good citizen would demand that the case be reopened." Myrick contended that his analysis provided such evidence.

While titled a letter, Myrick's report reads more like a lengthy academic study, consisting of forty-four pages of printed text, a three-page appendix of supplementary material, and six pages of endnotes, which indicate the source of statements in the text.[16] These sources reveal Myrick's considerable research for his analysis, which included interviews with Fukunaga's parents, work supervisors and fellow employees, Prof. Porteus, and Raymond Coll Jr., managing editor of the *Advertiser*. He also had conversations about the case with defense attorneys Eugene Beebe and Seba Huber. In addition, Myrick cited as references for his study printed material, including Fukunaga's confession, "Scenario," and letter to the *Star-Bulletin*, numerous articles from the *Star-Bulletin* and the *Advertiser*, and the trial transcript.

In the very first sentence of the cover letter of his "Open Letter," Myrick declared, "Everyone knows that Myles Fukunaga is abnormal: I herewith submit evidence showing that on and before September 18, 1928, he was not only highly abnormal but legally insane."[17] The reference to legal insanity is very likely because, in rejecting the motion for a new trial for Fukunaga, Judge Albert Cristy emphasized that, while Dr. Thompson attested that Fukunaga was mentally insane, he did not state that Myles was legally insane (see chapter 6). Myrick summarized how he came to his conclusion regarding Fukunaga's legal insanity, including working day and night to review, numerous times, the official version of the crime, Fukunaga's confession, the trial transcript, and information published in the newspapers. Since he was an assistant professor of philosophy, Myrick related that his qualifications for evaluating Fukunaga's mental condition included his training in "detecting, analyzing and removing the complexes of the insane" and his more than twenty years of first-hand experience with insanity, perhaps a reference to his mentally ill father.[18] He also raised the question that many asked about Fukunaga: "How could anyone so exceptionally fine do anything so exceptionally brutal? . . . Parents, school-mates, employers, fellow workers, acquaintances in general—without exception they have only words of the highest commendation."[19] Myrick ended his cover letter by recommending to the governor that he appoint a committee of highly regarded psychiatrists to establish by examining Fukunaga the validity of his conclusions, but Farrington chose not to.

Myrick began his analysis of Fukunaga's legal insanity by reviewing his life from his childhood to when he quit working at Queen's Hospital in March 1928.[20] From Fukunaga's mother, Myrick learned that when he first started school, he was "quiet, well-behaved, and good at his studies." However, in the fourth grade and possibly earlier, his teacher gave him numerous "whippings," which led to his abrupt aversion to school, and his mother also began to hit him when he refused to go to school. Myrick argued that these beatings affected Fukunaga deeply, making him afraid of his teachers and people in general, including other boys at school. Contributing to his fear of others was his small stature, such that Fukunaga generally kept to himself as a child, and Myrick attributed his acute loneliness later in life to his childhood beatings and the resultant fear instilled in him. As will become evident, Myrick employed a psychoanalytic approach, including consideration of the influence of Fukunaga's previous experiences on his later behavior, to analyze his mental status.

While Fukunaga graduated at the head of his eighth-grade class and said he was a very bright student, Myrick asserted that he was not as bright as he thought he was. Myrick partially accounted for Fukunaga's success in school as resulting from his seeking to compensate for his "physical inferiority"; he was also (at sixteen) of high school age when he graduated from the eighth grade. But once out of school, Fukunaga had no way to compare himself with the academic ability of others his age, and hence "the more he read and studied, the more [mentally] superior he thought himself to be." Myrick claimed that at the end of his formal education, Fukunaga was highly aware of his physical inferiority and mental superiority, both of which made him keenly desirous of continuing his education. As he observed: "School had not merely given him his only pleasure; it alone gave him any hope of escaping from lifelong drudgery. . . . Failure to realize his scholastic ambitions, therefore, meant far more to him than it would have to most of us. . . . Hence the keenness of his disappointment." In his confession, Fukunaga related that "the biggest disappointment" of his life was not being able to continue with his education because he had to work to help his parents support their large family. According to Myrick, his tedious and unchallenging work at the hospital and later the hotel, "by constantly reminding him of his own misery, was driving him mad."

In his psychological analysis of Fukunaga, Myrick argued that he displayed evidence of dissociation of personality, which could be traced back to his school days. He explained: "From home came his affections [emotions] and his character, from school his intellectual training and his ambitions; but from the first there has been little connection between the two. . . . We can begin to see how so sensitive a person could have planned so horrible a crime." Myrick maintained that this dissociation widened after Fukunaga left school.[21] Partly because of his avoidance of people and because his self-education had given him very different interests from those of his co-workers, he had no friends. As a lonesome boy with no one to confide in, Fukunaga could not bring his "imagination in touch with his affections." Myrick lamented that a single friend with whom he could have discussed his plans, ambitions, and dreams would have brought them into relation with his feelings and affections. But since he had no friends, "he was driven more and more to the unreal world of books, and his dissociation increased" over time. Fukunaga said of himself that books were his only friends, which only worsened his condition by leading him further away from reality. Myrick also contended that Fukunaga's dire poverty aggravated his dissociated personality because it precluded him from satisfying his simplest desires. After giving $35 of his monthly wages to his parents, he was left with only $5 to spend on his only pleasures in life—movies and magazines. Myrick asserted that these pastimes and the books he read only aggravated his dissociation because they provided "satisfaction through the experiences of others, never through his own experiences; they never brought his own desires nearer to realization, closer to the real world." Indeed, in an essay Fukunaga wrote about a year after Myrick finished his study, he related that books, magazines, and films led him to envy the lives of the persons he read about or saw on the screen and to despise his own life (see chapter 6).

Besides movies and books, Myrick argued that Fukunaga's work experiences also did not "bring together the world of his thoughts and the real world." Though he was praised by his employers for his courtesy, industry, and pleasant personality, Fukunaga did not enjoy his work at the hospital and hotel. He worked at Queen's Hospital for two-and-a-half years before finally quitting after twice not receiving a promised $5 raise. Fukunaga spoke of seeing the "suffering about [him]" at the hospital, including in the morgue, which Myrick maintained constantly reminded him of his own suffering. To emphasize the extent of Fukunaga's misery, Myrick cited Prof. Porteus as saying to him that, in all his clinical experience, he had never learned of a "life-history so painful."[22] Myrick argued that working at the hospital amid the sick and dying made the dissociation of Fukunaga's personality fully complete. He concluded his psychological analysis of him at the time he left the hospital in March 1928 by describing Fukunaga as "repressed and dissociated to an alarming degree, but he was not legally insane." That condition would not develop until after the confrontation with the rent collector in May.

Turning to the most significant question, in a section of his study titled "His Insanity," Myrick pronounced that Fukunaga was legally insane probably since May or June 1928, "when he first became split into two persons, one non-moral or even evil, the other good."[23] He contended that Fukunaga's strongest motive for his crime and the only one requiring that he commit murder was personal vengeance against the Hawaiian Trust Co., of which he was unaware. Emphasizing this unconscious desire for revenge as the key motivating factor for Fukunaga's killing of Gill Jamieson is another instance of Myrick's applying psychoanalysis in his evaluation of him. Myrick next cited Hawai'i law regarding insanity: "No person shall be held criminally responsible for any act, to the doing of which he is compelled by force which he cannot resist, or from which he cannot escape." He claimed that Fukunaga's unconscious desire for revenge against Hawaiian Trust was that force which drove him to kill Gill. Myrick thus concluded, "Myles Fukunaga is not legally responsible since he was driven by a force whose very existence was unknown to him." He therefore focused on the inability to resist a compelling force, rather than the inability to distinguish between right and wrong, as the principal criterion by which he adjudged Fukunaga as legally insane, although he also maintained that Fukunaga lacked the capacity to differentiate between right and wrong. In contrast, the prosecuting attorneys Davis and Brooks argued that Fukunaga was legally sane because he could make that differentiation. Judge Cristy also emphasized this factor when he rejected Dr. Thompson's contention that Fukunaga was insane because Thompson did not explicitly state that Fukunaga lacked the ability to distinguish between right and wrong. The failure of Davis, Brooks, Cristy, Steadman, and the three psychiatrists who examined Fukunaga to consider that he was legally insane when he killed Gill because he was compelled by a force which he could not withstand was yet another major racial injustice in his case.

To support his conclusion that Fukunaga was legally insane because he was subject to an irresistible force of which he was unaware, Myrick analyzed various "analogies" or "symbolisms" from Fukunaga's "Scenario" of his crime.[24] The Scenario is a three-page handwritten text called such by the press because it depicts the ransom payment as though it was a movie with a cast, including the father, the son, and the "Masked One" (Fukunaga collecting the ransom). Thus for Myrick, one of the most crucial of the analogies in the Scenario involves the Holy Trinity of the Father, the Son, and the Holy Ghost, with which Fukunaga is thought to have become familiar by watching films about the life of Christ.[25] Myrick elaborated that in Fukunaga's "crazy mind all three are compatible" because he identified himself with each person of the Trinity, which explains why he referred to himself as "The

Three Kings" and the "Three Walking Shadows" in the Scenario and in the letters to Frederick Jamieson and the *Star-Bulletin*. According to Myrick, like the Christian God, Fukunaga is "three persons in one—an author or creator, which enables him to use his literary skill and his brains and to plan his own death; a Son, which enables him to demonstrate the goodness of his character and to achieve his own death; and a ghost or shadow or actor, which enables him . . . to get vengeance" before he dies. Myrick asserted that through this Christian symbolism, Fukunaga believed that "what he was doing was thoroughly good and that he *himself* was also thoroughly good, even though he knew that as an actor bringing about this good he was a bad boy" (emphasis in original).

Myrick continued that Fukunaga was unaware of these analogies because their sole purpose was to confound his notions of right and wrong, and they thus "definitely prove that he was [legally] insane."[26] As for the persistent question of how could such a responsible and mild-mannered young man, who had never been in trouble before, commit such a violent homicide, Myrick contended that the analogies strikingly reveal the process which an insane person must undergo before he or she can do something totally contrary to his or her character. He argued: "Simply *because* his character was so deep, so strong, and so fine did he become insane" (emphasis in original). Otherwise, his impoverished life circumstances would have driven him to act like any criminal. But Myrick explained that Fukunaga "had not only to meet these crushing circumstances; he had to conform to his own fine character; and the only possible solution was insanity." This argument explains why more young Japanese American men did not engage in murder, since many (if not most) shared Fukunaga's destitute condition—their educational aspirations thwarted and their days spent in low-paid drudgery work; however, not as many of them shared his admirable character and hence did not go insane.

Summarizing his analysis of Fukunaga's legal insanity, Myrick asserted that when he left Queen's Hospital in March, he was "suppressed to an alarming extent"—without the education he deeply desired, without a single friend he could confide in, without any hope that his life would improve.[27] However, this suppression provided the "necessary energy" to carry out his crime. Before this suppressed energy could be unleashed, according to Myrick, Fukunaga first had to recognize that he had been unjust to his parents and that society had been the same to him, which provided the required motives for him. Before he could act upon them, his conscience had to be overcome, which Fukunaga did first by "splitting his already badly dissociated personality into two distinct selves—one a mere doer and as different from himself as if it had occupied an entirely different body, the other his true self, a self with the noblest of purposes." Second, he had to remove his human feeling, which Myrick claimed Fukunaga could do because he found it difficult to appreciate the humanity of others and because he was willing to give up his own life. Myrick thus concluded that Fukunaga's killing of Gill was due to two factors—the depressing conditions of his life and his insanity through which his conscience finally gave its approval. His insanity in turn was also due to two factors—the same agonizing circumstances of his life and the "sensitiveness of his conscience."

But then why did the three psychiatrists who examined Fukunaga find him legally sane? Myrick observed that they had two primary reasons: first, Fukunaga's explicit statements that he knew the difference between right and wrong, to which Myrick countered that such declarations after the killing did not establish that he was aware it was wrong on or before the day he did it.[28] Second, asked by the three psychiatrists if he knew right from wrong when he was planning his crime, Fukunaga said he did. But Myrick argued that by then his personality was completely dissociated; in his innermost self, Fukunaga was "good as ever" because he was unconscious of his motive of revenge. As for Fukunaga's unsolicited declaration during his interrogation—"I am not crazy. I am sane as ever"—Myrick explained that it was because he was afraid he was insane and hence would not be executed, given that his desire for death was one of the principal motives for his crime. Not noted by Myrick was another very significant reason that the three psychiatrists found Fukunaga legally sane—their examination was far too brief.

In a section on "His Motives," Myrick maintained that Fukunaga had four of them for committing his crime.[29] First, to have himself killed; second, to obtain money for his parents; third, "to express himself for once in his life [and] to realize himself" before dying—which included demonstrating his "power" through using his intellect to carry out his plan, enjoying himself by spending money freely for the first time in his life, and acting like an American; and fourth, to exact revenge against the Hawaiian Trust Co. for the shame and grief it brought to his parents. Myrick argued that these motives were connected with and reinforced one another; for example, only by expressing himself and getting revenge could he die feeling satisfied. He also asserted that because Fukunaga was unaware of his desire for vengeance, all of his motives seemed good to him: "Mere suicide was selfish and cowardly, but suicide through sacrificing oneself for others, that was truly noble. His conscience then had no difficulty in approving of his aims." Hence, he could act upon them and carry out the killing.

Concerning his desire to demonstrate his intellectual power by implementing his plan, Myrick cited Fukunaga's remark to a fellow Serene Rooms tenant: "Whoever's behind this [killing] must have brains, all right." He also noted the first sentence in his letter to the *Star-Bulletin*: "As a result of our recent exploits, we 'Three Kings' find the community all agog and in a state of suspense and terror," in which Fukunaga takes credit for the widespread fear he had created. Myrick did not mention statements in Fukunaga's confession that show Fukunaga viewed his crime as requiring concentrated thought—how he had "planned everything" in it and "studied" and not just read about the Leopold and Loeb case. As for quoting from Shakespeare and Walt Whitman, Fukunaga revealingly said he did so to demonstrate his literary knowledge, if not mental superiority, so that others would think that a person with a college education was responsible for Gill's murder.

With regard to Fukunaga's wanting to enjoy himself by spending money, which the prosecution and press emphasized as the main reason for his crime, Myrick countered that its importance was greatly exaggerated because a statement from his confession was highly misinterpreted: "Before midnight [Saturday] I was going to give up anyway. Because if I could not spend the money I might as well give up." Rather than on himself, Fukunaga wanted to use the ransom money to send his parents back to Japan, although he did spend some of it on a new pair of trousers, a fountain pen, a tryst with a prostitute, and his last visit to Waialua.

As for Fukunaga's desire to act like an American, Myrick claimed that "by imitating Americans, he could believe he really was an American." This argument supposedly explains why he copied Leopold and Loeb and Hickman so closely in kidnapping and killing Gill.[30] During the pre–World War II period in Hawai'i, it was very common to equate Americans with Whites, even among Japanese Americans. However, it does seem highly questionable to argue that the reason Fukunaga imitated three vicious White killers was so that he could truly feel he was an American. He could have acted like an American in numerous other ways besides murdering someone, such as improving his writing and speaking skills in English, as many nisei, including Fukunaga, sought to do. Calling himself by his American name was another means other nisei frequently used to assert their Americanness.

In the conclusion of his analysis, Myrick, by focusing on how Fukunaga was denied a "fair chance" before, during, and after his trial because he was not Haole, emphasized the racial injustices Fukunaga faced.[31] He elaborated that before his trial, Fukunaga did not have a fair chance because: "We did everything in our power to arouse in him an intense desire for education—only to deny him all means of satisfying it. We did everything in our power to turn him away from his own people and to make him want to be an American above everything else—only to have nothing to do with him thereafter. . . . It was we who denied him the simplest pleasures, except such as could come from books, movies and $5.00 a month of spending money." Obviously, the "we" that Myrick invoked referred to the dominant Haoles, who used their power to deny Fukunaga (and other non-Haoles) his fair chance in education and employment, his rights as an American, and his pursuit of the simplest pleasures. Myrick thus did not blame Fukunaga alone for his crime but found fault with Haoles as indirectly responsible by creating the depressing circumstances of his life and by denying him the means to change them. But Fukunaga was hardly alone in facing those agonizing conditions that many other non-Haoles also confronted on a daily basis without murdering young Haole boys. Racial oppression alone cannot account for his crime; his legal insanity was the decisive factor that drove Fukunaga to murder Gill.

During his trial, Myrick contended that Fukunaga did not have a fair chance because the "defense was woefully, needlessly, inexcusably weak." He related that defense attorney Seba Huber knew that Dr. Thompson could have testified on Fukunaga's behalf and that Huber had been strongly advised by another lawyer to call Thompson as a witness but Huber refused. Myrick also revealed a discussion he had with someone "who is in as good a position as anyone in the city . . . to know the inside of events," who told him, when complaining about the weakness of the defense, that Fukunaga would have been found guilty of murder no matter what the defense had been. Myrick continued that this person said that Fukunaga was "abnormal," and that "if he had been a haole, if the roles of murderer and murdered had been reversed," he would have been found not guilty. Myrick added, "This person now says that all he meant was that if Fukunaga's parents had been rich they could have hired alienists who would have saved Myles . . . ; it was, he says, a question not of race but of money." In short, this incident was another feeble attempt to obfuscate the salience of race in Fukunaga's conviction, in this case by class. In his report, Myrick did not identify this person but, after Fukunaga was hanged, the *Hochi* revealed that Myrick had informed them much earlier that it was Raymond Coll Jr., the managing editor of the *Advertiser*, who denied it was he.

Since the trial, Myrick maintained that Fukunaga had also been denied a fair chance. After sentencing, Fukunaga's attorney Eugene Beebe was not permitted to see him, nor was any psychiatrist. Myrick added, after first being interested in having him interview Fukunaga, Attorney General Hewitt changed his mind after the trial when he learned that Myrick's findings might be reported in the local newspapers. Myrick concluded his "Open Letter" by requesting that the governor grant executive clemency to Fukunaga because "it would silence the people who are saying that if Myles Fukunaga had been a haole of good family," he would have been acquitted. The racial significance of the Fukunaga case is hence confirmed by his eventual hanging because he was not "a haole of good family." Race enabled such Haoles to escape the gallows, while those who did not were all non-Haole except for one person.

Shortly after sending his "Open Letter" to Governor Farrington, Myrick shared a copy with Dr. Arthur L. Dean, who had been the previous president of the University of Hawai'i between 1914 and 1927. After discussing Myrick's report with him for an exhausting hour and a half, Dean returned it the next day with a letter in which he stated that he found Myrick's conclusions unconvincing, although he admitted not having any expertise in insanity.[32] Dean expressed stronger criticism of Myrick's study for its racial consequences than for its analysis of Fukunaga's insanity. "You, sir, are lending yourself to stir up hatred and strife," he wrote. "I believe that in fomenting race antagonism you are committing a terrible crime against society." Dean added that he had lived in Hawai'i for more than fourteen years and, in an assertion of emergent multiculturalism, informed Myrick that he knew of "no place where such diverse peoples dwell in a finer spirit." As an educator, he might have asked some of those diverse peoples if they shared his opinion about living together in Hawai'i.

Thompson's Affidavit

The other document that argued Fukunaga was insane when he killed Gill Jamieson was the affidavit submitted by Dr. Joseph Thompson on October 13 in support of a motion for a new trial for him. His qualifications as a psychoanalyst included having graduated with a medical degree from Columbia University in 1896, serving as a medical officer in the navy since 1897, and having conducted an intensive study of psychiatric cases in Honolulu, Guam, Washington, D.C., and Baltimore during the past seven years. Thompson became involved in the Fukunaga case as a result of representatives of the *Hawaii Hochi* approaching him. As the paper explained, they remembered there was a psychoanalyst who might have an opinion about Fukunaga, but by the time they called Thompson, the trial was over; nonetheless, they informed his defense attorneys about him.[33]

Contacted by Eugene Beebe, Thompson told him that he had been following the trial in the newspapers and concluded that Fukunaga was insane. According to the *Hochi*, navy regulations prevented Thompson from coming forward earlier with his opinion because the case was a civilian matter.[34] Thompson also made a lengthy presentation on Fukunaga's insanity to Attorney General Hewitt and offered his services as an expert in psychoanalysis. He told Hewitt that he was willing to conduct an intensive study of Fukunaga's mental condition if he could interview him, but Hewitt would not allow such.

As for Fukunaga being insane, Thompson stated in his affidavit that Fukunaga "showed to a thoroughly abnormal degree symptoms of dissociation, suggestibility, a vast amount of phantasy [*sic*], and hatred, component characteristics of the paranoid personality, confusion, identification, typical paranoid assertion of his sanity, marked introversion, regression, a suicide drive, which failed of accomplishment followed as it is so dangerously liable to be by murdering another . . . ; the testimony is filled with evidence relative to this lad's desire to die and for a youth without some serious physical illness, to desire to die is psychotic."[35] While he did not examine Fukunaga, Thompson attested in his affidavit that he had closely followed the testimony and read other evidence introduced at the trial, and that he had reviewed Fukunaga's confession and information concerning Fukunaga's behavior. However, as discussed in chapter 6, Thompson did not explicitly state that Fukunaga was legally insane.

Very similar findings are evident in Myrick's and Thompson's analyses of Fukunaga, including dissociation, suicide drive, fantasy, paranoid claims of sanity, and introversion, which lend credibility to their independent studies, despite their both not being allowed to interview him. While Myrick may have read Thompson's affidavit, he did not cite it among the many references of his study as a source or support for his own conclusions. Of the findings common between Myrick and Thompson, the only one mentioned by the three psychiatrists who testified for the prosecution at Fukunaga's trial was his suicide wish, which Faus claimed was "absolutely normal" for someone his age.

Mental vs. Legal Insanity

Unfortunately, the question of Fukunaga's sanity or insanity cannot be definitively resolved at this point in time because the necessary and sufficient information for such a conclusion does not exist and arguably did not exist when the case was still ongoing. The critical information required could have only resulted from a thorough examination of Fukunaga by an impartial committee of recognized experts in psychiatry, who could have been found in Hawai'i. The ninety-minute examination of Fukunaga conducted by the three psychiatrists was much too short, as Faus admitted in his testimony. The abbreviated questioning also contravened Hawai'i law, which stipulated that such evaluations should be conducted over a ten-day period and was the practice in the territory. Moreover, the three psychiatrists do not appear to have considered that Fukunaga might have been legally insane because he was compelled by a force he was unable to resist. Of the five experts who publicly expressed an opinion regarding Fukunaga's insanity, Myrick clearly produced the most detailed and intensive study and concluded that Fukunaga was legally insane.[36]

However, based solely on the legal criterion of being able to distinguish between right and wrong, Fukunaga may not have been legally insane when he killed Gill Jamieson, although he appears to have been mentally insane. By his statements and actions, Fukunaga demonstrated that he did know the difference between right and wrong and that killing Gill was wrong. In his ransom letter to Frederick Jamieson written the night before the murder, Fukunaga warned him not to notify or seek help from the police, which clearly indicates his awareness that he was planning a crime. In his confession, Fukunaga related that as he was riding in the taxi to Punahou School, "I kept thinking I am going to do this thing. I am going to be a bad boy from now on," as opposed to the good boy he previously had always been.[37] Before he killed Gill, Fukunaga also took actions to avoid being apprehended, such as wearing dark glasses so that he would not be recognized at the Seaside Hotel as he was taking Gill to the area behind it: "I used to work there. I didn't want the boys [workers] to see me."[38] He also wore those glasses when he went to Punahou to retrieve Gill from the school staff. In planning his misdeed, Fukunaga copied the kidnappings and murders by Leopold and Loeb and by Hickman and so was fully aware that they were crimes since those persons had already been convicted.

After the killing, Fukunaga again behaved in ways that showed he knew that he had committed a crime and hence wanted to avoid being caught. In his confession, he said in order for the police not to suspect him right away, he left cigarettes for three persons at the crime scene because he wanted them to suspect that three individuals were responsible.[39] He also signed the letters demanding the ransom payment and to the *Star-Bulletin*, "The Three Kings," so that the police would think three persons were involved. The night after the murder, Fukunaga related that he had trouble sleeping: "That night I couldn't sleep; all hours of the morning I kept thinking, 'I did it. I have to pay for this,'" which indicates his consciousness of his wrongful behavior.[40] In his letter to the *Star-Bulletin*, Fukunaga wrote that he would reveal himself to the police on September 25, "exactly a week after the crime had been committed, when we promise to mount on the scaffold of sin and to plead guilty and the death penalty we are to receive."[41] This statement demonstrates his knowledge that he had committed a crime and his intention to plead guilty for it and to accept the death penalty as his punishment. Last, in his confession, Fukunaga stated that when he was captured he was on his way home to tell his mother what he had done and was then going to turn himself in to the police.

Fukunaga also expressed remorse for killing Gill when asked by his interrogators how he felt about it, "I am sorry for what I did. I am sorry for Mrs. Jamieson."[42] In his interview at Oahu Prison the next day, Fukunaga added that he felt sorry for Gill[43] and "very ashamed and very sorry. . . . Now I realize terrible mistake."[44] During the interview, when asked why he sent flowers to Gill's parents, Fukunaga said he was sincere and thought about how the Jamiesons had suffered, and then he broke down and cried.

Furthermore, when questioned directly about his legal sanity during his interrogation—if he knew the difference between right and wrong—Fukunaga responded affirmatively. He also answered that he was sane when asked if he was sane or insane, and in his prison interview he asserted, "I am not insane. I am perfectly sane."[45] Admittedly, statements professing one's legal or mental sanity do not necessarily prove that is the case. Myrick observed that Fukunaga's repeated assertions of being sane were due to his fear that he was insane and thus would not be hanged, because he wanted to die.

As noted above, in concluding that Fukunaga was legally insane and therefore not guilty of murdering Gill Jamieson, Myrick emphasized the factor of compelling force, rather than the inability to differentiate between right and wrong, based on the Hawai'i Insanity Act. According to Myrick, this force was his desire for revenge against the Hawaiian Trust Co., which made him kill Gill. But to establish that this force existed in Fukunaga's mind would have required questioning him further because the three psychiatrists who examined him did not testify that they asked him any questions related to it. But even if Fukunaga was shown to be legally insane, that may not have precluded his conviction and execution because of the overwhelming desire that Haoles had to have him hanged as a demonstration of their supremacy, which would not tolerate any challenge to its rule.

After Fukunaga was captured, a neatly maintained scrapbook was found in his room at his parents' house.[46] Its contents included an essay titled "The Mystery We Call Life," which had been clipped from a magazine, with the first half underlined in black ink. The *Nippu Jiji* printed this marked portion of the essay that in many ways eerily describes Fukunaga and his self-admitted unhappy life, his reserved nature according to his parents and others, and his suppressed personality according to psychiatrists.

> Some people think that the world is cold and cruel.
> And they are often afraid to express themselves.
> They are usually depressed and unhappy, and they hide their true nature.
> They crawl into a figurative shell which encloses them from the outside world.
> Development is impossible to such people.
> They are shy and reserved; often afraid of everybody.
> Their own thoughts sometimes confuse them.
> Their own conclusions frequently scare them.
> Life is dishonest, even with themselves; and how can they be candid and openhearted to other people?
> These victims of repression have to go through life as hypocritical pretenders, and they are always afraid that they will unknowingly do something for which they will be penalized.
> God help the victims of this very grave mistake!

If Fukunaga kept and marked this essay because he thought that it applied to him, then it reveals much about his thoughts about his life and himself. Was he really afraid that he might "*unknowingly* do something for which [he] will be penalized?" (emphasis added). Did Fukunaga believe that he was not in full control of his actions and might commit an illegal act? While he would proclaim his sanity, did his "own thoughts sometimes confuse" him and his "own conclusions frequently scare" him? Sadly, did he consider "the world cruel and cold" and "life is dishonest"? We do know that he was "shy and reserved" and was "usually depressed and unhappy" and as a result tried to kill himself. Assuming that Fukunaga did keep a copy of this essay because it described himself, it lends credence to Myrick's analysis of his mental problems. He claimed that Fukunaga, because of his childhood beatings, was afraid of others, and that this fear resulted in his acute loneliness and being a "victim of repression" in his later life. The "figurative shell which encloses them from the outside world" can be related to Fukunaga's lonely existence and to his escape further and further into the unreal world of books and movies.[47] But then, what was his hidden "true nature," if he was "afraid to express" himself and went "through life as a hypocritical pretender?" Although Fukunaga did not write it, by his having kept and underlined this very short essay, he revealed more about his mental condition when he killed Gill than the equally short report and examination of him conducted by the three psychiatrists for his trial.

Thus, to establish that he was legally insane and therefore not responsible for murdering Gill Jamieson, for more than a year Fukunaga's supporters, led by the *Hawaii Hochi*, sought a complete psychiatric examination and a new trial for him, as the next chapter shows.

6. Aftermath of Death Sentence

Racial, Legal, and Community

While Myles Fukunaga was found guilty of first-degree murder and sentenced to be hanged, that hardly ended his case. The same day he was given the death penalty (October 8, 1928) the *Hawaii Hochi* published an editorial that referenced the racial dimensions of his conviction and death sentence.[1] It argued, "If we must kill this boy, let us be honest enough to admit we do it for revenge" because Fukunaga had murdered a Haole child from a prominent family. The editorial noted that until that point no question had been raised that would make a "racial issue" of Fukunaga's crime, but it had already become regarded as a "blot on the honor" of the Japanese American community. The *Hochi* was referring to the racial scapegoating of the community for Fukunaga's wrongdoing and the consequent intensification of the anti-Japanese movement. The newspaper itself would soon raise the racial issue in the case because of the concerted efforts by the press, the courts, and the *Nippu Jiji* to deny that race was a contributing factor in Fukunaga's rushed conviction and death penalty. I refer to this denial that race played a significant role in the case as incipient colorblindness because it was one of the first major such public assertions in the territory. Colorblindness is evident in the arguments by Haoles that Fukunaga was treated by the prosecution and court as an individual without consideration that he was of the "Japanese race" and thus had received a fair trial, the same as if he had been a Haole himself. More generally, colorblindness sustained Haole supremacy by refuting the salience of race by denying racial difference in the experiences of Haoles and non-Haoles. This chapter reviews events related to the Fukunaga case following his sentencing, including its racial dimensions, legal appeals of his conviction, Japanese American community resistance to his guilty verdict and death penalty, and, finally, his execution.

Colorblindness in the Case

As one of the leading advocates of the colorblind view of Fukunaga's conviction, the *Nippu Jiji* in a lengthy editorial on October 12 was quick to criticize the efforts to obtain a new trial for him.[2] Claiming that the initiatives originated with the *Hawaii Hochi*, the editorial described them as "deliberate and cunning attempts" to save Fukunaga from the gallows. The *Nippu Jiji* further charged that those efforts sought "to make a racial issue out of the case," as the *Hochi* had done in the language-schools dispute. As discussed in chapter 1, the *Hochi* and *Nippu Jiji* engaged in a heated conflict in the mid-1920s over laws the territorial legislature enacted to restrict the operations of Japanese language schools. In many ways, the Fukunaga case was a continuation of the fierce opposition between the two newspapers and their respective publishers, Fred Makino of the *Hawaii Hochi* and Yasutaro Soga of the *Nippu Jiji*.

I cite the *Nippu Jiji* editorial at length to delineate its early colorblind position on the Fukunaga trial and verdict, from which it did not waver very much, even after Fukunaga was hanged more than a year later.[3] It contended: "There is not, and must not be, any question of race discrimination in the Fukunaga case. This desperate little arch-fiend . . . was defended by two of the ablest lawyers of the Hawaiian bar. . . . It would be utterly impossible to conceive anything further that could have been done to give Fukunaga a fair and impartial trial." As for what could have been done, a jury consisting of fair and impartial jurors would have been a start instead of twelve men who had all read his confession in the newspapers. The editorial continued, "The particular argument in the Fukunaga case [is] that he is and was at the time of the murder insane. . . . In such cases as that of Fukunaga, however, races seem to have little weight—indeed, in view of such crimes as that committed by Loeb-Leopold and Hickman, it would seem that the white race suffers with the Japanese by comparison." The *Nippu Jiji* argued that the effort to reopen the case by the *Hochi* was a "disgraceful and utterly unwarranted attempt to provoke and breed racial animosity." Like the *Star-Bulletin* and Judge Alva Steadman (see below), the *Nippu Jiji* focused on Fukunaga's crime, in which, as it correctly stated, races seem to be of little consequence. However, the racial injustice in the Fukunaga case concerns not his crime but how he was convicted and sentenced to die because he was Japanese American and therefore subject to "race discrimination."

The *Nippu Jiji* followed its editorial with a statement asserting colorblindness in the case, which it had solicited from Judge Steadman four days after he sentenced Fukunaga to death. While he challenged the biologically based view of race, Steadman still revealed his limited understanding of the significance of race in the case. Denying racial difference in the experiences of Japanese Americans and Whites, he professed: "The Fukunaga case can be no stigma on the Japanese race any more than the Hickman and Loeb-Leopold cases can be a stigma on the Anglo-Saxon and Hebrew races. Such crimes are entirely an individual and not a racial characteristic of the particular defendant."[4] Steadman related that the people he knew, very likely Haole, did not consider the Fukunaga incident in any way a racial matter. He also defended the inclusion of Shinichi Maruyama as a juror, declaring that he was not selected for the jury as a representative of the *Nippu Jiji*. One cannot help but think that in requesting Steadman to issue his statement on the Fukunaga trial, the *Nippu Jiji* also asked him to address the issue of Maruyama as an employee of the paper serving on the jury.

As for Steadman's colorblind arguments, his contention that Fukunaga's crime was not a racial characteristic of his being Japanese is certainly valid. But his claim that "the case can be no stigma on the Japanese race" is fallacious since Japanese Americans were racially stigmatized by Fukunaga's misdeed. As the most powerful race in America in the 1920s, Whites could easily distance themselves from the vicious murders committed by Leopold, Loeb, and Hickman as the individual acts of three degenerate persons who happened to be White. But since Japanese Americans held a racially despised status in Hawai'i, they could not avoid being implicated in Fukunaga's crime, and Fukunaga could not escape being prosecuted as Japanese, instead of as an individual without reference to race. In arguing that the Fukunaga incident cannot be a stigma on Japanese Americans, Steadman was also ignoring that they were already racially stigmatized as the foremost political, economic, and cultural threat to Haoles, particularly the American-born generation like Fukunaga's. The claimed colorblindness of Haoles, like that of Steadman and his friends, was starkly contradicted by their race consciousness evident in their racialization of Japanese Americans as endangering their domination of Hawai'i. Fukunaga himself was racialized by the prosecution and some of their key witnesses when they emphasized his belonging to the "Japanese race" to account for his behavior. While the crime was obviously his, Fukunaga's speedy death penalty can be interpreted as directed not just to him but to the larger Japanese American community. It was being threatened with other harsh punishments, such as martial law or attacks against other cultural institutions besides the language schools, should it or any of its members seek to contest Haole supremacy. Like many others, Steadman was unwilling to acknowledge the primacy of race in Hawai'i and that its operation, rather than biology, resulted in differences among groups, including access to legal justice.

Another personal message from Haoles to Japanese Americans was published in the *Hawaii Hochi* from Chilton S. Childs, a "head [social] worker" at the Alexander House Settlement in Wailuku, Maui, on October 18.[5] Beginning "Dear Friends," Childs related that many "good true-hearted Japanese" had apologized to him and his friends because Gill Jamieson's murderer was Japanese and had expressed "deep racial regret and fear that other races would think all Japanese capable of such monstrosity." He thus wanted Japanese Americans to know "the way 'Haoles' think about" the issue. Childs offered that the murders by Fukunaga and Hickman "are not racial; they are the result of a twisted and distorted mind.... We haoles do not consider this question as one of race at all." Childs and the other Haoles he wrote for understood that Fukunaga's killing of Gill was not racial in the causal sense that being Japanese made him capable of doing it. However, he did not address that Fukunaga's swift conviction and death sentence were racial in motivation, again demonstrating how the racial injustices in the case were not recognized even by well-meaning Haoles.

Ongoing efforts in the Japanese American community led by the *Hawaii Hochi* to obtain a new trial for Fukunaga resulted in scrutiny by the *Honolulu Star-Bulletin* of what the *Hochi* was writing about the case. In mid-October, the *Star-Bulletin* had *Hochi* articles in Japanese translated and then maintained in its own article that "Japanese Daily Raises Race Issue in Fukunaga Case."[6] The article charged that the *Hochi* campaign was primarily an attack on the *Nippu Jiji* and that "racial aspects are emphasized very nearly to the exclusion of everything else." The paper was also very concerned that beyond Hawai'i the initiative would be "seen as racial, composed and led by Japanese," which it was to a large extent,[7] and hence would be "considered refutation of Hawaii's proud claim that here all races are as one." The latter claim was an expression of emergent multiculturalism or the false representation of Hawai'i as a racial paradise where, because "all races are as one," racial division did not exist, which was an absurd contention in the 1920s.

The same day it published its translation of *Hawaii Hochi* articles, the *Star-Bulletin* carried an editorial that criticized the campaign for a new trial for Fukunaga.[8] As though racial schism did not already prevail in the territory, it argued that seeking a new trial will "bring about race cleavage in Hawaii. It makes a racial matter of a murder that might have been committed by a person of any nationality." The editorial contended, "The Fukunaga murder

DOES NOT 'form a blot' on any class; no young Japanese has cause to be humiliated by it." Blinded by its colorblindness, the *Star-Bulletin* did not discern that the racial matter in the case did not pertain to the murder itself, which as it noted could have been committed by anyone. The racial element consisted of the quick conviction and death penalty Fukunaga received, which was far more likely for a Japanese American than a Haole. The newspaper also did not perceive how Fukunaga's conviction formed a racial blot on Japanese Americans as a result of their having become implicated in his crime through racial blame pinning, which led to many of them losing their jobs. While young Japanese may not have felt "humiliated" by Fukunaga's wrongdoing, they certainly needed to be concerned about it because nearly twenty young Japanese American men were picked up, interrogated, and detained by the police as suspects in the Jamieson murder due to racial profiling.

The very next day in another editorial, "Raising the Race Question," the *Star-Bulletin* continued to demonstrate its complete incomprehension of the racial issue in the Fukunaga incident by focusing on the crime rather than his conviction.[9] It contended, "There has been no general disposition in Hawaii—or anywhere else—to class Fukunaga's fiendish act as a racial crime. No responsible person, no responsible organization, has blamed the kidnapping and murder of Gill Jamieson on the Japanese race." Referring to the statement in a petition from Japanese American community leaders (see below) to the governor that if Fukunaga is sane his criminal action would form a "blot upon the good name of the Japanese community," the editorial asserted that it was a "clear and inexcusable attempt to use the fact of race to reopen the subject of Fukunaga's sanity." This argument is similar to those expressed decades later after colorblindness had been established as the dominant racial ideology in America that "any hints of race consciousness are tainted by racism,"[10] which serves to maintain the racial status quo of oppression and inequality.

The *Hawaii Hochi* responded to the *Star-Bulletin* editorial ("A Bad Situation Arises") with its own. The *Hochi* editorial maintained that the *Star-Bulletin* "fears the mainland reaction, which will destroy the carefully fostered illusion of racial harmony in Hawaii, so den[ies] that any racial interpretation had arisen locally" about the Fukunaga case.[11] As the *Hochi* observed, the case had attracted national and international scrutiny from leading magazines and scientific journals.[12] The editorial continued that the *Star-Bulletin* had previously sought "to make a racial issue of every important question," including the plantation strikes and Japanese American resistance against the attempt to close their language schools and hence "to stimulate race hatred and split the community wide open."

By referring to the 1920 strike and the very recent language-schools clash, the *Hochi* was framing the Fukunaga case in the larger racialized context of the ongoing anti-Japanese movement. It also was highlighting the hypocrisy of the *Star-Bulletin* in invoking race in those conflicts and then denying its significance in the Fukunaga incident. The *Star-Bulletin* represented both the strike and the language-schools lawsuit as the vanguard of the "Japanese racial menace" against Haole economic, political, and cultural domination of Hawai'i. Regarding the strike, a *Star-Bulletin* editorial asserted, "Is control of the industrialism of Hawaii to remain in the hands of Anglo-Saxons or is it to pass into those of alien Japanese agitators? . . . Given the choice . . . between destruction of the sugar industry or the Japanizing of this territory, we would prefer destruction."[13] The *Advertiser* concurred in its own editorial: "The strike is an attempt on the part of the Japanese to obtain control of the sugar industry . . . in line with Japanese policy wherever they colonize [in] Korea, Manchuria, Eastern Inner Mongolia, Shantung, and Formosa."[14] Together with the press, the dominant Haoles racialized both the strike and the language-schools dispute as strategic means by which Japanese in Hawai'i were creating opportunities for Japan to seize control of the territory from them.[15]

Less than two weeks after Fukunaga's sentencing, the *Hawaii Hochi* first presented its argument that his trial demonstrated that there were "two kinds of justice" in Hawai'i—one for Haoles and the other for non-Haoles.[16] In support of its contention that racial injustice prevailed, a *Hochi* editorial cited the killing in 1918 by "a husky haole" athlete, David Buick, who shot to death a Japanese taxi driver after robbing him of $1 yet was convicted of second-degree murder. The paper noted, unlike in the case of Fukunaga, there "was no hysterical demand for summary justice, no threats of lynching, no Vigilantes" because Buick had close connections with Haoles. After he was sentenced to prison, he was permitted to leave temporarily and work in town and eventually was pardoned by the governor after serving only part of his sentence. The *Hochi* also cited another case at Pu'unene plantation mill on Maui in which a Haole engineer poured gasoline on a Japanese worker and set him on fire to prove to him it was gasoline and not kerosene. The victim was horribly burned to death, while his killer was acquitted after being tried in court. As the *Hochi* editorialized a few days later, "Apparently in the eyes of the *Star-Bulletin*, hanging is not called for when the victim is only an Oriental! But when the son of a prominent Haole is killed, that is altogether different."[17] To underscore how the dual system of racial injustice also extended to other non-Haoles besides Japanese Americans, the *Hochi* related the case of a "lowly Porto Rican" who, acting in self-defense, stabbed and killed a member of a Haole established family and was then quickly convicted, sentenced, and hanged.[18]

Given its political significance, the Fukunaga case emerged as a contentious issue during the election campaign season in October 1928. At a Democratic Party rally in downtown Honolulu, the crowd almost broke into a riot when candidate for sheriff David K. Trask, a Native Hawaiian, "turned his guns on the alleged domination by the so-called 'silk-stockinged precincts.'"[19] Constantly interrupting Trask, the supportive crowd shouted to tell them more about the Fukunaga incident, and he responded that Sheriff Patrick Gleason should answer them. Trask unsparingly attacked his election opponent and claimed that Gleason had been berated by twenty major Republican leaders during the search for Gill Jamieson's killer. Also referring to the racial and class division between the two political parties, a Democratic territorial senate candidate proclaimed that the people could not expect an honest deal from the Republicans because the party was dominated by fifteen big businessmen on O'ahu. Such racial and class domination by Haole Republican elites was ultimately responsible for sending Fukunaga to the gallows because they wanted to maintain the unequal racial order.

Legal Appeals for Naught

Legal efforts to save Fukunaga from being hanged began the day after his death sentence. His attorney Eugene Beebe requested the territorial attorney general to have a full examination of Fukunaga's mental status conducted by navy psychiatrist Dr. Joseph Thompson.[20] The *Hawaii Hochi* contacted Thompson regarding his opinion about Fukunaga's sanity, and the paper immediately conveyed his conclusion that Fukunaga was insane to the latter's attorneys the day after the trial ended.[21] While Beebe agreed to pursue the matter with Thompson, his co-counsel, Seba Huber, was not so inclined because he had previously clashed with Thompson in a court case.

Beebe tried very hard to obtain permission from Attorney General Harry Hewitt and High Sheriff John Lane, who had jurisdiction over Fukunaga at Oahu Prison, for Dr. Thompson to examine him.[22] However, Hewitt denied his request, having conferred with Governor Farrington and Prof. Stanley Porteus, and announced that no one, including Dr. Thompson and Prof. Myrick, would be permitted to interview Fukunaga to determine his sanity or insanity. After the trial, Beebe also could no longer meet with Fukunaga, according to a statement issued by Lane, who also said that Fukunaga would not be allowed to write his life story, which might reveal evidence of his insanity, legal or otherwise. Furthermore, Huber was not participating anymore as defense counsel, having told Hewitt that he was not in favor of another mental evaluation of Fukunaga.[23] Obviously, measures were being taken to ensure that Fukunaga's conviction and death sentence would be upheld.

However, several days after Fukunaga received the death sentence, Fred Makino asked Robert K. Murakami to handle his case, and he readily agreed because he thought Fukunaga had been denied a fair trial.[24] One of just two nisei lawyers in Hawai'i, Murakami received his law degree from the University of Chicago in 1925 and was hoping for a position as an attorney with the city and county of Honolulu. A friend of his, Ralph Honda, recalled sixty years after Murakami took the Fukunaga case, "[He] told me that nobody would defend [Fukunaga] . . . because those were Republican days. . . . [Murakami] offered and that was the end for him. He was black-balled."[25] Murakami also would pay dearly for accepting the unpopular case, receiving many death threats and other menacing remarks while working on it.[26]

Undaunted, on October 15, Murakami filed a motion for a new trial for Fukunaga, just two hours after Governor Farrington had signed his death warrant.[27] Farrington set Fukunaga's hanging for October 23, the earliest date that it could be held because territorial law mandated a two-week waiting period after a death sentence was issued.[28] The primary argument of Murakami's motion was that new evidence, which demonstrated Fukunaga's insanity at the time of the killing, had been discovered since the verdict and was unavailable to the defense at the trial. This new evidence that Fukunaga was insane when he murdered Gill Jamieson was presented in an affidavit by Dr. Thompson sworn on October 13. He agreed to submit it when he was asked during a meeting with Makino, Murakami, and George Wright, the English-language section editor of the *Hochi*, the previous day.

The motion for a new trial included another affidavit from Eugene Beebe, who withdrew as Fukunaga's counsel together with Seba Huber the same day the motion was filed.[29] Beebe's affidavit stated that he was unaware Dr. Thompson was of the opinion that Fukunaga was insane when the youth killed Gill Jamieson, and that he only learned of Thompson's existence after the trial was over. Beebe also attested that he made every effort to determine if any psychiatrist or psychoanalyst would testify for Fukunaga and if any person qualified as an expert believed that Fukunaga was insane on the day of the murder. In addition, he asserted that he had consulted with Drs. Faus, Eckerdt, and Chung and with Dr. Paul Withington, Prof. Stanley Porteus, and other reputable doctors in Honolulu as to Fukunaga's sanity or insanity.

City and county attorney Charles Davis responded to Murakami's motion by filing an affidavit sworn by Dr. Faus, the city medical examiner.[30] Faus claimed that he was particularly trained in the study of mental illness, despite testifying during the trial that psychiatry was a "hobby" of his. He also stated that he and Drs. Chung and Eckerdt submitted a written report of their examination of Fukunaga to his attorneys and quoted from it: "We . . . find him to be of sane mind. We found him to be quiet, cooperative, entirely aware of his predicament, well oriented, with good foresight and apprehension. . . . We unreservedly concur in the opinion that he is mentally responsible." Faus did not mention in his affidavit that they examined Fukunaga for only ninety minutes.

In addition to his motion for a new trial, Murakami filed a notice of intention to sue out a writ of error from the circuit court to the territorial Supreme Court on October 18, the last day allowable under the law.[31] The notice automatically served as a stay of execution for thirty days, during which Murakami could file his writ of error, which was an appeal of the circuit court verdict, to the Supreme Court.

The next day, Murakami's motion for a new trial was heard by Judge Albert M. Cristy, who was ruling on criminal cases for Judge Steadman during his vacation. In arguing against the motion, deputy city attorney Francis Brooks sharply rebuked Fukunaga's previous attorneys Huber and Beebe.[32] As he declared, "The killing was admitted, no defense of insanity was offered," all jury instructions were given as requested by the defense, and the trial began on a date they had set. Brooks further accused the defense attorneys of "lack of due diligence," asking "What prevented them from going farther?" than to consult just "five alienists." He noted that there were ninety physicians listed in the telephone directory, including sixteen who were Japanese American. Brooks exclaimed, "All that counsel had to do was to pick up the telephone receiver and inquire. But none of them was called. Why not?" As a former defense attorney, Brooks possibly was indicating what he would have done if Fukunaga had been his client.

Brooks also emphasized that there was no testimony at the trial from Fukunaga's relatives and acquaintances that they had observed unusual behavior on his part.[33] "None of them called. No parents, no school teachers, no childhood friends. Why not?" he questioned again. The simple answer was that it would have prolonged the defense beyond nineteen minutes. Moreover, Brooks harshly criticized Dr. Thompson: "He talks about incipient regression, and I don't know what else [in his affidavit], but he doesn't say anywhere that this defendant was legally insane or that he didn't know the difference between right and wrong. Why, your honor, there isn't an Igorrote in the extreme limits of the Philippine Islands that doesn't know that 'Thou shalt not kill.'" He also made much of the absence of an affidavit from Huber in Murakami's motion, declaring it was because Murakami could not get one from him since Huber knew Thompson. Well beyond challenging the motion, Brooks's arguments were a powerful indictment of Beebe and Huber.

During a recess at the hearing, Murakami related to the press that Fukunaga was not consulted about the efforts to save him from being hanged by arguing that he might be insane, although "he knew what was being done."[34] While Fukunaga may have known about those efforts, with his death wish and insistence that he was sane, what did he really think about Murakami's appeal on his behalf?

The day after the hearing for a new trial, Judge Cristy denied the motion in a verbal decision in court.[35] In what was described as a "scorching, blistering oral opinion," Cristy directed his arguments particularly at Dr. Thompson and his affidavit, which maintained that Fukunaga was insane. Cristy proclaimed, "Insanity is no defense in the territory of Hawaii. The judge of this court, if properly reported by the press, probably would be found insane by this same doctor." He explained that insanity, as defined by the U.S. Supreme Court and the Hawai'i Insanity Act of 1925, meant the inability to differentiate between right and wrong. Cristy began with the Supreme Court definition, as given in *Davis v. U.S.*: "The term [insanity] . . . means such a perverted and deranged condition of the mental and moral faculties as to render a person incapable of distinguishing between right and wrong, . . . or when . . . able to distinguish between right and wrong, yet his will, by which I mean the governing power of his mind, has been otherwise than voluntarily as completely destroyed that his actions are not subject to it, but are beyond his control."[36] He emphasized that the Supreme Court definition was essentially incorporated into the territorial Insanity Act. Cristy then cited the relevant section of the act: "Any person acting under mental derangement, rendering him incompetent to discern the nature and the criminality of the act done by him, shall not be subject to punishment therefore."[37] However, he failed to mention the section of the act that refers to being compelled by a force that cannot be resisted as another criterion for being judged legally insane.

Cristy remarked that Thompson found Fukunaga was "either an incipient case of regression-dissociation, psychosis or a paranoid personality of a wide variant from the norm. What a 'wide variant from the norm' may mean has nothing to do with this court. And the further conclusion of Dr. Thompson that he believes Myles Fukunaga was insane on the eighteenth day of September, 1928 means nothing to this court."[38] Getting to his point in what was called his "unsparing denunciation" of him, Cristy bellowed, "If Dr. Thompson were to say that this man was insane because he did not know the difference between right and wrong, . . . this community would know what he meant." The legal problem with Thompson's affidavit was that he did not specifically state that Fukunaga lacked the ability to differentiate between right and wrong when he killed Gill Jamieson. One can ask why Murakami did not notice this crucial deficiency in the affidavit.

After denying the motion for a new trial, Judge Cristy fired a verbal warning shot at Murakami, virtually accusing him and implicitly the *Hawaii Hochi* of obstructing justice by making public comments about the case. He pronounced that the case was still pending in the territorial courts and that "some things [have been] called to the attention of the court, which indicates lack of observance of this fact. . . . If you want this institution to survive, then don't attempt to obstruct justice in any way by what you do."[39] Cristy's harsh criticism of Murakami can be understood as part of the ongoing threats directed to the Japanese American community, especially by the Honolulu dailies and government officials, not to contest the racial order, particularly by legal challenges.

Nonetheless, a month later, on November 17, Murakami filed an application for a writ of error with the Hawai'i Supreme Court requesting a review of the proceedings in Fukunaga's trial.[40] The court clerk issued the writ the same day, which postponed Fukunaga's execution, scheduled for two days later, for thirty days. Governor Farrington then rescheduled Fukunaga's execution for January 3, 1929, the second time his hanging was postponed.[41] As for Fukunaga, according to High Sheriff John Lane, he was in very good health, spending his time reading religious books and speaking with the prison chaplain, Father Valentin, and did not appear very different from when he entered the prison. Two weeks after he was sentenced to death, Fukunaga was baptized into the Catholic faith through Father Valentin's guidance and began his deep religious transformation.[42] He had spent the previous week studying basic lessons on Catholicism from books provided by the chaplain after he had requested his services. Fukunaga's devout faith would be quite apparent in his farewell letters written the night before he was hanged (see below).

A month after he applied for the writ of error, on December 18, Murakami filed a 132-page opening brief with the Hawai'i Supreme Court, which requested a new trial for Fukunaga.[43] He argued that sixteen errors were committed by the court during Fukunaga's trial, nine of which concerned the faulty jury-selection process.[44] Errors 1 to 4 and 6 to 8 included those that maintained the court erred in refusing to exclude from the jury Otto Meyer, George H. Swift, William L. Thoene, Victor Hurd, and William Kahilikolo, who the defense had claimed were biased or otherwise disqualified from serving as jurors.[45] Meyer, Swift, Thoene, and Hurd had all participated in the search for Gill Jamieson's killer, with Meyer and Hurd having been formally deputized, but the court denied the defense challenges for cause of them. As for Kahilikolo, the subject of errors 6, 7, and 8, Murakami asserted that the court erred when it refused the defense challenges of him for cause because, among several issues, Kahilikolo said he would find the defendant guilty if the prosecution merely proved Fukunaga killed Gill.

The fifth error Murakami assigned also pertained to jury selection and concerned the prosecution using one of its peremptory challenges to remove someone from the jury after it had previously waived the opportunity. The last error involving jury selection was number 9, which argued that "practically every one of the twelve jurors . . . had either expressed or entertained an opinion" regarding Fukunaga's guilt or innocence prior to their voir dire examination.

Errors 10 and 14 related to whether Fukunaga was given a fair and impartial trial because of prejudicial actions taken against him.[46] The first involved the court erring when it did not declare a mistrial after it learned that Fukunaga was being held at Oahu Prison with convicted felons, which meant that he was being treated as a felon before and during his trial, according to the brief. Also included as part of this error was that statements by Dr. Eckerdt, Dr. Faus, other witnesses, and the jurors themselves indicated that they considered Fukunaga guilty before his trial had started. As noted in chapter 4, several jurors clearly stated during jury selection that they believed Fukunaga killed Gill and should have been challenged either for cause or peremptorily. Regarding error 14, Murakami contended that the court erred in making prejudicial statements to the jury after the prosecution had rested its case and before the defense began its own, particularly that the trial would end before Saturday's primary election.[47]

Error 16 was the admission into evidence of the "alleged statements of the defendant"—Fukunaga's confession—despite defense objections.[48] Murakami claimed that there was insufficient evidence that the statements were made voluntarily, while there was proof that Fukunaga was not informed that he had a "right" to decline to speak with his interrogators and that what he said could be used against him. However, there was no such right until 1967.

Errors 9, 11, and 12 challenged the validity of Fukunaga's conviction. Error 9 was that the court erred in accepting the verdict of the jury, which was "contrary to law . . . and the weight of the evidence."[49] Error 9 also involved the court's instructions to the jury, which did not include the option of finding Fukunaga not guilty of murder, its acceptance of the defense stipulation that Fukunaga killed Gill, and its instructions to the jury to consider the stipulation as evidence in the trial. Error 11 followed from the ninth in asserting that the court erred in sentencing Fukunaga because the sentence was based on the erroneous verdict of an improperly constituted jury.[50] Error 12 was the court's entering a plea of not guilty for Fukunaga after he stated in court that he was pleading guilty, which deprived him of his rights to plead guilty to murder and to be tried by the court instead of a jury.

The ruling of the court against the motion for a new trial constituted errors 13 and 15. Regarding the former, Murakami argued that the court erred when it did not grant a new trial based on newly discovered evidence—Thompson's faulty affidavit.[51] Error 15 by the court was its instructions to the jurors that they could return home following jury selection until the next morning, when the trial proceedings began with opening statements.[52]

In his reply brief to Murakami's assignment of the sixteen errors, city attorney Charles Davis argued that Judge Steadman should have accepted Fukunaga's guilty plea to first-degree murder and then sentenced him to death.[53] His brief continued that the prosecution urged the judge to do such, but he wrongly interpreted the law, maintained that he could not admit a guilty plea to an indictment charging first-degree murder, and compelled them to proceed with the trial. Davis was referring to Steadman's ruling that Fukunaga's guilty plea to first-degree murder could not be accepted because the law provided that the degree shall be determined by a jury. He countered that Hawai'i law did not prohibit courts from accepting a guilty plea to first-degree murder and that it required the degree of murder to be decided by a jury only in cases where a jury trial was held.

Regarding Murakami's contention that the court committed reversible error by refusing to excuse the five named persons, Davis responded, "The defendant at the trial failed to exercise all of his peremptory challenges and . . . accepted the jury as satisfactory," waiving his four remaining challenges.[54] The reality was that defense counsel Beebe and Huber failed to use those remaining peremptory challenges to have Swift and Hurd removed from the jury, although they did challenge peremptorily the three others. Despite underscoring the failure of the defense attorneys to use all of their peremptory challenges, Davis's reply brief went so far as to claim: "It would be almost impossible in the history of criminal trials to find a case where a defendant was more fairly and impartially treated by the court and by the prosecution. . . . The judge and counsel representing the territory went a long way in this case to protect the defendant in every possible way." Significantly, Davis did not include Fukunaga's attorneys among those who went to great lengths to protect him, which was their legal duty.

The Hawai'i Supreme Court met on December 27 to consider Murakami's appeal of Fukunaga's conviction.[55] A week later on January 3, 1929, the court issued its thirty-five page opinion, which affirmed the guilty verdict and dismissed each of the sixteen errors specified by Murakami.[56] Claiming that Fukunaga had a fair trial and was defended by capable counsel, the court pronounced: "The murder was clearly characterized by malice, deliberateness and premeditation. The overwhelming weight of the uncontradicted evidence was that the defendant was sane at the time of the commission of the offense. We can find no prejudicial error in the proceedings had at the trial. The verdict, the judgment and the sentence are affirmed." Discussed below is the Hawai'i Supreme Court's dismissal of the errors—although not all of them, since some were less salient than others and had little chance of being confirmed by the court.[57]

With regard to Murakami's contention that the court erred in not excusing Meyer, Swift, Thoene, Hurd, and Kahilikolo from the jury, two of whom had been deputized, the Hawai'i Supreme Court ruled, "A defendant in a criminal case who fails to challenge a juror for cause cannot afterwards successfully claim that he should have been excused for cause." However, the defense had challenged Meyer, Hurd and Kahilikolo for cause. The court also emphasized that Huber and Beebe did not use all of their peremptory challenges: "An erroneous overruling of an objection to a juror avails nothing to the defendant if he does not finally exhaust his peremptory challenges,"[58] thus implicitly reprimanding them for failing to do so. As for Murakami's argument that some of the jurors were biased, the court asserted, "The mere fact that some of the persons examined on the voir dire proved to be biased or prejudiced or to be otherwise disqualified is not ground for setting aside a verdict, providing the persons thus disqualified were all excused from service."[59] But the problem was that many obviously biased jurors, particularly those who said they believed that Fukunaga killed Gill, were not considered disqualified and served on the jury. Concerning the verdict being a nullity (legally invalid) because the jury was illegally constituted, after briefly reviewing the voir dire examination of each of the thirty-seven potential jurors, the court declared, "We are satisfied that none of the jurors who sat in the case was disqualified; that they . . . were all in an attitude of mind of entire fairness."[60] This conclusion can be seriously questioned just from the short review in chapter 4 of the examination of five jurors—Swift, Fuller, Hurd, Maruyama and Wall. The court also noted that Beebe and Huber did not request a change of venue for the trial. Besides not seeking a change of venue, the failure of the defense attorneys to ask for a later start of the trial was a far more egregious error.

As for Murakami's argument that the court erred by not approving a new trial based on newly discovered evidence, the Supreme Court ruled that it would not be in accord with legal procedure to allow an out-of-court expert

(Dr. Thompson), who has never seen or spoken with the defendant, to decide what the facts and history of the person shall be and then assert an opinion about his sanity or insanity.[61] But Thompson was not given the opportunity to examine Fukunaga, and Murakami's appeal was intended to provide for a complete psychiatric examination.

Regarding the argument of both Murakami and Davis that the court erred when it refused to accept Fukunaga's guilty plea at his arraignment, the Hawai'i Supreme Court maintained: "The practice in these islands, under the monarchy, the provisional government, the republic and the territory, has been for trial judges to refuse to accept a plea of guilty to an indictment charging an offense punishable with death and to require the entry of a plea of not guilty and a trial by jury to determine the guilt or innocence of the accused."[62] While it may have been the practice in the past and at that time, the ruling avoided the more critical question of what the law was regarding a defendant pleading guilty.

Concerning Fukunaga not being advised that his statements to the police could be used against him, the court pronounced, citing law, "our statute does not so require," and the evidence showed that his statements were given voluntarily without any threats or inducements being made.[63] With regard to the judge not instructing the jury that they could find Fukunaga not guilty, if they believed he was sane when he committed the crime, the court asserted that such a verdict was legally impossible because Fukunaga through his counsel admitted that he did the killing, and no evidence was presented of absence of malice or of justification or extenuation.[64] The possibility of a straightforward not guilty verdict was precluded by the defense stipulation that Fukunaga killed Gill Jamieson, but it was extremely unlikely anyway.

Since the Supreme Court did not issue its decision on Murakami's motion for a new trial earlier, Governor Farrington on January 3, 1929, gave Fukunaga a third reprieve for thirty days.[65] The day after the court made its ruling, Murakami said he planned to appeal Fukunaga's conviction to the Ninth U.S. Circuit Court of Appeals in San Francisco.[66] At the end of January he announced that he would be leaving for San Francisco to work on the new appeal with attorneys Eric Lyders and W. D. Prideaux, who had offered their services.[67] Fukunaga's was the first criminal case from Hawai'i to be appealed to the Ninth Circuit Court and resulted in Farrington giving both Fukunaga and Vicente Kacal, the only other person on death row, both thirty-day reprieves to March 2.[68] The stay was the fourth granted to Fukunaga, and with each such action Kacal received a similar postponement, although it would be his last.

Lyders and Prideaux, who were the lead attorneys, and Murakami submitted their "Brief for Appellant" on May 1, 1929, to the Ninth Circuit Court of Appeals seeking a reversal of the territorial Supreme Court decision.[69] They argued that twenty-five errors were committed, including most of the sixteen cited in the previous appeal. These errors had to involve a violation of constitutional issues to be within the appeal court's jurisdiction. The general argument in nineteen of the errors was that the Supreme Court erred when it ruled that the trial court did not commit an error when it took or did not take a particular action, which had been specified as one of the previous sixteen errors.

In their brief, Fukunaga's lawyers also discussed the "Effect of Stipulating that Defendant Did the Killing." They argued that, according to Hawai'i law, it "threw upon the defendant the presumption that the killing was done with malice aforethought, and the burden of showing that malice did not exist, or that there was a legal justification or extenuation for said killing."[70] Legal justification could be self-defense, while extenuation could include legal insanity, but such arguments were not advanced by Huber and Beebe. Ultimately, the error regarding the stipulation that Fukunaga killed Gill Jamieson was one of gross incompetence by his attorneys at that time rather than a legal error committed by the territorial Supreme Court. In the conclusion of their brief, Fukunaga's attorneys emphasized the disastrous consequences for him of the stipulation that he did the killing. They maintained that Huber and Beebe made no attempt to overcome the burden thrust upon him by the admission.[71] Fukunaga's appeal was heard on June 3, 1929, by a three-judge panel of the Ninth Circuit Court of Appeals; two weeks later, the court issued its opinion dismissing it.[72] The court decided that Fukunaga's appeal did not involve any constitutional issues and hence was not within its jurisdiction. Murakami went to Oahu Prison to give Fukunaga the bad news in person, while Fred Makino negotiated with Lyders and Prideaux to file another appeal to the U.S. Supreme Court.[73]

As Fukunaga's last legal appeal, Lyders, Prideaux, and Murakami submitted a "Petition for Writ of Certiorari" to the U.S. Supreme Court on September 4, 1929.[74] Since the Ninth Circuit Court of Appeals had ruled that their appeal did not raise any constitutional issues, they specified four constitutional questions in their appeal seeking a reversal of the lower court's decision. First, the petition argued, since Fukunaga, at nineteen, was a minor when he killed Gill and when he went on trial, it was the duty of the court to provide him with the special protection to which he was entitled. Second, it contended that the trial court erred when it allowed the prosecuting attorney to state to the jury that Fukunaga at his arraignment said he was guilty. Third, the petition stated that the trial court committed another error when it permitted Fukunaga's attorneys to stipulate that he did the killing. And last, it asserted that, because the above errors violated Fukunaga's rights under the Fifth and Sixth Amendments to the U.S. Constitution, the Ninth Circuit Court of Appeals erred when it dismissed his appeal on the basis that it lacked jurisdiction. However, the U.S. Supreme Court on October 21 decided against hearing Fukunaga's case, bringing to an end his year-long quest for a new trial. At that point, the only legal recourse to save his life was to seek from Governor Lawrence Judd a commutation of his death sentence to life in prison.

Community Resistance against Conviction

At the same time that legal appeals were being submitted on Fukunaga's behalf, the Japanese American community was organizing opposition to his conviction and death sentence. In fact, the community financed those appeals by contributions to his defense fund that eventually totaled almost $7,000. But earlier, on the day that Fukunaga was sentenced to be hanged, a *Hawaii Hochi* editorial questioned if he was really sane and declared its very early resistance to his execution.[75] The *Hochi* would subsequently lead the campaign of the Japanese American community for racial justice for Fukunaga. While the paper conceded that Fukunaga's role in the death of Gill Jamieson was indisputable, it argued that major questions had been raised as to his "mental responsibility," particularly "grave doubts as to his complete sanity."

Shortly after Fukunaga was given his death sentence, the Japanese American community submitted a petition to Governor Wallace R. Farrington that requested a stay of execution and a psychiatric examination of Fukunaga by Dr. Thompson.[76] Noting Thompson's conclusion that Fukunaga was insane, the petition asserted that "if he [Fukunaga] is sane, his crime forms a blot on the good name of the Japanese community and is a humiliation which will be keenly felt by thousands of young Japanese." The Japanese American leaders who signed the petition thus recognized how Fukunaga's heinous crime, while an individual act, had racially stained their entire community, especially young nisei like him. The petition had seventy-one signatories, including more than fifty leaders of the local Japanese community, such as Buddhist and Shinto priests, Japanese language school principals, businessmen and professionals, and presidents and other officers of business and voluntary organizations. Based on what the press said were their "American" names and occupations, almost twenty of those signing the petition were Haoles, including Lockwood Myrick Jr. However, the governor swiftly denied the petition.[77]

Unlike the Honolulu dailies, the *Hawaii Hochi* reported that Myrick submitted his "An Open Letter" in early November and summarized his study.[78] Despite receiving copies from Myrick, the *Star-Bulletin* and *Advertiser* made no mention of his report. Two weeks later, a *Hochi* editorial accused the two newspapers of trying "desperately to hide the truth" about Fukunaga's insanity.[79] According to the *Hochi*, the editors of the *Star-Bulletin* and *Advertiser* offered, among their reasons for not publishing any news of Myrick's study, that it was not a legal document before the court, that the question of Fukunaga's sanity had already been settled, and that it would be unwise to provide information from his analysis to the public. Describing those reasons as "all rot," the *Hochi* maintained that the editors of the two papers refused to print anything about Myrick's report because it "convincingly establishes a point of view directly opposed" to that of their newspapers concerning Fukunaga's sanity. It added that another reason for their suppression of Myrick's study was because it reveals facts they had been trying to conceal. Myrick's lengthy analysis would be serialized in the *Hochi* in daily installments in December 1928 in Japanese and English.

As a staunch advocate of the Japanese American community, the *Hochi* compared its support of Fukunaga with that which it provided in the Japanese language schools litigation a few years earlier. A November 1 editorial proclaimed that it was prepared to fight Haole leaders as it had in the previous dispute. The *Hochi* observed, "Then, as now, the English press was violent in its opposition. . . . The same charges of race agitation were raised against us. . . . And then, as now, the *Nippu Jiji* sided with the English papers and attacked The *Hochi*."[80] To emphasize the close relation between the *Nippu Jiji* and the *Star-Bulletin*, the *Hochi* referred to the *Star-Bulletin* as the "Haole sister" of the *Nippu Jiji*. The racial reference reflects how the *Star-Bulletin* and *Advertiser* were both seen, including by Haoles themselves, as expressing the views and concerns of their community.

Besides regularly writing about the Fukunaga case, the *Hochi* convened an open meeting of the Japanese American community on December 9 at the Oahu Theatre in downtown Honolulu to present its position on the case.[81] The featured speakers were Makino and Kusaka Haga, managing editor of the *Hochi*, who addressed an enthusiastic capacity crowd estimated at nearly two thousand with another five hundred latecomers listening from the windows. Speaking for two hours, Makino reviewed the events of the case from the day of the kidnapping to the recent filing of an appeal with the territorial Supreme Court and explained the U.S. judicial system. He emphasized that, since doubts had been raised about Fukunaga's sanity, the youth should be given a complete psychiatric examination.[82]

The huge turnout, which would be repeated at subsequent gatherings concerning the Fukunaga case, clearly demonstrated the substantial support among Japanese Americans for the advocacy stance taken by the *Hawaii Hochi* on behalf of Fukunaga. Since it did not convene a comparable meeting to explain its stand on the Fukunaga case, it is highly doubtful that the *Nippu Jiji* could have attracted such a large audience to hear its speakers argue that Fukunaga should be hanged and had received a fair trial. As the *Hochi* described the *Nippu Jiji*, "Repudiated by the Japanese, this renegade newspaper crawls fawning to the feet of those it has always served [Haoles], and whimpers like a whipped dog. . . . It has lost face with the Japanese."[83] Indeed, the *Hochi* began to exceed the *Nippu Jiji* in circulation in fall 1928.[84]

In January 1929 Makino spoke in Hilo at the Yuraka-Kwan Theatre to nearly one thousand Japanese Americans about the *Hochi* campaign on behalf of Fukunaga.[85] He pledged himself and his newspaper to continue their efforts to provide Fukunaga a full psychiatric examination to determine if he was sane or not. Makino declared, "We admit that he did the crime. If he is proven sane, he should be hanged. If he is proven insane, then he is not responsible and should be put in an institution." Interviewed by a reporter from the *Hilo Tribune-Herald*, Makino related that virtually the entire Japanese American community backed the initiative led by his newspaper.

In a surprising editorial published in July 1929, the *Nippu Jiji* acknowledged the reason for the enormous support among Japanese Americans for Fukunaga's legal battle, to which it was strongly opposed.[86] The editorial related that the *Nippu Jiji* asked those who had contributed to Fukunaga's defense fund why they had, and the answer was "invariably because there is a feeling that he has been discriminated against on account of his nationality [race]. As one prominent Japanese said: 'Had the haole boy killed Fukunaga, he surely would have been adjusted [*sic*] insane and escaped punishment. Japanese boy, crazy as a bed-bug, kills haole boy and they hang him.'" The editorial concluded that, due to that widespread belief, a great amount of money had been spent to save Fukunaga from being executed.

In response to the U.S. Supreme Court deciding not to hear the Fukunaga appeal, the Japanese American community convened a large meeting at the Park Theatre in downtown Honolulu on November 4, 1929.[87] All of the speakers called for Governor Judd to grant executive clemency to Fukunaga and commute his death sentence to life imprisonment. The capacity audience unanimously adopted a resolution that requested the governor bestow clemency on Fukunaga since Judd had recently reprieved the convicted murderers of a Japanese American named Matsumiya (see below).

In an editorial a few days later, the *Hochi* argued that "racial discrimination" was the primary reason for Fukunaga's impending execution.[88] It contended that if Fukunaga is hanged, "it will not be because . . . he is a murderer. It will be because he killed the son of the vice-president of one of our big trust companies and because his victim was a white boy!" As evidence of the differential treatment of Fukunaga and other Asians, the editorial cited recent murders of Asians, including the beating and strangling of an elderly Japanese man for his money, the shooting death of an old Chinese storekeeper for no apparent reason, and the beating death with a hammer of an elderly Japanese man by a Haole man to steal his pocket money. The *Hochi* emphasized that none of the killers in those cases was executed, and two of them were not even in prison. It also reasserted its argument from more than a year previous that a dual system of racial justice prevailed in Hawai'i—"one for the murderers of Orientals and another for the murderer of a white person." The editorial concluded that Fukunaga's hanging would climactically "split the racial groups apart." Rather than Fukunaga's execution, the racial split between Haoles and non-Haoles resulted more directly three years later from the murder of Joe Kahahawai and the subsequent commuting of the ten-year sentences at hard labor given to his four convicted killers to one hour (see Conclusion).

The next day the *Hochi* followed with an editorial that highlighted another troubling racial injustice in the case—Fukunaga's quick trial and psychiatric examination.[89] It maintained that there had been an implicit time limit for the trial, which was supposed to end before Saturday's primary election. With regard to "speeding up so-called justice," the editorial provided examples of homicide cases after Fukunaga's in which the question of the possible insanity of the accused was raised. In the previously mentioned murder of the taxi driver Matsumiya, one of the defendants claimed to be insane; in this case the court set no time limit for the psychiatrists to examine him, so they took a month to find him sane. The week before in Hilo, the *Hochi* noted, the trial of a Native Hawaiian man for killing his wife was about to begin when he said he was insane. Instead of a ninety-minute examination, the judge postponed the trial and ordered the defendant sent to Honolulu for observation by experts at the territorial mental hospital to determine if he was sane or not, again with no period specified.

In another approach, the Japanese American community tried to halt Fukunaga's hanging by submitting petitions to Governor Judd. On November 9, a petition signed by seventy-two Japanese American community leaders was sent to him requesting that he reduce Fukunaga's death sentence to life imprisonment. The petition emphasized the "superficial examination" of Fukunaga and the independent analyses by Dr. Thompson and Prof. Myrick, which both found him insane when he committed his crime. In early November Fukunaga's family sent its own petition to Judd asking him to commute his sentence to life in prison "for that one terrible crime." A few days later, Robert Murakami presented three petitions from the Japanese Chamber of Commerce, two Buddhist missions, and other Japanese American community leaders to the governor.[90] Citing Fukunaga's youth as a reason he should not be hanged, all three petitions requested Judd to convert his death penalty to life behind bars.

One Sunday in mid-November, a group of five Japanese women circulated yet another petition and submitted it to the governor; it bore the signatures of more than a thousand Japanese American women—mothers and other residents of Honolulu.[91] Among the reasons they gave for Judd to grant executive clemency to Fukunaga was because he "was a good boy up to the time of the crime, which makes us believe that he was possibly out of his rational mind when the crime was perpetrated." The petition ended, "If your excellency will give weighty consideration to this petition, we will cherish and honor your name as a champion of justice and humanity in Hawaii forever." Judd ensured that he would never be honored or remembered as such by not commuting Fukunaga's sentence and then three years later drastically reducing the ten-year sentences of the murderers of Joe Kahahawai.

All of the above efforts were for naught because Judd signed Fukunaga's death warrant on November 12, setting the date of his execution for a week later.[92] In his statement to the press, Judd declared, "This is a dastardly crime, well planned and executed with exceptional brutality." Ignoring the study by Prof. Myrick and the affidavit by Dr. Thompson, Judd concluded, "I cannot perceive the circumstances surrounding this case are today any different than they were when my predecessor in office . . . signed the death warrant on October 15, 1928."

The day before Fukunaga was hanged, the *Hochi* underscored the larger racial significance of his execution for Hawai'i.[93] The paper asserted that Fukunaga had become the "symbol" of something much more important than any one person: "Myles Fukunaga, hanged to save the face of a little faction that controls the territory of Hawaii, becomes a martyr in the eyes of those who believe that his death proves there are two kinds of justice in Hawaii—one for the rich and powerful Haoles and another . . . for the poor Orientals." For the latter, the *Hochi* argued, Fukunaga had been transformed into an "emblem of racial inequality." The editorial captured how the Fukunaga case illuminated how race as the leading organizing principle of social relations operated in Hawaiʻi in the 1920s (and for at least another two decades). Rather than a colorblind society or multicultural paradise, race resulted in and enforced the racial inequality and racial injustice that prevailed in the territory. Fukunaga's execution, despite his likely insanity, fully demonstrated the power of race as wielded by Haoles to maintain their settler colonial rule over non-Haoles.

The Last Days

The day before Myles Fukunaga's short life would come to its tragic end, Father Bruno Bens, the acting chaplain of Oahu Prison, spoke to the press about Fukunaga's faith.[94] The kindly priest related that Fukunaga had never been to church, so he thought it was appropriate that Myles should take part in at least one Mass—his first and last. He added, "I am convinced that Myles' repentance is sincere. All my efforts have been to turn his face to the future, to strengthen his courage for the ordeal still before him . . . and to assure him that salvation is not beyond his reach." Asked about Fukunaga's sanity, Father Bruno replied that he would not conduct the last sacrament of the church for him unless he was certain Fukunaga could fully understand it.

Fukunaga was hanged on November 19 at 8:12 A.M. and pronounced officially dead twelve minutes later, fourteen months after he took the life of Gill Jamieson.[95] While more than a year had passed since his crime, his execution still commanded front-page headlines, such as the *Star-Bulletin*'s "Fukunaga Pays Final Penalty." Earlier on the last day of his life, Myles was visited by Father Bruno at 5 A.M. to celebrate Mass for him, the first time it was held for a single worshipper at Oahu Prison, and he returned at 7 A.M. to pray with him.[96] Kneeling and separated by the bars of his prison cell, Fukunaga and Father Bruno were reciting together the Sorrowful Mystery, the prayer for the dying, when High Sheriff John Lane and other prison officials came for him at 8 A.M. The sheriff waited a few minutes until they were finished and then read the five-page death warrant. As Lane went on, Fukunaga stood at attention next to his canvas cot with his head bowed, slowly counting the beads of a rosary while praying in silence. After the prison guards opened his cell door, Fukunaga knelt and implored Father Bruno, "Father, give me your blessing," so he splashed holy water on his forehead.[97] Those would be his last spoken words.

Just two minutes before his hanging, Fukunaga began walking calmly from his cell, led by prison officials and Father Bruno, who read from the Miserere, the prayers for the sick and dying, to the death chamber several steps away.[98] After mounting the gallows, three straps were fastened around his body, holding his arms, hands, and legs in place; a black bag was lowered over his head, and a thick rope noose was placed around his neck. Sheriff Lane pressed a button that set off a buzzer on the lower floor where three guards then each pushed a separate button, one of which sent an electric current that released the trap door, sending Fukunaga plunging eight feet to his death. His body swung on the rope, then slowly turned so that it faced the thirty-six spectators, including newspaper reporters and public officials. He was the last Japanese American executed in Hawai'i.

Rather than his prison uniform, Fukunaga, a dapper figure to the very end, wore a new gray suit, white shirt with no tie, and freshly polished black shoes. When he spoke to the press shortly after the execution, still clearly shaken, his voice breaking, Father Bruno observed that "Myles Fukunaga died a true penitent."[99] He related, "His last days were spent in the reading of that great work, *Life Everlasting*. . . . The mass this morning at 5 o'clock was an ordinary mass. . . . But afterward, ah afterward!" Perhaps Father Bruno was referring to the happiness that Fukunaga experienced after participating in his only Mass.

After his hanging, Fukunaga's body was immediately taken to the Japanese Crematory Co. in downtown Honolulu for Buddhist funeral services.[100] Dressed in a white kimono with his hands clutching a rosary, Fukunaga's body lay in the shrine room of the funeral parlor as thousands of grim mourners—men, women and children—who had never known him, filed past throughout the day in an endless stream. Offering their last respects, they paused briefly to bow before him with hands placed together following Buddhist practice.[101] Fukunaga's casket was surrounded by numerous floral offerings and gifts from sympathizers. His parents had earlier expressed their desire that only relatives and very close family friends attend the service, but their son's conviction and execution had transformed him into a public figure, if not a martyr, among Japanese Americans. In its description of Fukunaga's last rites, the *Hawaii Hochi* observed how his "remains had been returned to his own people after the principles of Anglo-Saxon justice had been vindicated." To emphasize this point, the paper described the solemn atmosphere of the "simple but profoundly impressive" traditional Japanese funeral service for him: "The fragrance of incense mingled with the soft, monotonous chanting of robed priests, the deep tones of a temple gong, and candles burning before the Buddhist shrine." Fukunaga may have died a Catholic, but his funeral service was Buddhist.

At 4:30 P.M., a half hour before the service was to begin, the shrine room was still crowded with mourners filing past Fukunaga's casket, while outside on the street a long line of people waited.[102] The service subsequently began with the striking of a brass gong and was led by the bishop of the Higashi Hongwanji temple with several priests from other Buddhist sects also participating. After the service, the funeral procession of fifty cars headed for the Japanese cemetery in Mo'ili'ili at the opposite end of Honolulu. As the procession left the funeral parlor, hundreds of people lined both sides of the streets. On Beretania Street in the financial section of the city, it was not crowded, nor was it in front of Washington Place, where resided Governor Judd.

Further along Beretania Street, the sidewalks and stores were crowded with thousands of "silent, dark-faced watchers."[103] Motorcycle and traffic police assisted by clearing Beretania Street and closing off side streets so that the cortege could proceed directly to Mo'ili'ili, a predominantly Japanese American community. Fukunaga would be buried in its Japanese cemetery, and thousands of them waited for him in silent solemnity, packing the grounds of the adjacent Kuhio School. At the cemetery, Fukunaga's casket was taken to a small shrine room and placed before the altar for further prayers. Two Buddhist priests began chanting sutras as Fukunaga's parents, sisters, and close relatives and friends came forward individually to offer three pinches of incense at the altar. They were followed by a seemingly unending line of men and women, perhaps including many who did not attend the earlier funeral. After the service, Fukunaga's flower-covered casket was carried to his final resting place, which is easily recognized by its distinctive tall, natural stone marker.[104] Although Fukunaga died a Catholic, and the Catholic church offered to conduct a service for him, his parents wanted to have a Buddhist funeral since it was their religion and that of their ancestors. But out of respect for their son's chosen religion, his body was not cremated.[105]

The *Hochi* editorial on the day of Fukunaga's hanging pointed out that Buddhists (Japanese) were the only ones who expressed opposition to his execution, despite being "branded as pagans, heathens and idolators by members of the 'civilized' western churches."[106] It observed how Fukunaga had renounced Buddhism and "tried desperately to become like the haoles," including converting to Catholicism, yet Christians did not oppose his hanging, while Buddhists did, remaining steadfast in their belief in the sacredness of life. The editorial cautioned the thousands of young nisei who were being encouraged to become "truly 'westernized' by joining the Christian churches" to take heed. This initiative to have Japanese Americans adopt Christianity and reject Buddhism was a major goal of the Americanization movement led by Haoles and supported by Yasutaro Soga and Rev. Okumura.

The *Star-Bulletin* did not have an editorial about Fukunaga's execution on the day it occurred. Instead, it had one titled "Where the 'Melting Pot' Melts," which reported on thirty Samoans who held a feast prepared in the manner of their traditional homeland a few days earlier.[107] The function was one of the first events organized by the newly formed Samoan Civic Association, which the editorial lauded, as it did similar gatherings held by "individual or united racial groups" for fostering "closer contact and friendlier understanding" among the races in Hawai'i. The editorial asserted that such organizations brought forth the "finer qualities of racial pride without stirring racial animosity." It can be interpreted as indirectly about the Fukunaga hanging insofar as it sought to chastise organizations such as the *Hawaii Hochi* for inciting "racial animosity," as the *Star-Bulletin* and others had earlier claimed. Instead, the *Star-Bulletin* expressed its preference for a racial melting pot in which races and organizations contribute their traditional cultures, notably food, toward "closer contact and friendlier understanding" but not necessarily toward racial justice and equality. The reference to the melting pot is yet another example of emergent multiculturalism in the Fukunaga case.

The *Hochi* editorial the day after Fukunaga's execution criticized an *Advertiser* editorial, "The Fukunaga Case," by *Advertiser* managing editor Raymond Coll Jr., which had appeared three days earlier.[108] Denouncing Coll's editorial as consisting of "falsehood and misrepresentation," the *Hochi* noted that Lockwood Myrick Jr. in his "An Open Letter" had quoted a knowledgeable person of events in the territory as saying to him that Fukunaga was "abnormal" and that, if he had been Haole, he would not have been found guilty.[109] The *Hochi* editorial then revealed that Myrick, before leaving on a trip to Asia in January 1929, gave a typewritten statement to the *Hochi*, which indicated that it was Coll who made the comments about Fukunaga to him.

In his editorial, Coll described the Fukunaga case in terms probably shared by many Hawai'i residents, except Japanese Americans and those who believed he was insane: "Never, in the history of Hawaii, has such a brutal, mercenary crime been committed as this one was! . . . It was the result of a carefully worked out scheme of a perfectly sane mind, with one animus only . . . to extort money!"[110] He continued that no evidence had been produced of any intent to deny Fukunaga his rights. This bold pronouncement ignored the numerous legal appeals, community petitions, and *Hawaii Hochi* editorials that all argued Fukunaga had been denied his due process rights to a fair trial and a full psychiatric examination. In yet another prime example of incipient colorblindness in the case, Coll claimed that "whether the crime were [*sic*] committed by a Japanese, an Hawaiian, or a white man has nothing whatever to do with the issue" and that the "nationality of the man" did not affect the "treatment of the case by the authorities or the . . . ultimate result." Coll's denial of racial difference in the treatment and ultimate outcome of the Fukunaga case was intended to counter the charges of racial discrimination and racial injustice against Fukunaga regularly made by the *Hochi*. Furthermore, his published statement completely contradicted his interview remarks to Myrick and hence demonstrated the superficiality of public assertions of colorblindness, then as now.

Obviously referring to the *Hochi*, Coll asserted that there was a deliberate effort by a "certain Japanese newspaper . . . to inject a racial issue into this case" and to emphasize that an injustice had been done to Fukunaga and Japanese Americans.[111] Again refuting the significance of race, he absurdly contended, "Nothing which can be asked by a white man or a Hawaiian in Hawaii is not available to every Japanese in this territory," which ignored the continuous denial of justice and equality. Coll further claimed, "If ever a lynching were justified, it would have been the lynching of Fukunaga immediately after the facts in the case came to light," and that Fukunaga had escaped such vigilante justice because "the Honolulu community is deeply imbued with the principles of Anglo-Saxon justice and the predominance of law." A little more than two years later, Joe Kahahawai would be lynched by the vigilante purveyors of such Anglo-Saxon justice and law (see Conclusion).

Three days after Fukunaga's execution, the *Star-Bulletin* revealed the contents of two of the four farewell letters he had left with Father Bruno.[112] One letter was to the "Catholic Church, Her Pastors and the Congregation" and the other to Father Valentin, the prison chaplain when he was incarcerated. Both letters were signed "Yours in Christ, James Myles Fukunaga," James being his baptismal name when he became a Catholic. Both have a deeply religious tone ("The holy sacrifice of our Lord has moved me as never before. I thank the Lord Jesus Christ that He should come to me, an unworthy sinner.") and express Fukunaga's heartfelt gratitude to the church and priests for their prayers for him.

In his letter to Father Valentin, composed the last night of his life, Fukunaga shared that his parents had visited him on Saturday for the last time and revealed his profound regret for the pain he had caused them, especially his mother: "It has grieved me much to have seen them suffer so, and it made me realize how much I have wronged them. Oh, if only I had known what mother love, true and pure was, I would not have come to meet such a fate as this."[113] Fukunaga's letter indicated that the composure with which he walked to the gallows was more than apparent because he wrote of looking forward to death: "The night seems to be dragging on so slowly, and I am a little impatient for the call to come. It is because the mind is so filled with thoughts of eternity that the soul longs for release." Fukunaga also remembered Vicente Kacal, his death-row mate who was hanged eight months earlier in March 1929: "I am wondering in this stillness where Vicente Kacal is this moment. . . . Where he is, I hope that I may be with him, soul to soul." While they were waiting together for their respective executions, Fukunaga and Kacal apparently became friends, perhaps one of the few friendships Myles had as an adult.

Fukunaga's letter to his nineteen-year-old sister Yuriko was delivered to her at home on the day he was executed.[114] She was said to have "read it with brimming eyes, clasped it to her breast and ran sobbing from the room," not showing it to her parents until much later. In the brief letter, Fukunaga asked his oldest sister to look after their parents, "as [he] would have cared for them had [he] been the son [he] should have been." He also requested that his sister and parents have no sympathy for him because he knew where his "soul was going and was content."

To attorney Robert Murakami, Fukunaga expressed heartfelt appreciation for having done much for him. He continued: "Even though I am not saved from the hangman's tree, we must rejoice in that there is a greater One that judges in Heaven. . . . I feel as if I was being freed today."[115] The four letters Fukunaga left behind show that he accepted his death as punishment for his crime and found great comfort in his Catholic faith. Unlike his letters to Frederick Jamieson and the *Star-Bulletin*, none of them quoted from Shakespeare.

Five days after his death, the *Hochi* printed Fukunaga's essay, "Let Your Light Shine! A Message from My Soul to the Younger Generation," which he wrote the previous month.[116] It was dedicated to Rev. Tokuji Komuro, pastor of Harris Memorial Methodist Church, who first gave him spiritual guidance and met with him at least ten times. The minister had suggested to Fukunaga that, if he felt regret for his crime, he might make some amends for it by sharing his thoughts about what he did with those younger than himself. Writing the essay also enabled Fukunaga to express how he viewed himself and his misdeed in ways that were much less possible in his confession to the police. No mention is made about having wanted to send his parents back to Japan or to die.

In his message, Fukunaga appeared to have a clearer understanding of what led him to commit murder than at the time of his capture. He attributed his wrongdoing to reading too much fiction, which made him desire a life like that of the characters in the books he read and to dislike his own life. He added that movies had the same negative effect upon him. Last, Fukunaga mentioned "envy" and that he "envied the rich and well-off people. It poisons your mind just as cheap magazines from the newsstands do."[117] At this near end of his life and possibly earlier, Fukunaga seemed to have come to the same conclusion that Myrick had concerning how books, magazines, and films had exacerbated his dissociated personality by providing enjoyment through the experiences of others, resulting in his own unhappy life. As for envy, Myrick did not include it among the four principal motives that Fukunaga had for killing Gill, and Fukunaga did not mention it in his confession or interview.

In another section of his essay, Fukunaga wrote about how a "block of marble" had been placed before him together with a "set of tools and a book of helpful hints and directions on how to sculpture the real likeness of myself out of that clean, spotless block of marble."[118] The latter represents Fukunaga's adolescence, while the tools and book of directions refer to the education he received. He continued: "My hands carved out a rough form of my figure. I followed the directions and my work was good so far. But the tedious labor began to tell on me; the tools were becoming dull." Fukunaga is referring to his employment at Queen's Hospital where he was considered a good worker, but the labor was tedious and dulled his intellectual tools. In consequence, "What's the use, I said, and gave it up. The result? Angry and discontented, I poured forth my wrath and with one last struggle I knocked the half-formed figure to the ground and there it lay in scattered pieces." Fukunaga is describing how he had destroyed his own half-formed young life by killing Gill in "one last struggle," although he had not mentioned previously that it resulted from being angry and his wrath. The latter may refer to Fukunaga's unconscious desire for revenge against the Hawaiian Trust Co., which Myrick claimed was his strongest motive for his crime.

Fukunaga continued: "After the deed, a new soul awakened in me and [I] finally came to regret the mistake I made. . . . I had been fortunate. They gave me material, tools and directions. I had every chance of making good. . . . Why didn't I ask for help or a little word of encouragement from those about me?" This last comment reminds one of Myrick's observation that if Fukunaga had a single close friend with whom he could have talked about his dreams and ambitions, it would have lessened his dissociation and subsequent insanity, but he had none.[119] Perhaps after a year of reading the Bible and finding spiritual comfort in prayer, Fukunaga had forgotten how unhappy and lonely rather than "fortunate" he had been. Also, instead of having "every chance of making good," he had earlier remarked that not being able to continue his education was the biggest disappointment of his life. Nonetheless, Fukunaga accepted full responsibility for his wrongdoing, describing himself as a "weak, discontented worker who brought about his own downfall. Are you going to be like him? No, not on your life! . . . Blame not they that gave him every opportunity and guidance, but blame him alone." However, "they," referring to the dominant Haoles, can be blamed for denying him the opportunity to succeed in life, as they did with other non-Haoles.

Commenting on Fukunaga's message, a *Hochi* editorial maintained that it revealed "the REAL Myles."[120] Rather than being a vicious murderer, he was, his essay showed, a "thoroughly good boy" and that Gill was killed by a totally different person. The editorial noted that, while Fukunaga wrote of the opportunities that were his, he was oppressed by the "terrible economic pressure that denies equality of opportunity" to Japanese Americans. It argued, "[Fukunaga] wanted so desperately to be regarded as an American that he failed to see the shallowness and insincerity of that imitation Americanism which violates its own principles by denying equal rights, equal opportunities and equal justice to all races." The *Hochi* was thus denouncing the nascent colorblindness professed by Haoles for its insincerity and falsity in contending that Fukunaga was provided with equal rights, opportunities, and justice as all races were but, in fact, were denied to non-Haoles. The *Hochi* criticism brings to mind the argument advanced decades later by Bonilla-Silva regarding "color-blind racism," particularly "abstract liberalism" as one of its central frames with its emphasis on equal opportunity and individual rights.[121] The editorial concluded that, by hanging Fukunaga, Haoles had transformed him into a "martyr in a great cause of every Oriental-American in Hawaii." That cause was resistance to anti-Japanese racism and discrimination, but they would persist during the 1930s and start to decline only after World War II.

Five days after Fukunaga's execution, the *Hawaii Hochi* convened an outdoor mass meeting on a Sunday evening at the Chuo Gakuin Central Japanese Institute language school in downtown Honolulu.[122] The announced purpose of the gathering was to provide a report on the Fukunaga case to the Japanese American community, particularly the *Hochi* campaign to save him from the gallows. Attended by an estimated six thousand persons, the meeting lasted three-and-a-half hours, from 6:30 to 10 P.M. It was probably held outdoors because of the lack of a building that could accommodate such a vast audience. The speakers included Fred Makino and Kusaka Haga, the managing editor of the newspaper, who spoke first and provocatively compared the *Hochi* campaign for justice for Fukunaga to the U.S. war of independence. During his nearly hour-and-a-half speech, Haga declared, "As in the Revolutionary War, we undertook the Fukunaga trial to do away with discrimination." In his two-hour address, Makino repeated the "two kinds of justice" argument advanced previously by the *Hochi*—"one for the haole Americans and the other for the Orientals." During the meeting, which was intended as the final statement of the *Hochi* on the Fukunaga incident, it was announced that the paper had raised nearly $7,000 for its legal campaign on his behalf.

The same day the mass gathering was held, the *Hochi* carried an editorial, "Racial Harmony," which disputed its proclaimed prevalence in Hawai'i by Haole leaders.[123] It argued that "Orientals" had long hoped for racial equality from the "occidental" community members, who assured them that there was no race discrimination in Hawai'i. The editorial remarked that this contention has been the "favorite theme of speakers at conventions, civic organizations, Rotary Club luncheons, inter-racial banquets and gatherings of all kinds" such that "many almost came to believe it!" This theme of racial harmony was still another early assertion of multiculturalism, which continues to be professed by government officials, community leaders and journalists, although at present most people in Hawai'i do believe in it.

Disparaging the accommodationist approach advocated by Soga and Okumura, the *Hochi* editorial continued that as long as Japanese Americans follow the "false leadership of those who fawn and curry favor with the Haoles," they will never be considered as equals by them. Directing its comments to the nisei such as Fukunaga, the *Hochi* proclaimed that for too long they believed the "hypocritical bunk about 'assimilation'" and listened to those who sought to keep them from "demanding what is theirs by right of their American birth." Instead, the nisei should "demand [equality] as a right and take it!" More realistically, the editorial urged the nisei to advance themselves politically by registering to vote and by voting, which they eventually did during the following decade when, at 25 percent, they became the largest group of voters in Hawai'i. However, Japanese American candidates tended to run as Republican, the party of the dominant Haoles that would remain in power until 1954.

Several days after the mass meeting organized by the *Hochi*, Governor Judd spoke at a Thanksgiving-eve dinner hosted by a group of Japanese, including representatives of the *Nippu Jiji*, which was reported in a *Hochi* editorial.[124] The editorial offered the paper's regret that the governor had publicly denounced the *Hochi* and expressed his displeasure about the role the paper had taken in the Fukunaga case. Summarizing the governor's remarks, the *Hochi* related that Judd accused the paper of "seeking to stir up race hatred" and of having come dangerously close to contempt of court in its editorials about the case. Ignoring his hosts and asserting agreement with the prevalent view of Japanese Americans as un-American, even at their Thanksgiving-eve dinner, the governor referred to them as "aliens" and "guests" of the government and hence claimed it was highly improper for them to criticize "American justice." The *Hochi* replied by emphasizing that it had demonstrated that racial inequality and discrimination exist in Hawai'i: "We did not create these conditions. We did not 'dictate' the dual standard of justice." As is evident, a frequently utilized tactic by the dominant Haoles to counter charges of racial discrimination and racial injustice was to dismiss them by accusing those who made those complaints of inciting "race hatred"—in short, blaming the victim.

Shortly after publication of the *Hawaii Hochi* editorial criticizing Judd's address, he appears to have requested a "legal analysis of the publicity in the Fukunaga case" by the territorial Office of the Attorney General. Judd may have been seeking retaliation against the *Hochi*, Fred Makino, and George Wright because of their persistent accusations of racial injustice and discrimination against Fukunaga and Japanese Americans in general. The analysis focused on whether the above parties had violated any laws in their editorials and articles on the Fukunaga case and was written and submitted by deputy attorney general H. T. Kay on February 4, 1930.[125] One of the laws that Kay reviewed was the anarchistic publications act, which was passed in 1921 by the territorial legislature to restrict what the Japanese newspapers could publish, after the support of some of them for the 1920 strike. He noted that the relevant portion of the act, which might apply to the *Hochi* coverage of the Fukunaga case, provided that "any person who shall print, publish, sell, distribute or circulate in the Territory any written or printed article . . . which shall be designed and intended to create or have the effect of creating distrust between people of different races or between citizens and aliens shall be guilty of a misdemeanor."[126] Kay observed that in its editorial of December 2, 1929, "A Word in Reply to Governor Judd's Speech," the *Hochi* "practically confesses that they have taken the view that the Fukunaga case involved racial discrimination and that they were making a race issue out of the same."[127] However, he concluded, from a practical perspective it was questionable if a conviction by a jury could be obtained and if the statute could withstand a constitutional challenge because it was very broad and ambiguous. Based on Kay's recommendation, which in effect upheld freedom of the press rights, Judd decided not to pursue the matter any further.

The hanging of Fukunaga in late November 1929 brought to a close the intensified anti-Japanese movement of the 1920s, a decade distinguished as the most racially hostile against Japanese Americans until World War II. It began in January 1920 with the outbreak of the sugar strike, which Japanese plantation workers together with Filipinos led and participated in. This well-organized and costly challenge to Haole domination resulted in the ensuing measures taken in retaliation against Japanese Americans to maintain their economic, political, and cultural subordination. Consequently, during the subsequent decade, Japanese Americans did not join Filipinos in their plantation strike in 1937 on Maui. But on the waterfront, labor leaders like Jack Kawano were recruiting dock workers into the Honolulu Longshoremen's Association, which he co-founded that same year, while other Japanese Americans, such as Bert Nakano, were doing the same with the Hilo Longshoremen's Association. Some Japanese Americans, including Kawano, Yasu Arakaki, Jack Kimoto, and other labor organizers, joined the newly established but small Communist Party in Hawai'i as a way to foster political and economic change in the islands. In electoral politics, Japanese Americans were first elected to public office in the 1930s, but most of them as Republicans, the party in power in Hawai'i since annexation.

Continuing their conciliatory approach to Haole supremacy, Soga and Okumura convened their annual New Americans Conference until 1941 for young, educated nisei, during which they mingled with Haole business, political, and educational leaders who advised them to remain on or return to the plantations. In general, Americanization became the primary goal of Japanese Americans, especially the nisei. Thus, except for labor organizing on the docks with other racial minorities, Japanese Americans assumed a much less activist and advocacy stance in the 1930s than in the previous decade, which can be attributed to the persisting anti-Japanese movement of which Fukunaga's hanging was its climax in the 1920s. But Haoles were not done enforcing the racial boundary by sending non-Haoles to their early death. The concluding chapter compares the execution of Fukunaga with the lynching of another young local male, Joe Kahahawai, who also was raced to death two years later.

Conclusion

Fukunaga and Kahahawai

In November 2016 I was invited to participate in a public forum with five other speakers on the topic of "What Can Hawai'i Teach America about Race" at a community center in downtown Honolulu.[1] It was organized by *Honolulu Civil Beat*, a liberal, online news site that focuses on public issues concerning Hawai'i, and attracted a capacity audience of more than a hundred persons. The event was part of the ongoing "Hawai'i Storytellers" series of *Civil Beat*, so the other speakers and I were instructed to tell a personal story related to race or ethnicity in Hawai'i. This approach detracted from how I otherwise would have addressed the topic, which would have been to criticize it as another example of privileging multiculturalism in Hawai'i. The story I told was about my experiences as a non-Haole professor at the University of Hawai'i at Mānoa, where I have been employed since 1989, due to the persisting stereotype that non-Whites are not faculty. I related how even while walking the picket line during the UH faculty strike in 2001 I was asked by a skeptical Haole professor if I was really a faculty member. I described other examples of this questioning of my faculty status, including by students from Hawai'i used to having predominantly White professors, which has occurred on a number of occasions on campus. In an effort to challenge the premises of the forum, I ended my talk by emphasizing that the stereotyping I have encountered as a Japanese American is far less demeaning and dehumanizing than that which Micronesians, the latest migrants to Hawai'i, have to contend with on a daily basis, especially through racist comments and jokes told about them.

Although I spoke at the *Civil Beat* gathering, the primary problem I have with its title and approach is that it implies that the people of Hawai'i have the expertise and ability to instruct a vastly more racially and ethnically complex and diverse continental United States how to solve its long-persisting problems with race and racism, as though we have solved our own.[2] This false claim has been around since the early 1990s when Hawai'i was represented by journalists and several academics as a "multicultural model" for other racially and ethnically divided societies.[3] The origins of this notion can be traced to the emergent multiculturalism revealed herewith in the Fukunaga case.

In this concluding chapter, I discuss the contemporary racial significance of the Fukunaga case by reviewing recent manifestations of multiculturalism and colorblindness in Hawai'i. But before that, I present a fuller comparison of the Fukunaga and Kahahawai cases from a racial perspective than has been advanced previously, and I emphasize how those two individuals as non-Haoles were both raced to death. As I noted in the book's introduction, the two cases have been juxtaposed by many of the leading historians and social scientists of race and ethnicity in Hawai'i. Their commentary about the cases tends to focus on how they both gravely threatened the supposed racial tolerance and harmony between Haoles and non-Haoles in the late 1920s and early 1930s. However, none of the discussions of the incidents provides an extensive comparative analysis of them, and the comparisons that do exist are somewhat superficial, gesturing toward one or the other case, depending on the scholar's primary concern. Also, when the two cases are reviewed together, emphasis tends to be on their very different legal outcomes—how Fukunaga was hanged for murdering Gill Jamieson, despite probably being insane, while the four convicted killers of Kahahawai had their ten-year sentences at hard labor commuted to one hour in custody of the sheriff. No doubt, blatant racial injustice differentiates the consequences for the defendants in the two homicide cases. However, rather than focus on the different results for their respective defendants, we can analyze the cases by viewing Fukunaga and Kahahawai as two local young men subject to the unbridled racial power of Haole supremacy, which resulted in their early deaths.[4]

Race was the decisive factor in their respective deaths—Fukunaga's execution and Kahahawai's lynching—because they both were considered by Haoles to have brazenly challenged their oligarchical rule in Hawai'i. This chapter hence supports the book's principal argument—that the Fukunaga case was a major component in a trajectory of racial injustice against other non-Haoles who had defied Haole domination—by extending the focus on the racial significance of the Fukunaga case to that of Kahahawai. It underscores the continuity of racial injustice and racism between the two incidents, which is not very surprising given the primacy of race as the foremost organizing principle of Hawai'i society at that time and into the first decade after World War II. To facilitate the comparison with the Fukunaga case, the chapter begins with a necessarily brief summary of how twenty-two-year-old Native Hawaiian Joe Kahahawai came to be kidnapped and shot to death by four Whites from the continental United States on January 8, 1932. The synopsis also manifests why his murder and its racial aftermath became so highly significant for the local people of Hawai'i.

The Lynching of Joe Kahahawai

The tragic end of Joe Kahahawai's short life began with the false accusation by a twenty-year-old White woman, Thalia Massie, that he and his four friends kidnapped and raped her early in the morning of September 13, 1931, in the Ala Moana area of Honolulu.[5] Kahahawai and his buddies since childhood were all local males in their early twenties—Native Hawaiian Ben Ahukuelo, Chinese Hawaiian Henry Chang, and Japanese Americans Horace Ida and David Takai. They had spent Saturday night at a neighborhood *lu'au* and later at the Waikīkī Park dance hall. Thalia, the wife of a navy lieutenant based at Pearl Harbor, had also been in Waikīkī that night with her husband and a group of navy officers and their wives at another dance venue, the Ala Wai Inn. Saturday night there had recently become navy night and hence avoided by non-Haoles. After an argument with one of the officers, Thalia left the dance shortly before midnight and walked off on her own, eventually onto John Ena Road. A few hours later, she told the police that a car drove up behind her, and she was forced into it and taken to nearby Ala Moana Road, where she was raped by "four or five Hawaiians." Thalia added that, because it was dark, she would not be able to identify her rapists, but she did not mention that, due to an eye affliction, without her glasses she was blind as a bat anyway. She was examined by a doctor at a hospital emergency room, who found no evidence that she had been raped, although she did have a broken jaw. Speculation about what really happened is that she was assaulted by a Haole man, possibly a former lover, who was seen walking several feet behind her, as though they had just had an argument, as one witness said, at about ten to fifteen minutes past midnight.[6]

Meanwhile, Kahahawai and his friends left the Waikīkī Park dance a little after midnight in a car owned by Horace Ida's sister but driven by Ida that night and headed home. They later conversed with some friends of theirs driving next to them on Beretania Street at about the same time that Thalia was seen on Ena Road. Shortly afterward, their car nearly collided with another vehicle occupied by a middle-aged couple, and the wife got out and engaged in a brief scuffle with Kahahawai. The couple then drove to the nearby police station to file a complaint about the altercation and gave them the car's license plate number. This minor incident led the police to focus on the five friends as those who had raped Thalia and to begin questioning them early Sunday morning, beginning with Ida. But the interaction with their friends along Beretania Street and the squabble with the couple provided a timeline that established the youths could not have raped Thalia.

Nonetheless, Haole elites led by corporate executive Walter Dillingham and his close friend Admiral Yates Stirling, commander of naval forces in Hawai'i, demanded the arrest and conviction of the five young men immediately after they learned of their possible involvement.[7] Few such magnates were as openly disdainful of non-Haoles as Dillingham, arguably the most powerful individual in the territory.[8] He soon convened an emergency meeting that included the governor, the mayor of Honolulu, Admiral Stirling, the local army commander, the city and county attorney, the territorial attorney general, the Honolulu sheriff, the chief of detectives, the editors of the *Star-Bulletin* and *Advertiser*, and twenty of the foremost businessmen. The editors of the two Honolulu dailies said they would write editorials advocating the conviction of the accused youths. The men, overwhelmingly Haole, agreed to create a $5,000 fund to obtain information that could be used by the prosecutor's office. They also decided that the attorney general's office would assist the city prosecutor and that funds would be raised to hire secretly a law firm to provide further assistance to the prosecutor's office.[9] This same strategy was used by the HSPA in the Japanese Federation of Labor and in the Manlapit and Basan conspiracy trials. One can readily see in the convening and strategizing by this group consisting of the most powerful and influential men in the territory that elite Haoles were absolutely determined to have the five youths found guilty of raping Thalia Massie, although they might be innocent.

The trial of what was being called the "Ala Moana case" began on November 16, 1931, with jury selection. The presiding judge, Alva E. Steadman, had the same role in the Fukunaga trial. After two days, the jury of twelve men was impaneled and consisted of six who were hapa Haole, or of White and Hawaiian admixture, two Chinese Americans, two Japanese Americans, one Portuguese American, and one Haole. The prosecution's case was not very convincing and rested primarily on the highly questionable if not perjured testimony of its star witness, Thalia Massie. She was able to recall information about the defendants that she initially told the police she could not, including being able to identify them in court. Thalia also changed the time she left the Ala Wai Inn to 11:35 P.M. from midnight in order to accommodate the timeline the youths provided about their activities. However, when defense attorney William Heen, who had played an active role in the Fukunaga case, pressed Thalia for details about the abduction and rape, she repeatedly replied, "I don't remember" or "I don't know."

The prosecution case further fell apart once the defense began to present its witnesses, including three of the defendants, who testified consistently about what they all did that night. Their testimony established that they did not have the time to commit the crime. Several police detectives and officers were witnesses for the defense, some unwillingly, and contradicted the testimony for the prosecution of their fellow officers and especially that of Thalia. As historian David E. Stannard observes in *Honor Killing*, "By the time the defense was preparing to wrap things up, almost nothing of the prosecution's case was still intact. In fact, all that did remain was Thalia's completely uncorroborated, and repeatedly contradicted, courtroom testimony."[10] Just how flimsy the prosecution case was is evident from their closing argument in which the prosecuting attorney offered that they had two "theories" about the timing of the rape—either it occurred between 11:35 and 12:30 or "somewhere around 11:10 and 11:45."[11] But the latter theory contradicted even Thalia's testimony about when she left the dance hall.

However, the jury deciding the case deliberated for four days before informing Judge Steadman they were inextricably deadlocked at six to six, so he declared a mistrial. The jurors in favor of acquittal remarked later that they were particularly troubled by the obvious attempts by the prosecution to create, withhold, and falsify evidence for the trial. Six days later, a group of Haole sailors tried to force a confession from Horace Ida by kidnapping and severely beating him. That having failed, Tommie Massie, his mother-in-law, Grace Fortescue, and two sailors, Edward Lord and Deacon Jones, concocted a plot to kidnap Kahahawai and threaten him with death so that he would admit raping Thalia. On January 8, 1932, they brazenly abducted him in front of the Ali'iolani Hale court building and took him to Fortescue's rented cottage in Mānoa, where he was shot to death after refusing to confess. The four conspirators were caught red-handed a few hours later as they were on their way to dispose of Kahahawai's body in the sea.

Two days after his killing, the funeral for Kahahawai was held at Our Lady of Peace Cathedral in downtown Honolulu. More mourners attended his last rites than any funeral in Hawai'i since the passing of the beloved Queen Lili'uokalani fifteen years earlier. After the requiem mass, a long procession walked more than a mile from the cathedral to the cemetery on School Street for his burial, where a reported three thousand persons gathered. While most of them were Native Hawaiian, many of them, like Joe's friends, were not, including Japanese Americans, Chinese Americans and other Asians, and a small number of Haoles.

The grand jury that would decide if Massie, Fortescue, Lord, and Jones would be indicted for murdering Kahahawai convened two weeks after his killing. The prosecutor presented convincing witnesses and evidence against them and asked the grand jury to return indictments for first-degree murder and kidnapping. However, after deliberating for a couple of hours, the jurors voted twelve to nine not to indict them on both charges. Aware that the accused might not be charged with any crime, despite the mountain of evidence against them, Judge Albert M. Cristy informed the jurors that they could also consider indicting them for second-degree murder. After two more votes against any charges being filed, the grand jury finally returned indictments for second-degree murder by a twelve to eight margin.

Fully realizing their legal predicament, the defendants hired Clarence Darrow, widely regarded as the best criminal defense attorney in America, to represent them. Defending White racists accused of murdering a person of color was hardly typical of the long and distinguished legal career of the seventy-five-year-old Darrow, who once described himself as an advocate "for the poor, for the weak, for the weary."[12] But he had lost his retirement investments in the recent stock market crash and badly needed the money, a whopping $40,000 (equivalent to almost $700,000 in 2018) plus expenses for an expected two months of work.

During jury selection for the trial, it became apparent that almost all potential jurors did not wish to serve because of the concern that, no matter how they voted, they might lose friends or their jobs as a result. Thus, in marked contrast to the Fukunaga trial, many of those called from the jury pool claimed that they had a fixed opinion about the guilt or innocence of the defendants and could not change it, whatever evidence might be presented.

After six days of trial testimony, the jury deliberated for two days before returning a guilty verdict for manslaughter for all four of the defendants. Several jurors spoke later to the press and revealed that at first the split among them was almost exactly along racial lines, with the six Haole jurors joined by one Native Hawaiian strongly in support of acquittal. The other five jurors—three Chinese Americans, one Portuguese American, and one Native Hawaiian—were equally committed to a guilty verdict for second-degree murder. As a way to break the deadlock between them, the manslaughter verdict was a compromise offered by those in favor of second-degree murder.

Following the verdict, Governor Lawrence Judd came under tremendous political pressure to grant the convicted killers a full pardon from leaders in Hawai'i, including Dillingham, Stirling, and the HSPA, and from the continental United States, including more than a hundred members of Congress. Contributing to the mounting pressure on Judd were newspaper editorials across the country, which condemned the verdict in racial if not racist terms. Hearst columnist Floyd Gibbons raged, "Are we no longer Americans? No longer free and white? Are all the mainland millions of us in a class with those seven white men of the Massie jury who let five yellow and brown men swing a verdict directly against the sympathies of the whole civilized world?"[13] Consistent with the racialization of Hawaii's non-Haole population in the Massie rape case as savages, they were not considered part of the civilized world, which was reserved for Whites, as was being an American.

Less than a week after being convicted, the four killers appeared in court before Judge Charles Davis at 10 A.M. He gave each of them the maximum sentence of ten years at hard labor at Oahu Prison as prescribed by territorial law. The Honolulu sheriff then took them into custody, but inexplicably all of them seemed to be smiling with delight. The reason was the previous evening a deal was struck among the convicted four, Darrow, Davis, the prosecutor, the attorney general, and Judd, by which Judd would commute their sentences to one hour. The governor had succumbed to the immense pressure exerted upon him, including the threat of martial law or a commission form of government led by the military. The sheriff escorted his prisoners across King St. to Judd's office at 'Iolani Palace, where he signed a petition for commutation, and the four were free to leave, having literally gotten away with murder.

Except for the "old-guard Haole elite," very few people in Hawai'i supported Judd's drastic reduction of the sentences, particularly Native Hawaiians. Princess Abigail Kawananakoa, who would have been queen if not for the overthrow, expressed the feelings of most of them in her statement: "With this commutation, . . . are we to infer from the governor's act that there are two sets of laws in Hawaii—one for the favored few and another for the people generally?"[14] The *Hawaii Hochi* made a direct comparison of Judd's granting of clemency with his ignoring the numerous pleas for similar consideration for Fukunaga. It noted that when a thousand Japanese American mothers signed a petition requesting Judd to commute Fukunaga's death sentence, "he turned a deaf ear to their pleas. But when a few powerful influences are brought to bear in behalf of society people who killed a Hawaiian youth, the governor is eager to grant the favor."[15] In making his decision, Judd also ignored the political alliance between Native Hawaiians and Haoles through the Republican Party.

Within five days, all of the convicted killers and Thalia Massie left Hawai'i, never to return. Massie's departure brought a formal end the next year to the pending retrial of the remaining four accused rapists. To settle the rape issue, the territorial legislature and the Honolulu Board of Supervisors shortly funded an investigation by the Pinkerton National Detective Agency of New York, which conducted an exhaustive three-month inquiry of the rape case in the summer of 1932. Its report concluded that the accused young men did not cause the kidnapping and assault and that they could not find adequate corroboration to establish that Thalia had even been raped.[16] The real tragedy and injustice in Joe Kahahawai's murder is that it began with that lie.

Comparing the Men and Their Cases

Before turning to a comparison of the Fukunaga and Kahahawai cases, I provide some personal background information about the two of them. They were both born in 1909 on neighbor islands—Myles on Kaua'i and Joe on Maui—and their families later moved to Honolulu.[17] Both young men were from working-class families and neighborhoods in the downtown area and lived about two miles from each other—Myles near the intersection of Beretania and Alapai Streets and Joe farther west in an area called Kauluwela, a multiracial community marked by "conditions of crowding and degradation equal to that of any city anywhere."[18] Myles's father worked as a gardener at Queen's Hospital, and Joe's dad was a streetcar motorman, although Joe was raised by his mother and stepfather after his parents divorced. Joe's mother, Esther Anito, sewed burlap bags at a fertilizer factory in nearby Palama, while Myles's mother, Hide, took daily care of her large family of seven children. Both Joe and Myles were Catholic, although Myles for only the last year of his life. Unlike Myles, who had no opportunity to attend high school, Joe was awarded a football scholarship to St. Louis High School, where he graduated in 1928, the year Myles's unhappy life began to fall apart even more. With the stock market crash the following year, as Myles sat on death row, Joe worked at odd jobs, including on the Honolulu docks, and occasionally earned money from boxing at military bases and other arenas. While Myles claimed to have no friends, Joe, as a well-known barefoot football player and boxer, had a close circle of friends of varied races and a larger group of admirers. Both young men were said to be shy and quiet but, unlike Myles, Joe was known to have a temper and had been convicted of assault.

While they were of the same age, class, and religion and lived very near each other, I doubt that they would have been close friends given their very different lifestyles and interests. But one can easily imagine the two of them walking past each other in downtown Honolulu, watching a movie at the same theater, and eating at the same café in Chinatown. As he read or heard about the Fukunaga case in September 1928, Joe had no idea how his life would be racially and historically intertwined with that of Myles, starting almost exactly three years later, and how being Native Hawaiian would contribute to his early death.

As non-Haoles, both Fukunaga and Kahahawai were racialized by the press and other White representatives, but in very different ways. Like other Native Hawaiians at that time and earlier, Kahahawai was likened as African American by the military, the press in the continental United States, and especially Grace Fortescue. Interviewed by Pulitzer Prize–winning journalist Russell Owen of the *New York Times*, she unashamedly confessed her complicity in the killing of Kahahawai and justified it based on her Southern upbringing. According to Owen, Fortescue said "she came from the South and that in the South they had their own ways of dealing with 'niggers,'" no doubt referring to the lynching of Kahahawai by her and her accomplices.[19] Stannard elaborates that "lynching—and all that it signified in terms of race and sexual honor—was an integral part of Kentucky [home state of Tommie Massie] culture, as it was in every other southern state."[20] The two navy sailors convicted of killing Kahahawai and the military in Hawai'i shared the same racist view of Native Hawaiians as "niggers," "savages," and "beasts" comparable to Blacks in the continental United States.

As for the press, *Time* magazine in its January 18, 1932, issue, published just ten days after Kahahawai was shot to death, confidently asserted that the primary reason Hawai'i had become a "restless purgatory of murder and race hatred" was miscegenation and "the lust of mixed breeds [presumably including Kahahawai and his two Native Hawaiian co-defendants] for white women."[21] This insatiable sexual desire was the same that African American men were assumed to have for White females. At the same time, University of Hawai'i sociologist Romanzo Adams glorified Hawaii's high interracial marriage rate as a principal feature of its "unorthodox race doctrine" based on racial equality. However, the completely contrary view on the continent was that intermarriage resulted in hybrid degeneracy and a population consisting of "half-castes" inherently inferior to Whites. Furthermore, as Stannard remarks, "Haole commentators both inside and outside Hawai'i, from Admiral Stirling to William Randolph Hearst, from the *Honolulu Times* to *Time* magazine, lumped nonwhites in the islands into catchall categories with noxious characteristics: 'savages,' 'mongrels,' 'mixed breeds,' and more."[22] This racialized lumping affirmed the dominant racial boundary by differentiating between Haoles and non-Haoles and underscored the presumed innate inferiority of the latter.

Regarding the racialization of Fukunaga, while the Honolulu newspapers referred to his killing of Gill Jamieson as "the most horrific crime in Hawaii's history," rather than demonizing him as a vicious murderer, he was regularly referred to as a "boy" by the press, prosecution, judge, and his attorneys during and after his trial. *Advertiser* reporter Thornton Hardy described Fukunaga as "this pretty boy with the soft round face, the soft arms, the soft hands, the girlish bones and the childish joints."[23] In a speech in August 1929, presiding Judge Alva Steadman referred to Fukunaga as "a delightful little boy and not a criminal."[24] These depictions can be attributed to his small stature, slight build, and his youthful age of nineteen, which legally made him a minor in Hawai'i. While it is understandable that his attorneys would portray their client as a boy to emphasize his lack of full responsibility for his actions, it is not clear why others did the same while seeking to have Fukunaga convicted and hanged as an adult. As a boy, Fukunaga was not represented as a sexual threat to Haole women as were Kahahawai and his friends, including Japanese Americans Horace Ida and David Takai. More generally and again in contrast to Fukunaga's being referred to as a boy, Japanese in Hawai'i were perceived by Haoles as "masculine," with qualities such as courage, assertiveness, and self-determination, which were partially due to Japan's militarism in China and Korea.[25]

Fukunaga may have been described as a boy more for personal rather than racial reasons. Nonetheless, he still was racialized as Japanese instead of being treated as an individual without reference to race by the prosecution, court, and press. While Fukunaga was Japanese American, prosecuting attorney Davis and his key witnesses Faus and Eckerdt racialized him as Japanese based on widespread stereotypes of Japanese as stoic and as constituting the racial other to Haoles. More significantly as Japanese, Fukunaga was seen as belonging to the group viewed as representing the greatest political, economic, and cultural threat to continued Haole supremacy. Therefore, they needed to be kept under control, particularly those like Fukunaga, who dared to cross the color line by murdering one of them. By executing Fukunaga, Haoles were sending a strong message to Japanese Americans not to disrupt the racial order by other ways more frequently employed, such as organizing plantation strikes and unions.

As non-Haole young men, Fukunaga and Kahahawai were both viewed by Haoles as defying their oligarchical rule in Hawai'i and hence were both raced to death. I have already discussed why Fukunaga was hanged, despite his probable legal insanity, because he was of the "Japanese race." Similarly, Kahahawai was lynched because he was Native Hawaiian by race and thereby racialized as African American by his White killers. One of the sailors who assisted Massie and Fortescue in Kahahawai's murder, Deacon Jones, thirty years later told a *Look* magazine writer that he was the one who shot him: "Here we are, we got a nigger sitting right there, and I got a gun."[26] After Massie started asking him questions about the rape, Kahahawai leaned forward, so Jones shot him, adding "I didn't hate the black bastard," but he killed him anyway. Kahahawai can also be said to have been rushed to his death because his killers could not wait for his retrial on the rape charge, which was scheduled for later in the year.

As for comparing the Fukunaga and Kahahawai cases, it reveals how the criminal justice system was subverted in both instances, given that race "has served as a fundamental organizing principle of injustice," as Omi and Winant argue.[27] Fukunaga was denied a full psychiatric examination and a fair trial with an impartial jury and competent defense attorneys. Kahahawai was deprived of justice, beginning with the false rape charge against him, by his killers being convicted of manslaughter instead of first-degree murder, and by their ten-year sentences being slashed to an hour. Flagrant racial injustice is evident in both incidents and also earlier in the unjust actions taken against Japanese and Filipino labor leaders in order to have them imprisoned because they had contested Haole settler rule by organizing plantation unions and strikes.

As discussed in chapter 1, more than a year after the 1920 strike had ended, Japanese Federation of Labor (JFL) secretary Noboru Tsutsumi and fourteen other union officials were charged with and subsequently convicted of conspiracy to dynamite a plantation interpreter's house based on likely perjured testimony. It was provided by two Japanese former plantation workers, who were initially indicted with the other defendants but soon granted immunity in exchange for testifying against them. Tsutsumi and the other JFL leaders were given sentences of from four to ten years at hard labor in Oahu Prison. After being released on parole, none of them engaged in labor organizing anymore, which is why the HSPA wanted them convicted and incarcerated.

Very similarly, Pablo Manlapit, president of Filipino labor unions during the 1920 and 1924 strikes, and another Filipino labor leader, Cecilio Basan, were convicted of conspiracy to suborn perjury in 1924, based again on very likely false testimony given by a Filipino former plantation laborer, Pantaleon Inayuda, and by a paid police spy, Enrique Montecillo. Inayuda later submitted an affidavit that he and five other Filipinos, including Montecilllo, had perjured themselves in court in exchange for $110 and a return trip to the Philippines provided by the HSPA. After serving more than two-and-a-half years in Oahu Prison, Manlapit was paroled on the condition that he leave Hawai'i, which he did for California, and he and Basan were later banished to the Philippines. Thus, two more labor leaders who had challenged Haole supremacy in the territory were imprisoned and exiled so Haoles could maintain their oligarchical rule over non-Haoles.

Four years later, subversion of the criminal justice system occurred again in the Fukunaga trial. He was unjustly rushed to his death sentence because the Haole community wanted him hanged as swiftly as possible for killing one of their own. On the first day of the two-day trial, his attorneys stipulated that Fukunaga killed Gill Jamieson, thus placing the burden upon them to establish that Fukunaga did not kill him with malice aforethought or that he was legally insane at the time, both of which they scarcely attempted to do. Another grave racial injustice inflicted upon Fukunaga was the seating of a highly biased jury. An overwhelming majority of the jurors claimed during jury selection that they had formed an opinion about his guilt or innocence but could somehow remove it and decide the case with an open mind. It is extremely unlikely that the opinion of those jurors was that Fukunaga was innocent, although he was legally entitled to that presumption. Nonetheless, they were allowed to sit on the jury, despite the four remaining peremptory challenges the defense could have used to remove them.

At the Massie rape trial in 1931, the prosecution presented witnesses, including Thalia Massie, a police detective, and a police officer who were strongly accused by the defense of perjuring themselves with the assistance of the prosecutor. But since the five defendants were innocent, the jury could not return a guilty verdict, although it was deadlocked. As shown previously, the Japanese Federation of Labor and Manlapit and Basan conspiracy trials, the Fukunaga murder trial, and the Massie rape trial all clearly manifest blatant racial injustices perpetrated against their non-Haole defendants. Thus, Governor Judd drastically reducing the ten-year sentences at hard labor of the four convicted White killers of Joe Kahahawai, and freeing them did not seem that preposterous to the die-hard Haole elite used to having their way. For them and Whites across the continental United States, Judd should have gone even further and granted them a full pardon. The Fukunaga case thus illuminates a trajectory of racial injustice against non-Haoles both before and after its occurrence, and its proximity and relation to those other major incidents of racial injustice confirm its larger racial significance.[28] As cultural critic Jeff Chang cogently observes, "Race makes itself known in crisis, in the singular event that captures a larger pattern of abuse and pain."[29] The unjust conviction and execution of Fukunaga is that extraordinary event that reveals the larger pattern of racial injustice and abuse against non-Haoles.

Comparison of the Fukunaga and Kahahawai cases also demonstrates the differential working of race as an organizing principle against non-Haoles. While the Fukunaga incident manifests the severe impact of race primarily against Japanese Americans, the Kahahawai case (including the Massie rape trial) shows how race affected non-Haoles more generally and not only Native Hawaiians. In the Fukunaga case, the Japanese American community was very much on its own, with a few significant exceptions, in seeking a new trial, a complete psychiatric exam, and later executive clemency for him. The limited assistance and support the community received came mainly from individual Haoles, notably Prof. Lockwood Myrick Jr. and Dr. Joseph Thompson. But collective expressions of support from Haole and non-Haole entities were for the most part nonexistent and reflected the generally antagonistic racial attitudes toward Japanese Americans, given fears about their eventual political domination of Hawai'i. In contrast, the Kahahawai case generated considerable support from non-Hawaiians, beginning with the Japanese Americans, Chinese Americans, other Asians, and some Haoles who attended his funeral and burial. The several thousands who gathered for his interment could be interpreted as a collective protest against his killing, although no such large multiracial demonstration appears to have occurred after his four murderers had their sentences slashed.

Soon after Kahahawai's killing, leaders of the Chinese American, Filipino American, Japanese American, and Native Hawaiian communities held a strategy meeting—notably at the private Pan-Pacific Club—and decided that they would request to see the governor and attorney general to express their concerns.[30] But even earlier, before Kahahawai and his friends went on trial for rape, as Stannard observes, two absolutely different versions of what happened to Thalia Massie on September 13, 1931, were circulating throughout Honolulu, and race determined which account one believed.[31] He elaborates, "Unlike the world of the plantation, where nonwhites of different nationalities and races were pitted against one another to prevent solidarity, the split in opinion that now was emerging cut right down the middle—haoles on one side, almost everyone else on the other." This "split in opinion" reflected the much deeper racial cleavage in island society between Haoles and "almost everyone else" who shared a racially oppressed political and economic status. This racial rupture is quite understandable, since the five youths represented several major local groups—Native Hawaiians, Japanese Americans, and Chinese Americans—while their accusers and their navy and Haole backers were all White. But the racial schism between Haoles and non-Haoles widened even more with the murder of Kahahawai and the freeing of his convicted killers.

It is undeniable that the Kahahawai case has had a far greater racial impact on Hawaii's people and society than the Fukunaga case has. Stannard's masterful book, *Honor Killing*, the most authoritative source on what I have been referring to as the Kahahawai case, is subtitled "How the Infamous 'Massie Affair' Transformed Hawai'i," to which he added "permanently" transformed in the text.[32] This argument is advanced in the book's concluding chapter, titled "Prelude to Revolution," which Stannard notes is how journalist Theon Wright depicted the Kahahawai case in his book, *The Disenchanted Isles: The Story of the Second Revolution in Hawaii.*[33] Wright contends that the "Democratic revolution" of 1954, when that party won control of both houses of the territorial legislature for the first time, directly resulted from the Massie rape and Kahahawai murder cases because they "widened the gap between the ruling oligarchy and those whom they regarded as second-class citizens."[34] While it can be agreed that the Kahahawai case contributed over time to the eventual rise to power of the Democrats, other more directly related events and processes intervened during the more than two decades between the freeing of Kahahawai's killers and the Democratic victory.

One of those critical processes was the organization by the International Longshoremen's and Warehousemen's Union (ILWU) of sugar and pineapple workers following the end of martial law in 1944. A short three years later, the union had a territory-wide membership of thirty-five thousand predominantly non-Haole men and women. Martial law, with its restrictions on plantation laborers being hired for the much higher-paying defense industry jobs, was itself an important factor in their substantially greater desire to join the ILWU, when they had been unwilling before the war. Beginning with the 1946 elections, the union became directly involved in local electoral politics by endorsing candidates, campaigning for those they favored, and holding voter registration drives.[35] The rise to power of the ILWU was a decisive factor in the Democratic victory in 1954 and was a far more critical and immediate preceding process than the Kahahawai case was. Besides martial law, World War II itself was also crucial in the Democrats' gaining control of the legislature because it enabled Japanese American veterans to obtain college and law degrees through the financial support provided by the GI Bill. Most of the newly elected Japanese American legislators in 1954 (primarily Democrats) were veterans who had used their GI Bill benefits to earn their degrees. Unlike unionization, the Democratic revolution could not occur shortly after the war because the veterans first had to go to college and law school.

Stannard expands on Wright's argument concerning the primarily political consequences of the Kahahawai case by discussing "the growing interracial solidarity" for which "the injustices of the Massie affair had provided the catalyst."[36] As a prime example of such developing racial unity, he cites the emergence in the fall of 1931 of "local" as a collective term used to differentiate the five defendants, all non-Haoles of different racial backgrounds, from their Haole accusers and supporters.[37] Later during that decade, non-Haoles began to refer to themselves as local and added to its meaning a significant class dimension of being working class besides the racial dimension of being non-Haole.[38] As Stannard cogently remarks, "A line was being drawn that signaled an emerging interracial and interethnic unity of consciousness among Hawai'i's various people of color."[39] Besides interracial unity, this color line represented the emerging categorical cleavage between locals and Haoles, which would become deeply embedded in Hawai'i society over the next several decades. In sum, the mutually felt racial injustices of the Kahahawai case fostered a common local identity with its shared racial and class components, which then contributed to the ILWU-led labor movement and its race- and class-based opposition of non-Haole workers to the Haole-owned Big Five companies that dominated Hawaii's economy. ILWU voters (including household members), endorsements, and financial contributions then enabled the Democratic revolution to arise, which also contributed to dismantling the racial hierarchy.

Contemporary Racial Significance

Beyond their historical legacies, the Fukunaga and Kahahawai cases can be compared in terms of their contemporary relevance for Hawai'i and its people. The lasting significance of Joe Kahahawai's murder was made starkly evident by the shooting death on November 5, 2011, of another young Native Hawaiian, twenty-three-year-old Kollin Elderts.[40] He was killed by another White representative of the U.S. government temporarily present in Hawai'i—twenty-eight-year-old State Department special agent Christopher Deedy. He had just arrived in Honolulu the day before to provide security for the upcoming Asia-Pacific Economic Cooperation conference. In the early morning hours at a McDonald's restaurant in Waikīkī, Deedy and Elderts had an argument that quickly escalated into a fist fight until Deedy pulled out his handgun and shot Elderts in the chest because, as he later testified, Elderts was reaching for his gun. The clash between them began when Deedy approached Elderts seated at a table at the McDonald's after he overheard Elderts addressing a young, White male patron, Michel Perrine, "Haole" several times in jest at the restaurant counter. Deedy had been told earlier by another State Department agent, who had previously worked in Hawai'i, that "f___ing Haole" was a "highly derogatory racial slur," although Elderts did not call Perrine that, according to witnesses. Despite his claim of self-defense, Deedy was put on trial for second-degree murder in July 2013.

The term "Haole" figures notably in the Deedy-Elderts case and in the confrontation between them. More than a year before Deedy's trial began, his attorney Brook Hart submitted a motion to be allowed to question potential jurors more thoroughly about their possible biases. Drawing unintended comparisons with the Kahahawai case, in his motion Hart asserted, "This case [Deedy] became a symbol of the federal government wrongfully exercising jurisdiction over the Hawaiian Kingdom; . . . it became an example of a mainland 'haole' allegedly expressing malice and prejudice towards a local Hawaiian. . . . Through in-depth media coverage, Special Agent Deedy's case raised deep-seated social, psychological, and philosophical issues, especially those particular to Hawaii, such as oppression, sovereignty, and racism."[41] Hart can be credited for being cognizant of the broader political implications of the case, including U.S. settler colonialism over Native Hawaiians and their continuing subjugation in their homeland, instead of it being about a fight between two drunken young men, which escalated into the death of one of them. In an interview, Hart continued that "some pretty strong anti-mainland, anti-haole sentiment" had emerged since the killing.[42] Interviewed for the same news article, I commented that Hart was racializing the incident but so were the news media and many other people from Hawai'i in their online comments about it. This extension of racial meaning to the case is not surprising since the confrontation between Elderts and Deedy intersects with much larger and more significant historical and contemporary conflicts between Native Hawaiians and U.S. settler colonialism and its primarily White representatives in Hawai'i.

Deedy's first trial in 2013 was described, in terms highly reminiscent of the Kahahawai murder case, as "one of the state's most highly publicized trials." The prosecution argued that a drunken and inexperienced Deedy shot Elderts without justification, failed to identify himself as a law enforcement officer, and aggravated the initial situation by kicking Elderts. Testifying in his defense, Deedy said he considered the verbal exchange between Elderts and Perrine a "hostile incident," very likely because he did not know the meaning of the term "Haole," and decided to intervene because he was a law enforcement officer. He also stated that he showed Elderts his federal agent badge and identified himself as such, although other witnesses testified that he did neither. Deedy also denied in court that he had threatened to shoot Elderts, although a prosecution witness, who was a U.S. Marine stationed in Hawai'i, testified that he heard and saw Deedy tell Elderts at least four times, "I'm going to shoot you in the face." This threat is certainly another way Deedy worsened the situation between him and Elderts.

Given the contradictory testimony, after almost five days of deliberation the jury was deadlocked, so the judge declared a mistrial. A coalition of advocacy groups promptly called for a "Justice for Kollin Elderts" protest march in Waikīkī and underlined the racial components of the killing: "Agent Deedy, a Caucasian agent . . . was drunk and armed with a gun. Kollin Elderts, a young Hawaiian man, was unarmed. Agent Deedy shot Kollin. Kollin is dead. Agent Deedy is guilty of murder." A year later, another trial was held to determine if that was the case.

In July 2014 Deedy was retried for second-degree murder, but in this trial the jury was also allowed to consider manslaughter and assault charges. After deliberating over parts of seven days, the jury acquitted him of murder but could not come to a unanimous decision on the manslaughter and assault charges, so another mistrial was declared. Shortly after the verdict was given, the Justice for Kollin Elderts Coalition again held a march through Waikīkī to protest the racial injustice of the acquittal of Deedy for murder. A third trial for the manslaughter and assault charges has been approved but not scheduled. Even if a third trial is held, Deedy already has been acquitted of murdering Elderts. But if no retrial is held, Deedy could get away with killing an unarmed, young Native Hawaiian man without spending any time in prison, just as Tommie Massie and his accomplices killed Joe Kahahawai and later were released.

Native Hawaiians and others have rallied in support of Elderts and his family and have emphasized the racial injustice in his killing. As Kalama Niheu, one of the Justice for Kollin Elderts Coalition leaders, asserted, "We understand that here in Hawai'i young men of color—*kanaka maoli*—cannot find justice. Police officers, [federal] agents can go with impunity and kill young men."[43] Unfortunately, the freeing of Joe Kahahawai's convicted killers after one hour in custody more than eighty years ago demonstrates how it still might be possible that Kollin Elderts's killer may also go unpunished. Unlike the similar tragic experiences of Elderts and Kahahawai, I cannot think of any Japanese American comparable to Fukunaga who has suffered from racial injustice to the extent that he did in the past or more recently.

As for contemporary assertions of colorblindness and multiculturalism in Hawai'i, the latter has continued to be expressed much more than the former and is the dominant ideology related to ethnicity and race in the islands. As noted above, since the 1920s and the emergence of a multicultural view of island society as a "melting pot" distinguished by "racial harmony," Hawai'i by the 1990s came to be advanced as a "multicultural model" for emulation by other nations divided by race and ethnicity.[44] Besides the forum I spoke at, another recent affirmation of this model was a public gathering with the same title, held in September 2015 in Honolulu but sponsored by another organization.[45] With their title and timing, both presentations can be viewed as responses to the Black Lives Matter movement in the continental United

States, in which its marches and demonstrations often were marred by racial violence in the streets, in contrast to the ethnic harmony and tolerance supposedly present in Hawaiʻi.

The 2015 forum featured four speakers—three Asian Americans and one Native Hawaiian—all of whom are relatively well known in the islands but none of whom would be considered as having any expertise on race.[46] The typical multicultural tropes about Hawaiʻi expressed by the panelists included that it is "the most racially harmonious place where you can live," and that it "offer[s] an example, maybe the only example, that it [a racially diverse society] can work." Not mentioned by any of them is that Hawaiʻi has the highest per capita rate of homelessness in the nation, which is highly racialized against Native Hawaiians and Micronesians and certainly not something about race we would like to teach other Americans. This obscuring of persisting inequality and systemic racism is precisely what multiculturalism is intended to accomplish, whether in Hawaiʻi or the continental United States, in the 1920s or at present. Consequently, the racial status quo is maintained, much to the detriment of indigenous and racial minorities. In the Fukunaga case, the *Honolulu Star-Bulletin* and the *Nippu Jiji* asserted emergent multiculturalism in their charge that the campaign by the Japanese American community for a new trial for him imperiled the racial harmony of Hawaiʻi, a classic example of blaming the victim.

With regard to colorblindness, the *Honolulu Advertiser*, the *Star-Bulletin*, the *Nippu Jiji*, the prosecuting attorneys, and judges invoked it in the Fukunaga case in their respective claims that he was tried and convicted as an individual without regard to his "Japanese race," despite his being racialized as such throughout the case. Nonetheless, those parties sought to deny the significance of race in the case by contending that Fukunaga was treated the same as any Haole would have been. Both incipient colorblindness and emergent multiculturalism were deftly employed in the Fukunaga case to mask Haole supremacy as the primary racial ideology in Hawaiʻi and hence the primary reason that he was so quickly convicted and sentenced to die.

While colorblindness as the dominant racial ideology in America has been far less prevalent in Hawaiʻi than multiculturalism has, it also surfaced in 2015. In August, Judicial Watch, a conservative Washington, D.C., foundation, filed a lawsuit on behalf of four Native Hawaiians and two non-Hawaiians as plaintiffs in the U.S. District Court in Honolulu against the state of Hawaiʻi and a few of its subsidiary agencies. The suit sought to stop what it alleged was a "racially exclusive election and constitutional convention designed to establish a sovereign Hawaiian nation."[47] The lawsuit claimed that the Native Hawaiian self-governance election organized for November 2015 by Naʻi

Aipuni, a private, nonprofit group,[48] with $2.6 million in funding from the state Office of Hawaiian Affairs, "violates the U.S. Constitution by pursuing a race-based and politically qualified election to establish a race-based nation." Only Native Hawaiians were eligible to vote in the election for delegates, also limited to Native Hawaiians, who would participate in a convention between February and April 2016 to draft a constitution for a Native Hawaiian government. As such, the election, convention, and government might be viewed as race-conscious, as opposed to colorblind, initiatives, although Native Hawaiians are not a race.

The Judicial Watch suit eventually resulted in a U.S. Supreme Court injunction issued on December 2, 2015, to stop ballot counting in the election.[49] So two weeks later, Na'i Aupuni, faced with the possibility of lengthy legal battles, announced that it was canceling the election and would hold a four-week constitutional convention in February 2016 and that all of the 196 candidates for delegate could participate.[50] Those who did produced a fourteen-page "Constitution of the Native Hawaiian Nation," which the delegates adopted by an 88 to 30 margin. However, it has yet to be put to a ratification vote by Native Hawaiians.

The Judicial Watch lawsuit might be considered comparable to others that similarly have been based on constitutional colorblindness, such as those that have challenged race-based affirmative-action programs in college admissions as racially discriminatory. However, a huge difference in the Judicial Watch suit is that most of the plaintiffs are persons of color rather than White, including four Native Hawaiians. This circumstance highlights the "contradictory" and "anti-racism 'lite'" nature of colorblindness as a racial project, according to Omi and Winant.[51] The superficial antiracism of the suit is evident insofar as it ignores ongoing systemic racism and discrimination against Native Hawaiians in education, employment, healthcare, housing, incarceration, and native rights, very similar to how colorblindness does not seek to resolve continuing racial inequality. Thus, Bonilla-Silva refers to colorblindness as "color-blind racism," which includes the "central frames" of abstract liberalism, naturalization, cultural racism, and minimization of racism that work together to maintain White power and privilege.[52] As a racial ideology, colorblindness has not taken hold in Hawai'i anywhere near to the same extent that it has in the continental United States, which can be attributed to the much greater belief in and support for multiculturalism by Hawaii's people, despite its shortcomings as a means to foster ethnic equality. Hence, of Bonilla-Silva's principal frames of colorblind racism, minimization of racism, which refers to the view that discrimination is no longer a primary factor affecting minorities' status in society,[53] is especially evident in multiculturalist perspectives of Hawai'i.

The previous major public assertion of colorblindness in Hawai'i was also a lawsuit against the state of Hawai'i, filed in 1995 by Harold "Freddy" Rice, a wealthy missionary descendant, for sponsoring the election for trustees of the Office of Hawaiian Affairs (OHA). Since OHA was created in 1978, only Native Hawaiians were allowed to vote in its elections for trustees, who also were restricted to Native Hawaiians, so Rice in his suit claimed reverse racial discrimination. In 2000 the U.S. Supreme Court agreed with him and ruled in *Rice v. Cayetano* that the state of Hawai'i was in violation of the Fifteenth Amendment of the Constitution by restricting voting in OHA elections only to Native Hawaiians. The courts have also declared that non-Hawaiians can run for OHA trustee, although none has been elected. Insofar as it has been deployed against Native Hawaiians, colorblindness continues to pose a legal and political threat to allegedly race-conscious programs for them, such as OHA, to a greater extent than against those for disadvantaged ethnic minorities, such as Filipino Americans and Samoans, because there are far fewer, if any, specific government programs and services for them.

Returning to the Fukunaga and Kahahawai cases, together they remind us about Hawaii's deeply troubled racial past when race determined so much of people's lives, including how they earned a living, where they lived, who their friends were, and even how they died. Through no fault of their own, Myles and Joe as local males were both raced to death unjustly. A lasting tribute to them would be to remember them as two young men who were made to sacrifice their lives for racial justice and equality for the people of Hawai'i.

Notes

Introduction

1. Former president Barack Obama would graduate from Punahou School fifty-one years later.

2. While Fukunaga confessed to killing Gill Jamieson that does not necessarily mean he was guilty of murder, since he could have been legally insane.

3. Stannard, *Honor Killing*, 31.

4. Omi and Winant, *Racial Formation*, 126.

5. Ibid., 264.

6. Omi and Winant, "Racial Formation Rules," 309. They also contend that the "prevailing ideology of colorblindness is a failed attempt to construct a new racial hegemony" and that it "cannot overcome the gap between the promises of reform and the realities of ongoing inequality and racial despotism" (323). Insofar as colorblindness is the dominant racial ideology in America, it is not clear how it has failed "to construct a new racial hegemony." Furthermore, colorblindness hardly seeks to address ongoing racial inequality and despotism.

7. Bonilla-Silva, *Racism without Racists*. In "Kill the Messengers," Gary Delgado also argues that colorblindness is a mode of racism (163).

8. Jung, *Reworking Race*, 71.

9. Jonathan K. Osorio contends that the Bayonet Constitution "was the very first time that democratic rights were determined by race in any Hawaiian constitution" (*Dismembering Lahui*, 244).

10. Fuchs, *Hawaii Pono*, 56.

11. Glenn, *Unequal Freedom*, 208.

12. Jung, *Beneath the Surface*, 95.

13. Fuchs, *Hawaii Pono*, 45. I thank Brian Chung for recommending that I emphasize the significance of Haole supremacy in this section.

14. Quoted in ibid., 153.

15. Reinecke, *Feigned Necessity*, 19.

16. Fuchs, *Hawaii Pono,* 65–67. As a result of the huge military buildup during the two previous decades, in 1940 almost 60 percent of employed White males in Hawai'i were in the armed forces.

17. Okamura, "Barack Obama," 150.

18. Stannard, *Honor Killing*.

19. Myrick, "Open Letter to Governor Wallace R. Farrington on Fukunaga's Insanity."

20. Fuchs, *Hawaii Pono*, 126.

21. "Fred Kinzaburo Makino."

22. Daws, *Shoal of Time*, 319.

23. Ibid.

24. Ogawa, *Jan Ken Po*.

25. Ibid., 147.

26. Ibid., 120.

27. Ibid., 136.

28. Ibid., 145.

29. In an October 8, 1928, editorial, "A Serious Question Is Raised," the *Hochi* argued, "If this crime was the act of a rational Japanese boy, . . . there will be a reasonable basis for the assumption of racial issues. . . . If he [Fukunaga] is insane, as many now believe, . . . there can be no possible stigma placed on the Japanese." The *Nippu Jiji* also presented its version of this argument (see "Professional Trouble-Makers"): "It is the contention of the Hochi that the Japanese race will be exonerated of the terrible crime that Fukunaga committed if he is insane, but that if he is sent to the gallows as a sane person his deed forms a blot on the Japanese community and Japanese race."

30. Lind, *Hawaii's People*, 141–43.

31. Ibid., 143.

32. Adams, "Unorthodox Race Doctrine," 148, 150.

33. Adams, "Hawaii as a Racial Melting Pot," 213–16.

34. Kotani, *Japanese in Hawaii*, 59–72.

35. Ibid., 65, 72.

36. Ibid., 72.

37. Okihiro, *Cane Fires*, 271–72.

38. Odo, *No Sword to Bury*.

39. Tsukiyama, a former labor arbitrator, wrote a highly informative essay, "Justice and the Case of Myles Fukunaga," for the *Hawai'i Herald* (January 1, 2010), the English language counterpart of the *Hawaii Hochi*, to mark the eightieth anniversary of Fukunaga's execution. As an attorney, he makes a significant contribution to an understanding of the legal aspects of the case by providing for the first time a concise review of the motions and appeals filed on behalf of Fukunaga.

40. Quoted in Odo, *No Sword to Bury*, 66–67. While Hawaiian Trust was not one

of the Big Five companies, Gill's uncles David Jamieson (American Factors) and William Jamieson (C. Brewer) were Big Five employees.

41. Tsutsumi, "Preserving Hawaii's Historic Cemeteries." The following year I was interviewed on Hawai'i Public Radio about the Fukunaga case ("Hanged in Paradise: The Life and Death of Myles Fukunaga"). In 2018, a play was presented locally on the Fukunaga case that focused on his insanity.

42. For comparison purposes with other convicted murderers in Hawai'i, in May 2015 I did a Google search for "Vicente Kacal," a Filipino who was on death row with Fukunaga and was hanged more than eight months before him on March 2, 1929, but there were no references at all.

Chapter 1. The Racial Setting of Hawai'i in the 1920s

1. Silva, *Aloha Betrayed*, 159. In chapter 4 of her book, Silva details concerted and organized Native Hawaiian opposition to Haole rule from the imposition of the Bayonet Constitution to annexation.
2. Fuchs, *Hawaii Pono*, 152.
3. Ibid., 161.
4. Haas, "Politics," 162.
5. Lind, *Hawaii's People*, 34.
6. Fuchs, *Hawaii Pono*, 159–60; Coffman, *Island Edge of America*, 10.
7. Fuchs, *Hawaii Pono*, 158.
8. Haas, "Politics," 162.
9. Coffman, *Island Edge*, 11.
10. Schmitt, *Historical Statistics of Hawaii*, 279.
11. Coffman, *Island Edge*, 11.
12. Fuchs, *Hawaii Pono*, 162.
13. Ibid., 69–70.
14. Lind, *Hawaii's People*, 85, 87.
15. Ibid.
16. Schmitt, *Historical Statistics*, 279.
17. Lind, *Hawaii's People*, 102.
18. Ibid., 85, 87.
19. Ibid., 34.
20. The Alexanders, Baldwins, Castles, and Cookes all were descended from missionaries to Hawai'i.
21. Fuchs, *Hawaii Pono*, 22.
22. Ibid., 243–45.
23. Omi and Winant, *Racial Formation*, 67.
24. Jung, *Reworking Race*, 59.
25. Jung, "Interracialism," 392.
26. Okamura, *From Race to Ethnicity*, 3.
27. This section on the anti-Japanese movement is adapted from Okamura, *From Race to Ethnicity*, 39–46.

28. The territorial legislature had a Native Hawaiian majority until the mid-1930s, but they belonged predominantly to the Haole-led Republican party.

29. Jung, *Reworking Race*, 82.

30. Porteus and Babcock, *Temperament and Race.*

31. The nonrating of Haoles in the study was an early manifestation of the view of Whites as the racially unmarked category. The overall average score for the six racial groups was 73.3.

32. Porteus and Babcock, *Temperament and Race*, 52.

33. Ibid., 326.

34. Jung, *Reworking Race*, 82.

35. Coffman, *Island Edge*, 25.

36. Okamura, *From Race to Ethnicity,* 43.

37. Lind, *Hawaii's People*, 85, 87.

38. Quoted in Beechert, *Working in Hawaii*, 215. As discussed in chapter 6, after Fukunaga was hanged in November 1929, Governor Lawrence Judd requested the territorial attorney general to determine if this law had been violated by the *Hawaii Hochi* in its coverage of the Fukunaga case.

39. Fuchs, *Hawaii Pono*, 132.

40. See Tamura, *Americanization*, 60.

41. Odo and Sinoto, *Pictorial History*, 128. The language schools operated by Christian groups emphasized subjects related to American culture, such as Christianity.

42. Tamura, *Americanization*, 146.

43. Ibid., 130.

44. Kotani, *Japanese in Hawaii*, 51.

45. Ibid., 49.

46. Quoted in Chaplin, *Presstime in Paradise*, 134.

47. Ibid., 139.

48. Chapin, *Shaping History*, 146.

49. Ibid., 143.

50. The information on the 1909 strike is from Kotani, *Japanese in Hawaii*, 27–33.

51. Beechert, *Working in Hawaii*, 214.

52. After Gill Jamieson was kidnapped, it was learned that the maximum penalty for "child stealing" was only two years in prison, so city and county attorney Charles S. Davis suggested the assumed kidnappers could be charged with conspiracy to kidnap.

53. Fuchs, *Hawaii Pono*, 120.

54. Ibid. Jung (*Reworking Race*, 95) concurs with Fuchs: "Japanese newspapers, Japanese language schools, and virtually anything else Japanese came under intensified attack after the 1920 strike."

55. Takaki, *Pau Hana*, 174.

56. Okamura, *From Race to Ethnicity*, 36.

57. Alcantara, "Filipino History before 1946."

58. Most of the information in this section on the dynamiting of Sakamaki's house and the trial of the JFL leaders is from Duus's *Japanese Conspiracy*.

59. Coffman, *Island Edge*, 25.

60. The attorney for two of the defendants was thirty-three-year-old Charles S. Davis, who would be the prosecuting attorney in the Fukunaga trial, while another defense attorney, fifty-six-year-old Francis M. Brooks, would serve as the deputy prosecuting attorney in the trial.

61. Duus, *Japanese Conspiracy*, 199.

62. Quoted in ibid., 216.

63. Ibid.

64. Most of the information on Manlapit and the 1920 and 1924 strikes in this section is from Reinecke, *Filipino Piecemeal Sugar Strike*, and Kerkvliet's biography, *Unbending Cane*.

65. Quoted in Kerkvliet, *Unbending Cane*, 17.

66. Ruben R. Alcantara, "1920 Hawaii Plantation Strike," 188.

67. Quoted in ibid.

68. Reinecke, *Filipino Piecemeal Sugar Strike*, 30.

69. Ibid., 89.

70. Ibid., 90.

71. Ibid., 76–78.

72. Jung, *Beneath the Surface*, 134.

73. Ibid., 133.

74. Quoted in ibid., 132.

75. Kerkvliet, *Unbending Cane*, 51.

76. Reinecke, *Filipino Piecemeal Sugar Strike*, 84–85.

77. Jung, *Beneath the Surface*, 135–36.

78. Quoted in Kerkvliet, *Unbending Cane*, 54.

79. Reinecke, *Filipino Piecemeal Sugar Strike*, 103.

80. Ibid., 107.

81. Ibid.

82. Ibid., 103.

83. Ibid., 108.

84. Ibid., 35.

85. Ibid., 113.

86. Kerkvliet, *Unbending Cane*, 70.

87. Reinecke, *Filipino Piecemeal Sugar Strike*, 117.

88. Ibid., 125.

89. Kerkvliet, *Unbending Cane*, 76.

90. Reinecke, *Filipino Piecemeal Sugar Strike*, 127.

91. After the war, Manlapit was employed as a land superintendent for the National Land Settlement Administration in Mindanao, ran unsuccessfully for the Philippine Congress as a Labor Party candidate in 1953, and later served as a technical adviser to

the Philippine Labor Unity Movement. He died of throat cancer in 1969 (Kerkvliet, *Unbending Cane*, 88, 111).

92. Beechert, *Working in Hawaii*, 230. As the labor movement led by the International Longshoremen's and Warehousemen's Union (ILWU) conducted successful strikes in sugar, pineapple, and longshore after World War II, the "technique" of filing criminal charges against union leaders would culminate with arrests for violating the Smith Act in 1951.

93. This Haole was an illiterate Irish laborer, John O'Connell, who deserted his cargo ship and in 1906 brutally murdered the young son of a prominent Haole family. Probably mentally ill, he also was known as Frank Johnson, after the ship he had jumped (Theroux, "Short History," 151).

94. Okamura, *Ethnicity and Inequality*, 160. Filipinos began immigrating to Hawai'i in December 1906 and numbered only 2,361 in 1910 (Lind, *Hawaii's People*, 34).

95. Ibid.

96. Theroux, "Short History," 157–158.

97. Okamura, *Ethnicity and Inequality*, 165.

98. In chapter 6, I cite cases of Haole killers of non-Haoles, who were charged with second-degree murder rather than first and sentenced to prison instead of the gallows.

99. Reinecke, *Filipino Piecemeal Sugar Strike*.

100. Native Hawaiians also were viewed as racially inferior by Haoles, particularly in being unable to govern themselves.

101. Porteus and Babcock, *Temperament and Race*, 67, 70.

102. Lind, *Hawaii's People*, 85.

103. Alcantara, "Filipino Community in Waialua," 15.

104. Du Bois, *Souls of Black Folk*.

Chapter 2. Kidnapping, Killing, and Racial Profiling

1. "Fukunaga Tried to Join," 1.

2. The engagement of the Jamiesons was announced on the "Society" page of the *Star-Bulletin* (June 28, 1916, 5).

3. Shortly after his retirement, Fred and Lulu moved to California and lived there for about ten years before returning to Honolulu where he died in 1958 and she four years later ("F. W. Jamieson Dies," B6).

4. After being arrested, Fukunaga gave a lengthy statement to the police in which he admitted he killed Gill Jamieson. It was printed in full in the *Star-Bulletin* on the first day of testimony in his trial ("Fukunaga Sane," 1, 8–9).

5. Ibid., 1.

6. Ibid., 8.

7. Ibid.

8. Linder, "Leopold and Loeb Trial."

9. "Check Story."

10. "Fukunaga Sane," 8.

11. Welton, "Fox or 'Moral Imbecile'?" Hickman resorted unsuccessfully to California's newly established plea of "not guilty by reason of insanity," leading to concerns in Hawai'i that Fukunaga might do the same.

12. A few days before his execution on October 19, 1928, at San Quentin Prison, Hickman told reporters he had written a "confession" letter to the father of Marion Parker in which he stated, "It hurts me to feel that I was an example for that Japanese youth [Fukunaga]." ("Hickman Has Remorse," 1).

13. "Boy Taken in Car," 1.

14. "Slayer Moved Deliberately."

15. "Lad Taken to Beach Hotel," 4.

16. "Fukunaga Sane," 8.

17. Ibid.

18. "Boy Relates Receipt," 4.

19. "Boy Taken in Car," 2.

20. "Heen and Godbold," 11.

21. Stannard, *Honor Killing*, 141.

22. "Heen and Godbold," 1.

23. Ibid., 11.

24. "Child Taken Away," 1.

25. Ibid. The actual words are "All the world's a stage/And all the men and women merely players."

26. "Fukunaga Sane," 8.

27. "Child Taken Away," 1.

28. Ibid.

29. "Meeting of Father," 4.

30. "3 Men," 1.

31. "Heen and Godbold," 1.

32. "Boy Taken in Car," 2.

33. "Two Poses of Gill Jamieson," 1.

34. The *Advertiser* headline referring to the victim by his full name, despite his young age, indicates the prominence of his family.

35. "Special Deputy Group," 1.

36. "Urge $20,000 Reward," 2.

37. As an indication of the kind of "military problem" requiring martial law, it would be declared in Hawai'i on the day Pearl Harbor was attacked, December 7, 1941.

38. "Martial Law Proposal," 4.

39. "Special Deputy Group," 1.

40. "Auto Firms," 3.

41. "Automotive Men."

42. "Assistance Offered."

43. "School Head."

44. "Net Closing In," 1, 3.

45. "Hilo Police."
46. Ibid.
47. Ibid., 3.
48. "Japanese Consular Officials."
49. "Search Ends," 3.
50. "Chu Describes," 3.
51. Ibid.
52. "Kaisan under Influence," 1.
53. "Ransom Note," 2.
54. "Crude Scrawl," 5.
55. "Kaisan's Wrong Handwriting."
56. "Police Grill Youngster," 2.
57. "Kaisan Tells His Story."
58. "So-Called Kaisan Case."
59. Ibid.
60. Stannard, *Honor Killing*, 85–88.
61. Ibid., 88.
62. It seems a bit odd that Kaisan, as the former chauffer of the Jamiesons, did not recognize Gill in the photo.
63. Quoted in "So-Called Kaisan Case."
64. "Kaisan Glad to Be Out," 1.
65. "Expert Testimony."
66. Porteus and Babcock, *Temperament and Race.*
67. Stannard, "Honoring Racism," 91.
68. Ibid., 90.
69. Ibid., 115. In 1997, Stannard was requested by the University of Hawai'i Vice President for Academic Affairs to submit a report on Porteus's writings for a university faculty-student committee that was considering removing Porteus's name from a new building named for him in 1974. In 1998, based in part on the committee's recommendation, the UH Board of Regents voted to delete his name.
70. Ibid., 86.
71. "Rent Driver," 1.
72. Quoted in Joseph Theroux, "Walking Shadow," 76.
73. "S. K. Nakamura Identified," 2.
74. Ibid.
75. "Did He Give Ransom Note?" 3.
76. Quoted in Tsukiyama, "Justice and the Case," C3.
77. "Police Seek Ex-Waiter," 1.
78. Richards, "Testimony," 1.
79. Ibid., 9.
80. Quoted in ibid.
81. "Slayer Moved Deliberately," 11.
82. "Boy Choked and Beaten," 1.

83. "Thousands Go to Spot," 2.
84. "City Search," 1.
85. "Throngs Jam Streets," 1.
86. "Weird Letter," 1.
87. "Fukunaga Sane," 8.
88. Ibid.
89. "Text of 'Death Letter,'" 1.
90. "Urge $20,000 Reward," 1.
91. "$20,000 Community Fund," 1.
92. "Committee Is Organized," 1.
93. "Victim Cut Up," 1.
94. "Japanese Pledge Aid," 2.
95. "Famous Hickman Case," 1.
96. "Revolting Crime," 2.
97. "All Eyes Out," 16.
98. "Net Closing In," 1.
99. "Lone Fox."
100. "Slayer Sorry," 4.
101. "Fukunaga High in Classes," 7.
102. Ibid.
103. "Killer Visited," 3.
104. During his interrogation by the police the next day, Fukunaga made a point of telling them he bought and read the newspaper every day.
105. "Fukunaga High in Classes," 7.
106. "Kidnapper in Card Game," 5. The address of the hotel was 67 N. Kukui St.
107. Quoted in ibid.
108. "Fukunaga Tried to Join," 13.
109. "Simple Rites Held," 1, 4.
110. "Police Follow Trail," 1–2.
111. "Lone Fox."
112. "Police Follow Trail," 1.
113. "Kirrie Boy Murdered."
114. "Flags at Halfmast," 2.
115. "Feelings Run High," 4.
116. "3 Still Held," 1.
117. "Let Us Have Law," 6.
118. "Text of 'Death Letter,'" 1.
119. "Galt Denies Rumors," 1.
120. "Public Asked to Watch," 4.
121. "Committee Is Organized," 2.
122. Quoted in ibid.
123. "Oriental Civic Organizations," 4.
124. "Japanese Civic Club," 1.

125. "$20,000 Community Fund," 3.
126. "Reward Fund," 1.
127. "Community Fund Swells," 1.
128. "Terrible Menace," 1.

Chapter 3. Capture, Confession, and Court

1. The plan includes calling Punahou to say that a hospital attendant would be coming to pick up Gill because his father had been injured in an accident, although Fukunaga changed his mind and referred to Gill's mother instead.
2. Myrick, "Open Letter," 47.
3. Ibid., 38.
4. "Fukunaga, on Arrest," 1.
5. "Lone Foxs."
6. "Fukunaga, on Arrest," 5.
7. Ibid.
8. "Father Wanted to Give," 12.
9. I am not certain why several private detectives were involved with the investigation—perhaps because of the reward money—but they worked closely with the police.
10. "Fukunaga, on Arrest," 5.
11. In another *Advertiser* version, which appeared the same day, of what Fukunaga allegedly said as he was being taken to the police station, he was asked if he had killed Gill. His very lengthy reply, which seems much too long to remember verbatim, was: "I killed the boy. I am a bad, bad boy. I am very sorry that I have put you folks to so much trouble. I have watched you as you searched for me. If you had let me alone I was just on my way home to confess the whole story to my mother. Then I was going down to the police station to give myself up. When you got me, I was waiting for a Punahou street car to take me home to mother" ("How Police Headquarters Appeared," 1).
12. "Miles [*sic*] Fukunaga Arrested," 1.
13. "Mob Gathers," 1.
14. "Justice Will Be Speedy," 1.
15. "Grand Jury to Meet," 1.
16. "Death Penalty Predicted," 5.
17. Hardy, "Revenge Motive," 3. Tom Coffman, in *The Island Edge of America* (146–47), has described Heen as "one of the most influential figures of the 1920s, 1930s, and 1940s. If Hawai'i then had been a state, Heen's popularity would have made him a top contender for governor or congressman."
18. "Fukunaga Sane," 1, 8–9.
19. Quoted in Hardy, "Revenge Motive," 1.
20. "Fukunaga Sane," 8.
21. Quoted in Hardy, "Revenge Motive," 1.
22. "Fukunaga Sane," 8.

23. "Cleverness," 13.
24. "Grief-Stricken Parents," 1.
25. "Dramatic Scene."
26. "Marked Dates," 5.
27. "Honolulu's Peril," 6.
28. "Eradicate the Gangsters."
29. Unless otherwise indicated, the information from Fukunaga's confession is from the official version published in the *Star-Bulletin* ("Fukunaga Sane," 1, 8–9).
30. Ibid., 1.
31. Ibid., 8.
32. Ibid.
33. Ibid.
34. Ibid.
35. Ibid.
36. Ibid., 9.
37. Ibid.
38. Ibid., 8.
39. Ibid.
40. Ibid., 9.
41. Ibid.
42. Ibid., 8.
43. Ibid.
44. Ibid.
45. Ibid.
46. Ibid.
47. Ibid.
48. Ibid.
49. Ibid.
50. Ibid.
51. Ibid.
52. Ibid.
53. Ibid.
54. Ibid.
55. Ibid.
56. Ibid.
57. Ibid.
58. Ibid.
59. Ibid.
60. Ibid., 9.
61. "Sorry for Act," 1–2.
62. Duus, *Japanese Conspiracy*, 179.
63. I refer to this second questioning of Fukunaga as "the interview" to differentiate it from "the confession."

64. "Sorry for Act," 1.

65. The information and quotations from the interview are from its printed version, which appeared in the *Honolulu Advertiser* on September 24 (ibid.).

66. What is noticeable in the interview is Fukunaga's ungrammatical English—for example, omitting "I," compared to his generally correct English in the confession. This difference might be attributable to different stenographers taking notes during the two interrogation sessions.

67. While this expressed desire for vengeance appears to contradict Myrick's argument that Fukunaga was unaware of it (see chapter 5), this assertion was made after the killing.

68. White, "Hoped," 1.

69. Hardy, "Love of Money," 1.

70. Ibid., 2. In his article about the interview, White displayed a tendency to embellish if not add to Fukunaga's statements. Asked if he "meant it" when Fukunaga sent flowers to the Jamieson family, White wrote that Fukunaga replied, "Oh, yes, yes! I meant it with every petal of their blossoms," which does not appear in the printed version of the interview. He also corrected Fukunaga's grammatical errors evident in the interview.

71. "Swift Justice Assured," 13.

72. Ibid., 13.

73. "Not Guilty Plea," 2.

74. "Swift Justice Assured," 1.

75. "Not Guilty Plea," 1–2.

76. Ibid.

77. "Public Denied Confession," 2.

78. "Parents Voice Deepest Regret," 1.

79. The Fukunagas likely received assistance in writing their statement.

80. "Parents Make Public Apology."

81. "Public Denied Confession," 1.

82. "Swift Justice Assured," 13.

83. "Utmost Speed," 1.

84. "Letter to the Editor," 6.

85. "Not a Racial Crime," 6.

86. Ibid.

87. "Say Race Is Not Factor."

88. "Huber, Beebe," 1.

89. "Here from Mainland," 1.

90. In his arguments in court against the motion for a new trial for Fukunaga on October 19, 1928, deputy city attorney Francis Brooks stated the defense counsel proposed the date when the trial should start ("Cristy Says No," 1).

91. "Lessons."

92. "Embarrassment to Japanese."

93. "Damon Denies Rumor," 1.

94. "3 Claims for Reward," 1.
95. "Suggest Other Uses," 1.
96. "Six Claims on File." Several Japanese Americans did receive small amounts from the reward fund, including Ethel Takahashi, waitress at the Sea View Inn ($100), and Mr. I. Sato, the inn's owner ($200), who said he would donate the money to the Waialua Young Men's Club and the United Welfare Drive.
97. "Looking to the Future," 6.
98. "Better Police Service," 1.
99. "Board Favors Additions."
100. "Better Police Service," 1.
101. Ibid., 3.
102. "Reduce Crime."
103. "In a New Guise."
104. Ibid.
105. "Citizens' Vigilance Corps."
106. "Nicoll Speaks."
107. "7 Recognize Fukunaga."

Chapter 4. Racial Bias and Injustice in Jury Selection and Trial

1. Stannard, *Honor Killing*, 160.
2. Ibid. Steadman would be the judge in the Massie rape trial three years later, during which doubts arose about his fairness after he dismissed every pretrial motion by the defense. In 1948, Steadman, then president of Cooke Trust Co., intervened in a case in which a prominent Haole woman, Therese Wilder, for whom he was executor of her estate, was killed. Two young Native Hawaiians, James Majors and John Palakiko, were charged with second-degree murder in her death, but Steadman had the mayor of Honolulu replace the acting prosecutor with a permanent prosecutor, who had the two youths indicted for first-degree murder and rape. They were both found guilty and sentenced to be hanged but eventually had their sentences commuted to life in prison.
3. "Examination of Talesmen," 2.
4. "Faces Trial Today," 1.
5. "Nine Jurors," 4.
6. "Selection of 12."
7. "Murder Trial," 1.
8. Unless otherwise noted, the information and page references concerning jury selection in this chapter are from the official "Transcript of Examination of Jurors" (1928), *The Territory of Hawaii v. Yutaka Fukunaga*, also known as Myles Yutaka Fukunaga, also known as Myles Fukunaga, in the Circuit Court of the First Judicial Circuit, Territory of Hawaii. In Tsukiyama Fukunaga Case Files, box 1, ms M005, Archives Collection, Hamilton Library, University of Hawai'i.
9. Ibid., 3.
10. Ibid., 58.

11. Ibid., 170–78.
12. Ibid., 152–58.
13. Ibid., 77–100.
14. "Nine Jurors Are Passed," 4.
15. "Transcript of Examination," 251–59.
16. "Famous Hickman Case," 1.
17. "Confession of Myles Y. Fukunaga."
18. "Japanese Daily Raises," 1–3.
19. "Transcript of Examination," 259–64.
20. In the *Advertiser* account of Wall's questioning by Huber ("Jury Panel Accepted," 3), no mention is made of his offering his services, car, and driver to Davis.
21. "Transcript of Examination," 211–31.
22. "Jury Panel Accepted," 3.
23. "Fukunaga Jury Chosen," 3.
24. "The 11 Jurors," 1.
25. I thank Noel Kent for emphasizing to me the significance of class, in addition to race, in the selection of the jury.
26. Lind, *Hawaii's People*, 100.
27. Stannard, *Honor Killing*, 164.
28. "Examination of Talesmen," 2.
29. The prosecution used two of its six peremptory challenges to remove potential jurors, both Native Hawaiian, and waived two others.
30. "Fukunaga Sane," 1.
31. Unless otherwise indicated, the information on the trial in this chapter is from the official "Transcript" of Fukunaga's trial, which was published in 1929, the year after it occurred. The page references are to those in the transcript. In *Transcript of Record,* Supreme Court of the United States, October Term, 1929. Yutaka Fukunaga, also known as Myles Yutaka Fukunaga, also known as Myles Fukunaga, Petitioner, vs. Territory of Hawaii, Respondent, 139–247. In Tsukiyama Fukunaga Case Files, box 1, ms M005, Archives Collection, Hamilton Library, University of Hawai'i.
32. Ibid., 144.
33. Faus had been the city medical examiner for about three years; Eckerdt was the superintendent of the "territorial hospital for the insane;" and Chung, who was a graduate of Punahou School, had been practicing psychiatry for three years in Hawai'i.
34. "Transcript," 156, 192.
35. Ibid., 200.
36. Ibid., 235.
37. Faus's competence as a psychiatrist can also be questioned by his response to Beebe, who inquired if it was "absolutely normal" for someone of Fukunaga's age to attempt suicide, and Faus replied with an incredible "yes."
38. "Dr. Faus Sees Hospital," 5.
39. Quoted in ibid.

40. UH professor Lockwood Myrick Jr. also argued that Fukunaga suffered from suppression, which contributed to his killing Gill (see chapter 5).
41. Quoted in "Dr. Faus Sees," 5.
42. "Transcript," 163.
43. "Not Guilty Plea," 1–2.
44. "Transcript," 197.
45. Ibid., 206.
46. Ibid., 202. Fukunaga was regularly referred to as a "boy" by his attorneys, the prosecution, the judge, and the press because of his youth and small stature. See the concluding chapter for more discussion of this issue.
47. By stating Fukunaga was not Japanese, Beebe may have been referring to him being Japanese American.
48. "Transcript," 171–77.
49. Ibid., 179.
50. Ibid., 182.
51. Ibid., 158.
52. Ibid., 159.
53. Hardy, "State Rests," 1.
54. "Transcript," 208.
55. Ibid., 208–10.
56. Ibid., 211–18.
57. Hardy, "State Rests," 7.
58. The suitcase contained 482 $5 bills, indicating that Fukunaga spent or took $90 of the ransom payment.
59. "Transcript," 225.
60. Ibid.
61. Ibid., 226.
62. Ibid., 227.
63. Ibid., 228.
64. Ibid., 229.
65. Ibid.
66. Coll, "Death Only Penalty," 7.
67. "Transcript," 232.
68. Ibid., 234.
69. Ibid., 235.
70. "Fukunaga Case," 1. In a motion to the Ninth U.S. Circuit Court of Appeals in San Francisco in February 1929, his new attorneys argued Fukunaga was denied due process of law because the entire defense at his trial took only nineteen minutes.
71. "Slayer's Fate," 1.
72. "Attorneys," 1.
73. "Final Plea."
74. "Attorneys," 1.
75. Ibid.

76. Despite successfully prosecuting Fukunaga to a first-degree murder conviction, city and county attorney Charles Davis lost his bid for reelection two days later in the primary election. In the "biggest upset" and "hottest race" in the primary, Davis lost to fellow Republican James F. Gilliland by about nine hundred votes ("Pacheco," 1).

77. "Transcript," 237.

78. Ibid., 240.

79. Ibid., 242.

80. Ibid., 244.

81. Ibid., 245.

82. Ibid.

83. Ibid., 246.

84. Ibid., 247.

85. Coll, "Death Only Penalty," 7.

86. "Hold Fukunaga Guilty," 8.

87. "Death Noose," 2.

88. Ibid., 1.

89. I base this conclusion on my review of the forty-two executions in Hawai'i occurring between 1900 and 1944, when the last civilian was hanged. See Okamura, *Ethnicity and Inequality in Hawai'i*, 160.

90. "Miranda Hanged," 1.

91. Ibid., 5.

92. "Miranda's Defense In," 5.

93. "Miranda Hanged," 5.

94. Ibid.

95. "Medicos Deny Agreement," 1.

96. "Fukunaga Turns to Bible."

97. "Myles Fukunaga Calls."

98. Ikei, "Myles Fukunaga Case Review," C7-C8.

Chapter 5. The Insanity Question

1. "Death Letter," 1.

2. Myrick, "Open Letter," 1; "Death Letter," 1.

3. In the 1935 update on the Harvard class of 1915 for its "vicennial," or twentieth anniversary, Myrick said he was living in West Newbury, Massachusetts, "writing [his] doctor's dissertation" and had been teaching previously.

4. Myrick, "Open Letter," 1.

5. Ibid., 1–2.

6. "Letter on the Fukunaga Case," 2.

7. "Fukunaga Letter Suppressed," 2.

8. "Kidnapper and Murderer."

9. "When Fukunaga Was Pupil," 1.

10. "Fukunaga High," 7.

11. Myrick, "Open Letter," 49. During his interrogation at the police station, U.S. Marshal Oscar Cox mentioned to Fukunaga that his daughter and son were in the same eighth-grade class at Waialua School as he was. His response was that Cox then should remember that he gave the opening address at their graduation ceremony ("Fukunaga Sane," 9).

12. "Fukunaga Gifted."

13. "Fukunaga Work."

14. Quoted in Myrick, "Open Letter," 49.

15. Ibid., 2.

16. While the publisher of the "Open Letter" is not indicated, it might be the *Hochi* since a portion of the bound copy is in Japanese.

17. Myrick, "Open Letter," 10.

18. Myrick's father had been a patient at the New Jersey State Hospital (Theroux, "Walking Shadow," 54).

19. Myrick, "Open Letter," 10–11.

20. The information in this section is from pages 11–18, titled "His Life," in Myrick's report.

21. Myrick, "Open Letter," 14.

22. Porteus later wrote to Myrick, "I did not make this statement except in relation to the whole tragedy"; however, Myrick ("Open Letter," 2) noted that Porteus's use of the term "life-history" indicates he was referring to Fukunaga and not to the larger Jamieson murder case.

23. Ibid., 27–36.

24. "Fukunaga Scenario," 1, 7. Like the "Schedule of Undertaking Okay!" the Scenario was pieced together from torn sheets of paper found in the wastebasket of Fukunaga's room at the Serene hotel.

25. Myrick, "Open Letter," 35.

26. Ibid.

27. Ibid., 40–41. At Fukunaga's trial, Faus and Eckerdt testified he suffered from suppression of his emotions.

28. Ibid., 39–40.

29. Ibid., 18–27.

30. Ibid., 24.

31. Ibid., 41–44.

32. Arthur L. Dean, Letter to Lockwood Myrick Jr., November 19, 1928. Hawai'i State Archives, Series 203, box 6, folder 152. RECORD OF QUASI-JUDICIAL EXECUTIVE ACTIONS. Record of Gov., Terr. of Hawai'i, Re: Quasi-Jud. Ex. Actions, Death Warr., Repriv., Re Docs.: Myles Yutaka Fukunaga 1929, November 1930.

33. "Justice, Not Mercy," 2.

34. "Cowardly Attack," 1.

35. "Argument Set," 7.

36. After Judge Cristy pointed out in his ruling against the motion for a new trial

that Thompson did not state that Fukunaga was legally insane, he did not issue a public statement maintaining that was the case.

37. "Fukunaga Sane," 2.
38. Ibid., 8.
39. Ibid., 2.
40. Ibid., 8.
41. "Death Letter," 1.
42. "Fukunaga Sane," 8.
43. "Sorry for Act," 2.
44. Those who believe Fukunaga could not differentiate between right and wrong might seize on this statement, especially the reference to "now" after he had killed Gill rather than when or before he did. However, his other actions before the killing, such as trying not to be recognized, demonstrate that he knew killing Gill was more than a "mistake."
45. "Sorry for Act," 2.
46. "Reads Editorial."
47. The "shell" could also refer to the *kiawe* trees under which Fukunaga liked to spend his free time reading.

Chapter 6. Aftermath of Death Sentence

1. "Serious Question," 1–2.
2. "Obstructing Justice."
3. Ibid.
4. "Fukunaga's No Racial Crime," 1.
5. Childs, "Open Letter," 2.
6. "Japanese Daily Raises," 1.
7. The contributions of Lockwood Myrick Jr. to the understanding that Fukunaga was legally insane cannot be discounted.
8. "Bad Situation Arises," 6.
9. "Raising the Race Question," 6.
10. See Omi and Winant, *Racial Formation*, 257.
11. "Running True to Form," 1.
12. "This Is Not a Fight," 1.
13. Quoted in Wakukawa, *History of the Japanese*, 248–49.
14. Editorial, *Honolulu Advertiser*, February 2, 1920.
15. Okamura, *From Race to Ethnicity*, 38.
16. "Desperate Expedient," 2.
17. "Cry of the Blood-Hound," 1.
18. "Desperate Expedient," 2.
19. "Fireworks Fly," 2.
20. "Authorities Deny Request," 1.
21. "Is Myles Fukunaga Insane?"

22. "Authorities Deny Request," 1.

23. "Relative of Fukunaga."

24. "Japanese Daily Raises," 1.

25. Quoted in Tamura, *Americanization*, 82.

26. Tsukiyama, "Justice and the Case," C6. In 1953 Murakami was appointed the first Japanese American circuit court judge on O'ahu (Tamura, *Americanization*, 242).

27. "New Trial Sought," 1.

28. Farrington at the same time signed the death warrant for Vicente Kacal, who was convicted of first-degree murder in July 1928 and had been waiting notification of his execution, another indication of the rush to execute Fukunaga ("Fukunaga Will Hang," 1).

29. Ibid., 7.

30. "Murderer Gets Stay," 1–2.

31. Ibid., 1.

32. "Cristy Says No," 1.

33. Ibid.

34. Ibid., 15.

35. Hardy, "Judge Refuses Appeal," 1.

36. Quoted in ibid., 15. The second part of this definition referring to "the governing power of [one's] mind" being "completely destroyed" so that one's "actions . . . are beyond [one's] control" is comparable to the notion of being "compelled by [a] force which [one] cannot resist" in the definition of insanity in the territorial Insanity Act.

37. Quoted in ibid.

38. Quoted in ibid.

39. Quoted in ibid.

40. "Writ of Error," 1.

41. "Fukunaga and Vicente Kacal," 1.

42. "Reprieves," 1.

43. "Opening Brief" 1928. In Supreme Court of the Territory of Hawaii, no. 1860. Fukunaga Case Files, box 2, ms M005, Archives Collection, Hamilton Library, University of Hawai'i.

44. Ibid., 44–58. The brief includes a nearly seventy-page "Argument" section that discusses in detail each of the sixteen errors. The page numbers refer to those in the brief.

45. Only Swift and Hurd served on the jury, while the others were eventually dismissed.

46. "Opening Brief," 50.

47. Ibid., 51.

48. Ibid., 51–52.

49. Ibid., 53.

50. Ibid., 56.

51. Ibid., 56–57.

52. Ibid., 58. I do not know if the practice was to sequester juries in murder trials immediately after they had been finalized, but it seems very unlikely that this claimed error would have resulted in an overturned guilty verdict.

53. "Court Erred," 1.

54. "Retrial Plea."

55. "Fukunaga Case to High Court."

56. "Court Backs Up Sentence," 1.

57. "Opinion of Supreme Court."

58. Ibid., 80.

59. Ibid., 90.

60. Ibid., 91.

61. Ibid., 114.

62. Ibid., 91.

63. Ibid., 107.

64. Ibid., 101.

65. "Fukunaga Gets Third Reprieve."

66. "Fukunaga to Take Case."

67. "Murakami."

68. "Fukunaga Gets New Reprieve."

69. "Brief for Appellant."

70. Ibid., 11.

71. Ibid., 26.

72. "Proceedings."

73. "Yutaka Fukunaga Appealed."

74. "Petition for Writ of Certiorari."

75. "Serious Question," 1–2.

76. "Argument Set," 1, 7.

77. "Mind Study."

78. "Prof. Myrick Makes Report," 1.

79. "Afraid of the Truth," 1.

80. "Why Should We Worry."

81. "Full History," 1.

82. "Hochi Editor Explains," 6.

83. "Newspaper Trials."

84. Fuchs, *Hawaii Pono*, 131.

85. "Sanity Issue," 2.

86. "Near the End." Besides discrimination, another reason Japanese supported Fukunaga was because he said he committed his crime in order to help his parents return to Japan, which they viewed as an expression of *oya koko* (filial piety), a dominant cultural value.

87. "Japanese in Strong Plea," 1.

88. "Thin Wedge of Distrust," 1.

89. "No Time Limit," 1–2.

90. "Too Young to Hang."
91. "1000 Japanese Women," 1.
92. "Death Warrant," 1.
93. "Shadow of Death," 1.
94. "Fukunaga to Receive."
95. "Walks to the Gallows," 1.
96. Ibid., 3.
97. "Fukunaga Case Finale," 1.
98. "Walks to the Gallows," 1.
99. "Fukunaga Case Finale," 1.
100. "Buddhists to Hold Funeral," 1.
101. "Fukunaga Is Given," 1.
102. Ibid.
103. Ibid., 1–2.
104. Fukunaga's gravestone is a brown stone slab inscribed with three *kanji* and is more than five-and-a-half feet high. According to several native speakers of Japanese, who also are fluent in English, with whom I consulted, the inscription can be loosely translated as "the gravestone of someone whose outcome in life was the result of a bad deed." It is implanted in a light reddish-colored concrete square about two-and-a-half feet high, making the grave marker one of the tallest in the cemetery. This base is also inscribed with *kanji* that indicate Fukunaga's Buddhist name given upon his death and the dates of his birth and death. I do not know when the grave marker was erected, but donations from the Japanese American community paid for it. I was told that the use of natural, unpolished stone for the gravestone indicates that it was intended as a memorial and not merely a grave marker. For more than twenty years until 2010, I lived across from the cemetery and used to visit Fukunaga's grave around Christmas to see if his relatives had left the usual flowers and other offerings they did every year. For Christmas 2014 they brought him a potted poinsettia plant and miniature pine tree, an apple and wrapped candy. These relatives of Fukunaga include the children of his many siblings.
105. "Buddhists to Hold," 1. Anti-Buddhism was another major component of the anti-Japanese movement.
106. "Law's Triumph," 1.
107. "Where the 'Melting Pot' Melts," 6.
108. "Fukunaga Case," 22.
109. "Hymn of Hate," 1.
110. "Fukunaga Case," 22.
111. Ibid.
112. "Fukunaga's Final Letters," 1–2.
113. Ibid., 1–2.
114. "Fukunaga Asks Sister," 1.
115. Quoted in Tsukiyama, "Justice and the Case," C8.
116. Fukunaga, "Let Your Light Shine!"

117. Ibid.
118. Ibid.
119. Myrick, "Open Letter," 15.
120. "Message from the Dead," 1–2.
121. Bonilla-Silva, *Racism without Racists*, 76.
122. "Fukunaga Is Discussed," 1.
123. "Racial Harmony," 1.
124. "Heart to Heart Talk," 1–2.
125. Kay, "Memo."
126. Quoted in ibid., 6.
127. Ibid.

Conclusion: Fukunaga and Kahahawai

1. The notion that Hawai'i can teach other places about race can be traced to at least 1961 by Lawrence Fuchs in *Hawaii Pono*: "Great changes were taking place in Hawaii, and the peoples of the Islands did have much to teach the world" (448). The other speakers are all relatively well known in Hawai'i, including novelist Lois-Ann Yamanaka, journalist Denby Fawcett, and kumu hula instructor Hina.

2. Another problem I have with the forum title is that we do not really talk about race in Hawai'i. Local residents are far more likely to mention "ethnicities" rather than "races" as comprising the constituent groups in the islands. The reason for this practice is because race is much less socially constructed than ethnicity is in Hawai'i.

3. To my knowledge, no other state or nation has ever sought to have representatives from Hawai'i teach them about race.

4. I fully realize that framing Kahahawai as local de-emphasizes his status as *Kanaka Maoli*, but it was during this period, and especially as a direct result of his murder and his convicted killers later being released, that local identity began to emerge and gain significance among non-Haole, working-class people like Kahahawai and Fukunaga.

5. Readers interested in a full description and analysis of Kahahawai's killing should consult David E. Stannard's authoritative book on the case, *Honor Killing: How the Infamous "Massie Affair" Transformed Hawai'i*, from which the information about the case has been drawn.

6. Thalia's story about being raped very likely was to provide an explanation of why she had a broken jaw.

7. The Dillingham Corporation had millions of dollars annually in contracts with the U.S. Navy in Hawai'i.

8. Stannard, *Honor Killing*, 117.

9. The firm hired was Thompson, Beebe & Winn; Eugene Beebe had been one of Fukunaga's attorneys, and Frank Thompson was the attorney for the HSPA.

10. Stannard, *Honor Killing*, 198.

11. Quoted in ibid., 210.

12. Quoted in ibid., 295.

13. Quoted in ibid., 384.
14. Quoted in ibid., 392.
15. Quoted in ibid., 384.
16. Ibid., 396–97.
17. The information in this section on Kahahawai is from Stannard's *Honor Killing*.
18. Stannard, *Honor Killing*, 72.
19. Quoted in ibid., 301. In her memoirs, Fortescue recalled how she prepared the night before the killing of Kahahawai by studying a newspaper photo of "that brutal, repulsive black face," so she would be able to identify him (quoted in ibid., 243).
20. Ibid., 155.
21. Quoted in ibid., 269.
22. Ibid., 413.
23. Hardy, "Love of Money," 2.
24. Quoted in "Delightful Little."
25. Jung, "Interracialism," 383.
26. Quoted in Stannard, *Honor Killing*, 402.
27. Omi and Winant, *Racial Formation*, 263.
28. The trajectory certainly continued further into the 1930s, as is evident in the Hilo Massacre on August 1, 1938, in which fifty union members and supporters were shot and wounded by the Hilo police in five minutes of gunfire. They were part of more than two hundred demonstrators who had peacefully assembled on the Hilo docks to protest the arrival and unloading of a ship, which was operated by a scab crew, in support of striking workers in Honolulu. No police were indicted by the grand jury for firing upon and wounding the demonstrators, who were overwhelmingly Native Hawaiian, Japanese American, and Portuguese American (Puette, *Hilo Massacre*).
29. Chang, *We Gon' Be Alright*, 3.
30. Stannard, *Honor Killing*, 274.
31. Ibid., 137.
32. Ibid., 210.
33. Wright, *Disenchanted Isles*, 83. The son of *Hawaii Hochi* English-language section editor, George Wright, Theon covered the Kahahawai murder trial as a reporter for the *Honolulu Advertiser* and later wrote his own book about the case, *Rape in Paradise*.
34. Quoted in Stannard, *Honor Killing*, 421.
35. Okamura, *From Race to Ethnicity*, 97.
36. Stannard, *Honor Killing*, 415.
37. Stannard (ibid., 413) states that in fall 1931 "people of color" began to describe the five defendants as "local," but Andrew Lind said it was initially the *Advertiser* that did so in its reporting of the Massie rape case (Okamura, "Local Culture," 119–37).
38. Okamura, *Ethnicity and Inequality*, 113.
39. Stannard, *Honor Killing*, 413.
40. The information in this section is from Okamura, "Race and/or Ethnicity," 94–113.

41. Quoted in Grube, "Can a White Federal Agent."
42. Quoted in ibid.
43. Quoted in Tsai, "March Decries Deedy Acquittal," B1.
44. Okamura, "Illusion of Paradise," 264–84.
45. "What Can Hawai'i Teach?"
46. The participants were former Kamehameha Schools trustee Corbett Kalama, venture capitalist Guy Kawasaki, actor Daniel Dae Kim, and UH Peace Institute director Maya Soetoro-Ng, who is the sister of Barack Obama.
47. Quoted in Essoyan, "Lawsuit Challenges," A21.
48. Na'i Aipuni states that it is a "not-for-profit organization, independent of any government or government agency or any Hawaiian community organization" ("Native Hawaiians Our Future," 28), although it was funded by OHA grants through the Akamai Foundation (Essoyan, "Lawsuit Challenges," A21).
49. Hurley, "U.S. High Court," B1.
50. Hurley, "Native Vote," A1.
51. Omi and Winant, *Racial Formation*, 259.
52. Bonilla-Silva, *Racism without Racists.*
53. Ibid., 29.

References

Adams, Romanzo C. "Hawaii as a Racial Melting Pot." *Mid-Pacific Magazine* 32, no. 3 (1926): 213–16.

———. "The Unorthodox Race Doctrine of Hawaii." In *Race and Culture Contacts*, edited by E. B. Reuter, 143–60. New York: McGraw-Hill, 1934.

"Afraid of the Truth." Editorial. *Hawaii Hochi*, November 21, 1928, 1–2.

Alcantara, Ruben R. "The Filipino Community in Waialua." PhD diss., American Studies, University of Hawai'i, 1973.

———. "Filipino History before 1946: The Sakada Years of Filipinos in Hawaii." 1988. http://scholarspace.manoa.hawaii.edu/bitstream/handle/10125/17988/alcantara_ch_4.pdf?sequence=1.

———. "The 1920 Hawaii Plantation Strike: Ethnicity and Class in Hawaii Labor Organizing." In *Festschrift in Honor of Dr. Marcelino Foronda, Jr.*, edited by Emerita S. Quito, 182–206. Manila: De La Salle University Press, 1987.

"All Eyes Out for the Boy." Editorial, *Honolulu Advertiser*, September 20, 1928, 16.

"Argument Set for Friday on Fukunaga Plea." *Honolulu Star-Bulletin*, October 16, 1928, 1, 7.

"Assistance Offered by General Conner." *Honolulu Star-Bulletin*, September 19, 1928.

"Attorneys in Fukunaga Case Present Arguments to Jury." *Honolulu Advertiser*, October 5, 1928, 1.

"Authorities Deny Request for Inquiry." *Hawaii Hochi*, October 10, 1928, 1.

"Auto Firms Offer Cars to Help in Search for Boy." *Honolulu Advertiser*, September 20, 1928, 3.

"Automotive Men Join Hands, Offer Aid in Kidnapping." *Honolulu Star-Bulletin*, September 19, 1928.

"A Bad Situation Arises." Editorial. *Honolulu Star-Bulletin*, October 17, 1928, 6.

Beechert, Edward D. *Working in Hawaii: A Labor History*. Honolulu: University of Hawai'i Press, 1985.

"Better Police Service Seen as Vital Need." *Honolulu Star-Bulletin*, September 25, 1928, 1, 3.

"Board Favors Additions to Police Force." *Honolulu Star-Bulletin*, September 27, 1928.

Bonilla-Silva, Eduardo. *Racism without Racists: Color-Blind Racism and the Persistence of Racial Inequality in America*. 4th ed. Lanham, Md.: Rowman and Littlefield, 2014.

"Boy Choked and Beaten, Faus Finds." *Honolulu Advertiser*, September 20, 1928, 1.

"Boy Relates Receipt of Ransom Note." *Honolulu Advertiser*, September 20, 1928, 4.

"Boy Taken in Car after Telephone Tale of Accident." *Honolulu Advertiser*, September 19, 1928, 1.

"Brief for Appellant." United States Circuit Court of Appeals for the Ninth Circuit, No. 5730, 1929. Fukunaga Case Files, box 1, ms M005, Archives Collection, Hamilton Library, University of Hawai'i.

"Buddhists to Hold Funeral for Fukunaga." *Hawaii Hochi*, November 19, 1929, 1.

Chang, Jeff. *We Gon' Be Alright: Notes on Race and Resegregation*. New York: Picador, 2016.

Chapin, Helen Geracimos. *Shaping History: The Role of Newspapers in Hawai'i*. Honolulu: University of Hawai'i Press, 1996.

Chaplin, George. *Presstime in Paradise: The Life and Times of The* Honolulu Advertiser, *1856–1995*. Honolulu: University of Hawai'i Press, 1998.

"Check Story That Fukunaga Clipped Out Murder Yarn." *Honolulu Star-Bulletin*, September 27, 1928.

"Child Taken Away on Ruse: Father Receives Letter Asking for Money." *Honolulu Star-Bulletin*, September 18, 1928, 1.

Childs, Chilton S. "An Open Letter to the Japanese." *Hawaii Hochi*, October 19, 1928, 2.

"Chu Describes How He Found Ex-Chauffer." *Honolulu Advertiser*, September 20, 1928, 3.

"Citizens' Vigilance Corps Nonpartisan Organization Says Chairman Balch." *Honolulu Advertiser*, September 30, 1928.

"City Search by 2000 Men Reaches End." *Honolulu Advertiser*, September 20, 1928, 1.

"Cleverness and Stupidty [*sic*] Shown in Murder Case." *Honolulu Star-Bulletin*, September 24, 1928, 13.

Coffman, Tom. *The Island Edge of America: A Political History of Hawai'i*. Honolulu: University of Hawai'i Press, 2003.

Coll, Raymond, Jr. "Death Only Penalty Law Will Allow." *Honolulu Advertiser*, October 5, 1928, 7.

"Committee Is Organized to Help Sheriff." *Honolulu Star-Bulletin*, September 21, 1928, 1–2.

"Community Fund Swells to $27,830.25." *Honolulu Advertiser*, September 23, 1928, 1.

"Confession of Myles Y. Fukunaga." *Nippu Jiji*, September 23, 1928.

"Court Backs Up Sentence of Fukunaga." *Honolulu Star-Bulletin*, January 3, 1929, 1.

"Court Erred in Fukunaga Case, Davis Asserts." *Honolulu Star-Bulletin*, December 21, 1928, 1.

"A Cowardly Attack." Editorial. *Hawaii Hochi*, October 26, 1928, 1.
"Cristy Says No to New Trial Bid for Fukunaga." *Honolulu Advertiser*, October 20, 1928, 1, 15.
"Crude Scrawl, Wierd [*sic*] Figures in Kidnappers Letter." *Honolulu Star-Bulletin*, September 19, 1928, 5.
"The Cry of the Blood-Hound." *Hawaii Hochi*, October 24, 1928, 1.
"Damon Denies Rumor." *Honolulu Star-Bulletin*, September 25, 1928, 1.
Daws, Gavan. *Shoal of Time: A History of the Hawaiian Islands*. Honolulu: University of Hawai'i Press, 1968.
Dean, Arthur L. Letter to Lockwood Myrick Jr., November 19, 1928. Hawai'i State Archives. Series 203, box 6, folder 152, Record of Quasi-Judicial Executive Actions. Record of Gov., Terr. of Hawai'i, Re: Quasi-Jud. Ex. Actions, Death Warr., Repriv., Re Docs.: Myles Yutaka Fukunaga 1929, November 1930.
"Death Letter Forecasts End of Boy's Life." *Honolulu Star-Bulletin*, September 2, 1928, 1.
"Death Noose for Fukunaga Court Decree." *Honolulu Advertiser*, October 9, 1928, 1–2.
"Death Penalty Predicted for Young Murderer." *Honolulu Star-Bulletin*, September 24, 1928, 5.
"Death Warrant for Murderer Is Approved." *Honolulu Star-Bulletin*, November 12, 1929, 1.
Delgado, Gary. "Kill the Messengers: Can We Achieve Racial Justice without Mentioning Race?" In *Racial Formation in the Twenty-First Century,* edited by Daniel HoSang, Oneka LaBennett, and Laura Pulido, 162–82. Berkeley: University of California Press, 2012.
"A Delightful Little Boy." Editorial, *Hawaii Hochi*, August 6, 1929.
"A Desperate Expedient." Editorial. *Hawaii Hochi*, October 20, 1928, 1–2.
"Did He Give Ransom Note?" *Honolulu Advertiser*, September 20, 1928, 3.
"Dramatic Scene Enacted at Oahu Prison When Parents See Slayer." *Nippu Jiji*, September 29, 1928.
"Dr. Faus Sees Hospital Need as Great Here." *Honolulu Star-Bulletin,* October 3, 1928, 5.
Du Bois, W. E. B. [1903]. *The Souls of Black Folk*. Mineola, NY: Dover, 1994.
Duus, Masayo Umezawa. *The Japanese Conspiracy: The Oahu Sugar Strike of 1920*. Berkeley: University of California Press, 1999.
Editorial. *Honolulu Advertiser*, February 2, 1920.
"The 11 Jurors." *Honolulu Advertiser*, October 1, 1928, 1.
"Embarrassment to Japanese." *Nippu Jiji*, September 27, 1928.
"Eradicate the Gangsters." *Nippu Jiji*, September 23, 1928.
Essoyan, Susan. "Lawsuit Challenges Native Hawaiian Election." *Honolulu Star-Advertser*, August 14, 2015, A21.
"Examination of Talesmen Occupies Day." *Honolulu Advertiser*, October 2, 1928, 1–2.
"Examinations Reveal Little of Importance." *Honolulu Star-Bulletin*, September 21, 1928, 1, 4.

"Expert Testimony." Editorial. *Hawaii Hochi*, October 1, 1928.
"Faces Trial Today." *Honolulu Advertiser*, October 1, 1928, 1.
"Famous Hickman Case Repeated Here; Kidnappers Cut Open Boy's Abdomen on Both Sides: Rip Open His Back and Strangle Him until Tongue Hangs Out." *Nippu Jiji*, September 20, 1928, 1.
"Father Wanted to Give All Aid in Son's Capture." *Honolulu Star-Bulletin*, September 24, 1928, 12.
"Feelings Run High as Body Is Found." *Honolulu Star-Bulletin*, September 21, 1928, 4.
"Final Plea for Youthful Slayer." *Nippu Jiji*, October 4, 1928.
"Fireworks Fly at River St. Meeting." *Honolulu Advertiser*, October 19, 1928, 1–2.
"Flags at Halfmast, Business Houses Are Closed Today." *Honolulu Star-Bulletin*, September 21, 1928, 2.
"Fred Kinzaburo Makino: A Biography." 2010. http://www.discovernikkei.org/en/journal/ 2010/11/29/fred-kinzaburo-makino/.
Fuchs, Lawrence H. *Hawaii Pono: A Social History*. New York: Harcourt, Brace and World, 1961.
"Fukunaga and Vicente Kacal, under Sentence to Die, Reprieved to January 3." *Honolulu Star-Bulletin*, November 19, 1928, 1.
"Fukunaga Asks Sister to Watch Over his Parents." *Honolulu Star-Bulletin*, November 20, 1929, 1.
"Fukunaga, on Arrest, Says 'I Am Guilty.'" *Honolulu Advertiser*, September 23, 1928, 1.
"The Fukunaga Case." Editorial. *Hawaii Hochi*, June 18, 1929, 1.
"The Fukunaga Case." Editorial. *Honolulu Advertiser*, November 17, 1929, 22.
"Fukunaga Case Finale an Anti-Climax after 14 Months of Legal Fighting." *Honolulu Star-Bulletin*, November 19, 1929, 1.
"Fukunaga Case to High Court." *Honolulu Star-Bulletin*, December 27, 1928.
"Fukunaga Is Discussed at Mass Meeting." *Honolulu Star-Bulletin*, November 25, 1929, 1, 7.
"Fukunaga Gets New Reprieve until March 2." *Honolulu Star-Bulletin*, February 1, 1929.
"Fukunaga Gets Third Reprieve, Pending Opinion." *Honolulu Star-Bulletin*, January 3, 1929.
"Fukunaga Gifted in a Literary Way." *Honolulu Star-Bulletin*, September 24, 1928.
"Fukunaga High in Classes at Waialua School." *Honolulu Star-Bulletin*, September 24, 1928, 7.
"Fukunaga Is Given Solemn Burial Rites." *Hawaii Hochi*, November 20, 1929, 1–2.
"Fukunaga Jury Chosen: Trial on Wednesday." *Honolulu Star-Bulletin*, October 2, 1928, 1, 3.
"Fukunaga Letter Suppressed." *Hawaii Hochi*, October 13, 1928, 2.
Fukunaga, Myles Y. "Let Your Light Shine! A Message from My Soul to the Younger Generation." *Hawaii Hochi*, November 24, 1929.
"Fukunaga to Receive Final Church Rites." *Hawaii Hochi*, November 18, 1929.

"Fukunaga Sane When He Slew Youth, Doctor Says: Confession Given to Court." *Honolulu Star-Bulletin*, October 3, 1928, 1, 8–9.

"Fukunaga Scenario Shows Slayer Thought of Crime as Motion Picture Plot." *Honolulu Advertiser*, October 5, 1928, 1, 7.

"Fukunaga to Take Case to Ninth Circuit." *Hawaii Hochi*, January 4, 1929.

"Fukunaga Tried to Join in Man Hunt for Self." *Honolulu Star-Bulletin*, September 25, 1928, 1.

"Fukunaga Turns to Bible: Reads it in his Cell." *Honolulu Star-Bulletin*, October 6, 1928.

"Fukunaga Will Hang at Oahu Prison October 23." *Honolulu Star-Bulletin*, October 15, 1928, 1.

"Fukunaga Work at Hospital and Hotel Regarded as Steady." *Honolulu Star-Bulletin*, September 24, 1928.

"Fukunaga's Final Letters to Church, Clergyman, Tell Attitude toward Death." *Honolulu Star-Bulletin*, November 22, 1929, 1–2.

"Fukunaga's No Racial Crime, Steadman Says." *Honolulu Star-Bulletin*, October 13, 1928, 1.

"Full History of Fukunaga Case Is Told." *Hawaii Hochi*, December 10, 1928, 1–2.

"F. W. Jamieson Dies at Oahu Avenue Home." *Honolulu Advertiser*, August 23, 1958, B6.

"Galt Denies Rumors of Threatening Notes: Asks Common Sense, Coolness." *Honolulu Star-Bulletin*, September 22, 1928, 1.

Glenn, Evelyn Nakano. *Unequal Freedom: How Race and Gender Shaped American Citizenship and Labor*. Cambridge, Mass.: Harvard University Press, 2002.

"Grand Jury to Meet Monday on Fukunaga." *Honolulu Advertiser*, September 23, 1928, 1.

"Grief-Stricken Parents Tell of Fukunaga's Life." *Honolulu Advertiser*, September 23, 1928, 1.

Grube, Nick. "Can a white federal agent who killed a Hawaii local get a fair trial?" *Honolulu Civil Beat*, June 19, 2012. http://www.civilbeat.com/articles/2012/06/19/16103-can-a-white-federal-agent-who-killed-a-hawaii-local-get-a-fair-trial/.

Haas, Michael. "Politics." In *Multicultural Hawai'i: The Fabric of a Multiethnic Society*, edited by M. Haas, 147–64. New York: Garland, 1998.

Hardy, Thornton. "Judge Refuses Appeal in Blast of Indignation." *Honolulu Advertiser*, October 20, 1928, 1.

———. "Love of Money, Romance Led Boy to Commit Deed." *Honolulu Advertiser*, September 24, 1928, 1.

———. "Revenge Motive of Murder, Says Slayer of Boy." *Honolulu Advertiser*, September 23, 1928, 3.

———. "State Rests in Fukunaga Murder Case." *Honolulu Advertiser*, October 4, 1928, 1, 7.

"A Heart to Heart Talk." Editorial. *Hawaii Hochi*, December 2, 1929, 1–2.

"Heen and Godbold Refuse Recompense for Their Services to Jamiesons." *Honolulu Star-Bulletin*, September 25, 1928, 1, 11.

"Here from Mainland to Practice at Bar." *Honolulu Advertiser*, November 25, 1921, 1.

"Hickman Has Remorse for Bad Example." *Hawaii Hochi*, October 17, 1928, 1–2.

"Hilo Police Gets KKK Note, Rumor." *Nippu Jiji*, September 22, 1928.

"Hochi Editor Explains Stand on Fukunaga." *Honolulu Star-Bulletin*, December 11, 1928, 6.

"Hold Fukunaga Guilty of First Degree Crime." *Honolulu Star-Bulletin*, October 5, 1928, 1, 8.

"Honolulu's Peril." Editorial. *Honolulu Star-Bulletin*, September 23, 1928, 6.

"How Police Headquarters Appeared." *Honolulu Advertiser*, September 23, 1928, 1.

"Huber, Beebe Are to Defend Young Slayer." *Honolulu Star-Bulletin*, September 25, 1928, 1.

Hurley, Tim. "Native Vote Is Called Off in Reaction to Top Court." *Honolulu Star-Advertiser*, December 15, 2015, A1.

———. "U.S. High Court Halts Balloting for Delegates to Hawaiian Body." *Honolulu Star-Advertiser*, December 2, 2015, B1.

"The Hymn of Hate." Editorial. *Hawaii Hochi*, November 20, 1929, 1–2.

Ikei, Clayton. "Myles Fukunaga Case Review." *Hawai'i Herald*, January 1, 2010, C7–C8.

"In a New Guise." Editorial. *Nippu Jiji*, September 28, 1928.

"Is Myles Fukunaga Insane." Editorial. *Hawaii Hochi*, October 10, 1928.

"Japanese Civic Club Gives $200 in Murder Case." *Nippu Jiji*, September 21, 1928, 1.

"Japanese Consular Officials Will Aid in Fukunaga Hunt." *Honolulu Star-Bulletin*, September 19, 1928.

"Japanese Daily Raises Race Issue in Fukunaga Case: Backs Petition." *Honolulu Star-Bulletin*, October 17, 1928, 1, 3.

"Japanese in Strong Plea for Fukunaga." *Hawaii Hochi*, November 5, 1929, 1.

"Japanese Pledge Aid in Search for Lost Youth." *Hawaii Hochi*, September 20, 1928, 2.

Jung, Moon-Kie. *Beneath the Surface of White Supremacy: Denaturalizing U.S. Racisms Past and Present*. Stanford: Stanford University Press, 2015.

———. *Reworking Race: The Making of Hawaii's Interracial Labor Movement*. New York: Columbia University Press, 2006.

———. "Interracialism: The Ideological Transformation of Hawaii's Working Class." *American Sociological Review* 68 (2003): 373–400.

"Jury Panel Accepted by Both Sides." *Honolulu Advertiser*, October 3, 1928, 1, 3.

"Justice, Not Mercy." Editorial. *Hawaii Hochi*, October 18, 1928, 1–2.

"Justice Will Be Speedy Says Davis." *Honolulu Advertiser*, September 23, 1928, 1.

"Kaisan Glad to be Out of 'All This,' He Says." *Honolulu Star-Bulletin*, September 25, 1928, 1.

"Kaisan Tells His Story." *Nippu Jiji*, September 24, 1928.

"Kaisan under Influence of Serum Tells Details of Penning Death Note." *Honolulu Advertiser*, September 20, 1928, 1.

"Kaisan's Wrong Handwriting Gets into Newspaper." *Nippu Jiji*, September 25, 1928.

Kay, H. T. Memo re Legal Analysis of the Publicity in the Fukunaga Case. Office of the Attorney General. Hawai'i State Archives. Series 203, box 6, folder 153, Record of Quasi-Judicial Executive Actions. Record of Gov., Terr. of Hawai'i, Re: Quasi-Jud. Ex. Actions, Death Warr., Repriv., Re Docs.: Myles Yutaka Fukunaga 1929, November 1930.

Kerkvliet, Melinda Tria. *Unbending Cane: Pablo Manlapit, a Filipino Labor Leader in Hawai'i*. Honolulu: Office of Multicultural Student Services, University of Hawai'i, 2002.

"Kidnapper and Murderer Made Fine Record at Kauai School, Says Teacher." *Nippu Jiji*, September 26, 1928.

"Kidnapper in Card Game at Hotel Friday." *Honolulu Star-Bulletin*, September 24, 1928, 5.

"Killer Visited the Scenes of Happier Days." *Honolulu Star-Bulletin*, September 24, 1928, 3.

"Kirrie Boy Murdered." *Dundee Courier*, September 28, 1928.

Kotani, Roland M. *The Japanese in Hawaii: A Century of Struggle*. Honolulu: Hawaii Hochi, 1985.

"Lad Taken to Beach Hotel, Driver Tells." *Honolulu Advertiser*, September 20, 1928, 1, 4.

"The Law's Triumph and Hawaii's Shame." Editorial. *Hawaii Hochi*, November 19, 1929, 1–2.

"Lessons from the Jamieson Case." Editorial. *Nippu Jiji*, September 25, 1928.

"Letter to the Editor." *Honolulu Star-Bulletin,* September 24, 1928, 6.

"Let Us Have Law." Editorial. *Honolulu Star-Bulletin*, September 21, 1928, 6.

"A Letter on the Fukunaga Case." *Hawaii Hochi*, October 12, 1928, 2.

Lind, Andrew W. *Hawaii's People*. 4th ed. Honolulu: University of Hawai'i Press, 1980.

Linder, Douglas O. "The Leopold and Loeb Trial: A Brief Account." 1997. http://law2.umkc.edu/faculty/projects/ftrials/leoploeb/Accountoftrial.html.

"Lone Fox Spends Most of the Time in Movie Theatres and Reading Room at Central 'Y' after Murder." *Nippu Jiji*, September 24, 1928.

"Looking to the Future." Editorial. *Honolulu Star-Bulletin*, September 25, 1928, 6.

"Marked Dates on Calendar in His Room." *Honolulu Advertiser*, September 23, 1928, 5.

"Martial Law Proposal Turned Down." *Honolulu Advertiser*, September 20, 1928, 3.

"Medicos Deny Agreement to Keep Silence." *Hawaii Hochi*, October 17, 1928, 1.

"Meeting of Father and Thug Who Slunk Away with Bills Told by Two Eye-Witnesses." *Honolulu Advertiser*, September 20, 1928, 4.

"The Message from the Dead." Editorial. *Hawaii Hochi*, November 26, 1929, 1–2.

"Miles [*sic*] Fukunaga Arrested as Jamieson Murderer: Makes Full Confession." *Honolulu Advertiser*, September 23, 1928, 1.

"Mind Study of Fukunaga Not to Be Allowed." *Honolulu Star-Bulletin*, October 10, 1928.

"Miranda Hanged." *Hawaiian Star*, October 26, 1904, 1, 5.

"Miranda's Defense In." *Hawaiian Star*, October 6, 1904, 1, 5.
"Mob Gathers at Station after Arrest." *Honolulu Advertiser*, September 23, 1928, 1.
"Morbid Crowd Sees Slayers Hanged Today." *Honolulu Star-Bulletin*, August 12, 1927, 1.
"Murakami to Take Fukunaga Case to Coast." *Hawaii Hochi*, January 31, 1929.
"Murder Trial of Fukunaga Begins Today." *Honolulu Advertiser*, October 1, 1928, 1–2.
"Murderer Gets Stay of Month." *Honolulu Advertiser*, October 19, 1928, 1–2.
"Myles Fukunaga Calls in Pastor." *Nippu Jiji*, October 9, 1928.
Myrick, Lockwood, Jr. "An Open Letter to Governor Wallace R. Farrington on Fukunaga's Insanity." Honolulu: No publisher is indicated in the copy at Hamilton Library of the University of Hawai'i, 1928.
"Native Hawaiians Our Future, Your Vote." *Honolulu Star-Advertiser*, September 13, 2015, 28.
"Near the End." Editorial. *Nippu Jiji*, July 20, 1929.
"Net Closing In on Abduction Gang, Investigators Say." *Honolulu Advertiser*, September 20, 1928, 1, 3.
"Newspaper Trials." Editorial. *Hawaii Hochi*, October 31, 1928.
"New Trial Sought for Murderer." *Honolulu Advertiser*, October 16, 1928, 1, 3.
"Nicoll Speaks to Noon Crowd of Vigilantes." *Honolulu Star-Bulletin*, October 3, 1928.
"Nine Jurors Are Passed in Murder Trial." *Honolulu Star-Bulletin*, October 1, 1928, 1, 4.
"Not a Racial Crime." Editorial. *Honolulu Star-Bulletin*, September 25, 1928, 6.
"Not Guilty Plea Entered for Fukunaga." *Honolulu Advertiser*, September 25, 1928, 1–2.
"No Time Limit." Editorial. *Hawaii Hochi*, November 8, 1929, 1–2.
"Obstructing Justice." Editorial. *Nippu Jiji*, October 12, 1928.
Odo, Franklin S. *No Sword to Bury: Japanese Americans in Hawai'i during World War II.* Philadelphia: Temple University Press, 2004.
Odo, Franklin S., and Kazuko Sinoto. *A Pictorial History of the Japanese in Hawai'i 1885–1924*. Honolulu: Bishop Museum Press, 1985.
Ogawa, Dennis. *Jan Ken Po: The World of Hawaii's Japanese Americans.* Honolulu: Honolulu Japanese Chamber of Commerce, 1973.
Okamura, Jonathan Y. "Barack Obama as the Postracial Candidate for a Postracial America: Perspectives from Asian America and Hawai'i." *Patterns of Prejudice* 45, no. 1–2 (2011): 132–51.
———. *Ethnicity and Inequality in Hawai'i*. Philadelphia: Temple University Press, 2008.
———. *From Race to Ethnicity: Interpreting Japanese American Experiences in Hawai'i*. Honolulu: University of Hawai'i Press, 2014.
———. "The Illusion of Paradise: Privileging Multiculturalism in Hawai'i." In *Making Majorities: Constituting the Nation in Japan, Korea, China, Malaysia, Fiji, Turkey, and the United States*, edited by D. C. Gladney, 264–84. Stanford, Calif.: Stanford University Press, 1998.
———. "Local Culture and Society in Hawaii." *Amerasia Journal* 7 (1980): 119–37.
———. "Race and/or Ethnicity in Hawai'i: What's the Difference and What Dif-

ference Does It Make?" In *Beyond Ethnicity: New Politics of Race in Hawai'i*, edited by Rudy Guevarra Jr. et al., 94–113. Honolulu: University of Hawai'i Press, 2018.

Okihiro, Gary Y. *Cane Fires: The Anti-Japanese Movement in Hawaii, 1865–1945*. Philadelphia: Temple University Press, 1991.

Omi, Michael, and Howard Winant. *Racial Formation in the United States*. 3rd ed. New York: Routledge, 2014.

———. "Racial Formation Rules." In *Racial Formation in the Twenty-First Century*, edited by Daniel HoSang, Oneka LaBennett, and Laura Pulido, 302–31. Berkeley: University of California Press, 2012.

"1000 Japanese Women Sign Fukunaga Plea." *Honolulu Star-Bulletin*, November 12, 1929, 1.

"Opening Brief for Defendant and Plaintiff in Error." In Supreme Court of the Territory of Hawaii, No. 1860, 1928. Fukunaga Case Files, box 2, ms M005, Archives Collection, Hamilton Library, University of Hawai'i.

"Opinion of Supreme Court." In *Transcript of Record*, in United States Circuit Court of Appeals for the Ninth Circuit, no. 5730, 65-115. San Francisco: FilmerBros. Co., 1929. Fukunaga Case Files, box 1, ms M005, Archives Collection, Hamilton Library, University of Hawai'i.

"Oriental Civic Organizations Join in Moves to Find Criminals." *Honolulu Star-Bulletin*, September 21, 1928, 4.

Osorio, Jonathan K. *Dismembering Lahui*. Honolulu: University of Hawai'i Press, 2002.

"Pacheco, and Perhaps Wright, Elected to Board in the Primary." *Honolulu Star-Bulletin*, October 7, 1928, 1.

"Parents Make Public Apology through Press." *Nippu Jiji*, September 24, 1928.

"Parents Voice Deepest Regret for Occurrence." *Honolulu Star-Bulletin*, September 24, 1928, 1.

"Petition for Writ of Certiorari." In Supreme Court of the United States, 1929. Fukunaga Case Files, box 1, ms M005, Archives Collection, Hamilton Library, University of Hawai'i.

"Police Follow Trail Left by Slayer of Boy." *Honolulu Star-Bulletin*, September 22, 1928, 1–2.

"Police Grill Youngster in Murder Case." *Honolulu Star-Bulletin*, September 22, 1928, 2.

"Police Seek Ex-Waiter as Gang Member." *Honolulu Advertiser*, September 20, 1928, 1.

Porteus, Stanley D., and Marjorie Babcock. *Temperament and Race*. Boston: Badger, 1926.

"Proceedings Had in the U.S. Circuit Court of Appeals for the Ninth Circuit." In *Transcript of Record*, in United States Circuit Court of Appeals for the Ninth Circuit, No. 5730, 1929, 329–39. Fukunaga Case Files, box 1, ms M005, Archives Collection, Hamilton Library, University of Hawai'i.

"Professional Trouble-Makers Seeking to Exploit Fukunaga Case as Business Proposition." *Nippu Jiji*, October 29, 1928, 1.

"Prof. Myrick Makes Report on Fukunaga." *Hawaii Hochi*, November 6, 1928, 1.
"Public Asked to Watch These Numbers." *Honolulu Star-Bulletin*, September 21, 1928, 4.
"Public Denied Confession until Trial." *Honolulu Advertiser*, September 25, 1928, 1.
Puette, William J. *The Hilo Massacre: Hawaii's Bloody Monday*. Honolulu: University of Hawai'i College of Continuing Education and Community Service, 1988.
"Racial Harmony." Editorial. *Hawaii Hochi*, November 24, 1929, 1–2.
"Raising the Race Question." Editorial. *Honolulu Star-Bulletin*, October 18, 1928, 6.
"Ransom Note Written by an Oriental Hand." *Honolulu Star-Bulletin*, September 19, 1928, 2.
"Reads Editorial on Life Mystery." *Nippu Jiji*, September 23, 1928.
"Reduce Crime Will be Aim of Vigilantes." *Honolulu Advertiser*, September 28, 1928.
Reinecke, John E. *Feigned Necessity: Hawaii's Attempt to Obtain Chinese Contract Labor, 1921–1923*. San Francisco: Chinese Materials Center, 1979.
———. *The Filipino Piecemeal Sugar Strike of 1924–1925*. Honolulu: Social Science Research Institute, University of Hawai'i, 1996.
"Relative of Fukunaga in Japan Insane." *Hawaii Hochi*, October 12, 1928.
"Rent Driver Tells How He Picked Up Boy." *Honolulu Star-Bulletin*, September 19, 1928, 1.
"Reprieves for Fukunaga and Kacal Granted." *Honolulu Star-Bulletin*, October 22, 1928, 1.
"Retrial Plea for Fukunaga Held Frivolous." *Honolulu Star-Bulletin*, December 24, 1928.
"A Revolting Crime." Editorial, *Nippu Jiji*, September 20, 1928, 2.
"Reward Fund Far Over Top: Total $23,558." *Honolulu Star-Bulletin*, September 21, 1928, 1.
Richards, R. "Testimony Given by Suspects Throws New Light on City Youth." *Honolulu Star-Bulletin*, October 3, 1928, 1, 9.
"Running True to Form." Editorial. *Hawaii Hochi*, October 19, 1928, 1.
"Sanity Issue in Fukunaga Case, Makino Declares." *Honolulu Star-Bulletin*, January 21, 1929, 2.
"Say Race Is not Factor in Crime of Myles Fukunaga." HCN, October 5, 1928.
Schmitt, Robert C. *Historical Statistics of Hawai'i*. Honolulu: University Press of Hawai'i, 1979.
"School Head Asks Principals, Students to Aid in Search." *Honolulu Star-Bulletin*, September 19, 1928.
"Schoolmates on Kauai Say Lad Was Quiet." *Honolulu Star-Bulletin*, September 24, 1928, 5.
"Search Ends When Body of Boy Is Found." *Honolulu Star-Bulletin*, September 20, 1928, 3.
"Selection of 12 Talesmen Begins." *Nippu Jiji*, October 1, 1928.
"A Serious Question Is Raised." Editorial, *Hawaii Hochi*, October 8, 1928, 1–2.

"7 Recognize Fukunaga at Oahu Prison." *Honolulu Advertiser*, September 26, 1928.

"The Shadow of Death." Editorial, *Hawaii Hochi*, November 18, 1929, 1.

Silva, Noenoe K. *Aloha Betrayed: Native Hawaiian Resistance to American Colonialism.* Durham, N.C.: Duke University Press, 2004.

"Simple Rites Held Today for Murdered Boy." *Honolulu Star-Bulletin*, September 21, 1928, 1, 4.

"Six Claims on File for Reward Fund." *Honolulu Advertiser*, September 26, 1928, 1.

"S. K. Nakamura Identified by Messenger Boy." *Honolulu Star-Bulletin*, September 20, 1928, 1–2.

"Slayer Moved Deliberately in Entire Crime." *Honolulu Star-Bulletin*, September 25, 1928, 11.

"Slayer Sorry; Shows Little Other Emotion." *Honolulu Star-Bulletin,* September 24, 1928, 1.

"Slayer's Fate in Hands of Twelve Men." *Honolulu Star-Bulletin,* October 4, 1928, 1.

"The So-Called Kaisan Case." *Nippu Jiji*, September 27, 1928.

"Sorry for Act Fukunaga Tells Interviewers." *Honolulu Advertiser*, September 24, 1928, 1–2.

"Special Deputy Group to be Used in Hunt." *Honolulu Star-Bulletin*, September 19, 1928, 1.

Stannard, David E. *Honor Killing: How the Infamous "Massie Affair" Transformed Hawai'i*. New York: Viking, 2005.

———. "Honoring Racism: The Professional Life and Reputation of Stanley D. Porteus." *Social Process in Hawai'i* 39 (1999): 85–125.

"Suggest Other Uses for $28,000 Now in Public Reward Fund." *Honolulu Star-Bulletin*, September 25, 1928, 1.

"Swift Justice Assured for Young Slayer." *Honolulu Star-Bulletin*, September 24, 1928, 1, 13.

Takaki, Ronald T. *Pau Hana: Plantation Life and Labor in Hawaii, 1835–1920*. Honolulu: University of Hawai'i Press, 1983.

Tamura, Eileen. *Americanization, Acculturation, and Ethnic Identity: The Nisei Generation in Hawaii.* Urbana: University of Illinois Press, 1993.

"A Terrible Menace." Editorial. *Hawaii Hochi*, September 21, 1928, 1.

"Text of 'Death Letter' Mailed Thursday Morning." *Honolulu Star-Bulletin*, September 21, 1928, 1.

Theroux, Joseph. "A Short History of Hawaiian Executions, 1826–1947." *Hawaiian Journal of History* 25 (1991): 147–59.

———. "Walking Shadow." *Honolulu*, July 1990, 52–55, 75–78.

"The Thin Wedge of Distrust." Editorial. *Hawaii Hochi*, November 7, 1929, 1–2.

"33 Men, 2 Women Watch Hanging of Two Filipino Slayers at Oahu Prison." *Honolulu Star-Bulletin*, May 27, 1927, 1.

"This Is Not a Fight." Editorial. *Hawaii Hochi*, October 13, 1928.

"Thousands Go to Spot Where Boy Was Found." *Honolulu Star-Bulletin*, September 21, 1928, 2.

"3 Claims for Reward Money Given Chamber." *Honolulu Star-Bulletin*, September 25, 1928, 1.

"3 Men Believed to Be Involved in Kidnapping." *Honolulu Star-Bulletin*, September 19, 1928, 1.

"3 Still Held by Police, 4 in Oahu Prison." *Honolulu Star-Bulletin*, September 21, 1928, 1.

"Throngs Jam Streets near Police Station." *Honolulu Star-Bulletin*, September 21, 1928, 1.

"'Too Young to Hang' Third Plea." *Hawaii Hochi*, November 10, 1929.

"Transcript." In *Transcript of Record,* Supreme Court of the United States, October Term, 1929. Yutaka Fukunaga, also known as Myles Yutaka Fukunaga, also known as Myles Fukunaga, Petitioner, vs. Territory of Hawaii, Respondent, 139–247. In Tsukiyama Fukunaga Case Files, box 1, ms M005, Archives Collection, Hamilton Library, University of Hawai'i.

"Transcript of Examination of Jurors." The Territory of Hawaii vs. Yutaka Fukunaga, also known as Myles Yutaka Fukunaga, also known as Myles Fukunaga. In the Circuit Court of the First Judicial Circuit, Territory of Hawaii, 1928. In Tsukiyama Fukunaga Case Files, box 1, ms M005, Archives Collection, Hamilton Library, University of Hawai'i.

Tsai, Michael. "March Decries Deedy Acquittal." *Honolulu Star-Advertiser*, August 16, 2014, B1.

Tsukiyama, Ted. "Justice and the Case of Myles Fukunaga." *Hawai'i Herald* 31, no. 1 (2010): C1-C8.

Tsutsumi, Cheryl Chee. "Preserving Hawaii's Historic Cemeteries." *Honolulu Star-Advertiser,* January 25, 2015.

"$20,000 Community Fund of Chamber of Commerce for Reward Half Raised." *Honolulu Star-Bulletin*, September 21, 1928, 1, 3.

"Two Poses of Gill Jamieson." *Honolulu Advertiser*, September 19, 1928, 1.

"Urge $20,000 Reward for Boy's Slayer." *Hawaii Hochi*, September 20, 1928, 1.

"Utmost Speed in Trial Urged by 'Vigilantes.'" *Honolulu Star-Bulletin*, September 24, 1928, 1.

"Victim Cut Up: Head Knocked In." *Nippu Jiji*, September 20, 1928, 1.

Wakukawa, Ernest K. *A History of the Japanese People in Hawaii*. Honolulu: Toyo Shoin, 1938.

"Walks to the Gallows with Calm Bearing." *Honolulu Star-Bulletin*, November 19, 1929, 1, 3.

"Weird Letter Placed upon Victim's Face." *Honolulu Advertiser*, September 20, 1928, 1.

Welton, Benjamin. "Fox or 'Moral Imbecile'? William Edward Hickman and the Murder of Marion Parker." 2014. http://www.crimemagazine.com/fox-or-%E2%80%9Cmoral-imbecile%E2%80%9D-william-edward-hickman-and-murder-marion-parker.

"What Can Hawai'i Teach America about Race." 2015. http://www.whatitmeanstobeamerican.org/events/what-can-hawaii-teach-america-about—race/.

"When Fukunaga Was Pupil on Kauai." *Honolulu Star-Bulletin*, September 26, 1928, 1.

"Where the 'Melting Pot' Melts." Editorial. *Honolulu Star-Bulletin*, November 19, 1929, 6.

White, E. "Hoped to Make Parents Happy, Fukunaga Says." *Honolulu Star-Bulletin*, September 24, 1928, 1–2.

"Why Should We Worry?" Editorial. *Hawaii Hochi*, November 19, 1928, 1.

Wright, Theon. *The Disenchanted Isles: The Story of the Second Revolution in Hawaii*. New York: Dial, 1972.

———. *Rape in Paradise*. New York: Tower, 1966.

"Writ of Error Delays Death of Fukunga." *Honolulu Star-Bulletin*, November 17, 1928, 1.

"Yutaka Fukunaga Appealed." *Tokyo Asahi Shimbun*, June 20, 1929.

Index

JONATHAN Y. OKAMURA is a professor in the Department of Ethnic Studies at the University of Hawaiʻi. He is the author of several books, most recently *From Race to Ethnicity: Interpreting Japanese American Experiences in Hawaiʻi.*

The Asian American Experience

The Hood River Issei: An Oral History of Japanese Settlers in Oregon's Hood River Valley *Linda Tamura*

Americanization, Acculturation, and Ethnic Identity: The Nisei Generation in Hawaii *Eileen H. Tamura*

Sui Sin Far/Edith Maude Eaton: A Literary Biography *Annette White-Parks*

Mrs. Spring Fragrance and Other Writings *Sui Sin Far; edited by Amy Ling and Annette White-Parks*

The Golden Mountain: The Autobiography of a Korean Immigrant, 1895–1960 *Easurk Emsen Charr; edited and with an introduction by Wayne Patterson*

Race and Politics: Asian Americans, Latinos, and Whites in a Los Angeles Suburb *Leland T. Saito*

Achieving the Impossible Dream: How Japanese Americans Obtained Redress *Mitchell T. Maki, Harry H. L. Kitano, and S. Megan Berthold*

If They Don't Bring Their Women Here: Chinese Female Immigration before Exclusion *George Anthony Peffer*

Growing Up Nisei: Race, Generation, and Culture among Japanese Americans of California, 1924–49 *David K. Yoo*

Chinese American Literature since the 1850s *Xiao-huang Yin*

Pacific Pioneers: Japanese Journeys to America and Hawaii, 1850–80 *John E. Van Sant*

Holding Up More Than Half the Sky: Chinese Women Garment Workers in New York City, 1948–92 *Xiaolan Bao*

Onoto Watanna: The Story of Winnifred Eaton *Diana Birchall*

Edith and Winnifred Eaton: Chinatown Missions and Japanese Romances *Dominika Ferens*

Being Chinese, Becoming Chinese American *Shehong Chen*

"A Half Caste" and Other Writings *Onoto Watanna; edited by Linda Trinh Moser and Elizabeth Rooney*

Chinese Immigrants, African Americans, and Racial Anxiety in the United States, 1848–82 *Najia Aarim-Heriot*

Not Just Victims: Conversations with Cambodian Community Leaders in the United States *Edited and with an introduction by Sucheng Chan; interviews conducted by Audrey U. Kim*

The Japanese in Latin America *Daniel M. Masterson with Sayaka Funada-Classen*

Survivors: Cambodian Refugees in the United States *Sucheng Chan*

From Concentration Camp to Campus: Japanese American Students and World War II *Allan W. Austin*

Japanese American Midwives: Culture, Community, and Health Politics *Susan L. Smith*

In Defense of Asian American Studies: The Politics of Teaching and Program Building *Sucheng Chan*

Lost and Found: Reclaiming the Japanese American Incarceration
Karen L. Ishizuka

Religion and Spirituality in Korean America *Edited by David K. Yoo and Ruth H. Chung*

Moving Images: Photography and the Japanese American Incarceration
Jasmine Alinder

Camp Harmony: Seattle's Japanese Americans and the Puyallup Assembly Center *Louis Fiset*

Chinese American Transnational Politics *Him Mark Lai; edited and with an introduction by Madeline Y. Hsu*

Issei Buddhism in the Americas *Edited by Duncan Ryûken Williams and Tomoe Moriya*

Hmong America: Reconstructing Community in Diaspora *Chia Youyee Vang*

In Pursuit of Gold: Chinese American Miners and Merchants in the American West *Sue Fawn Chung*

Pacific Citizens: Larry and Guyo Tajiri and Japanese American Journalism in the World War II Era *Edited by Greg Robinson*

Indian Accents: Brown Voice and Racial Performance in American Television and Film *Shilpa S. Davé*

Yellow Power, Yellow Soul: The Radical Art of Fred Ho
Edited by Roger N. Buckley and Tamara Roberts

Fighting from a Distance: How Filipino Exiles Helped Topple a Dictator
Jose V. Fuentecilla

In Defense of Justice: Joseph Kurihara and the Japanese American Struggle for Equality *Eileen H. Tamura*

Asian Americans in Dixie: Race and Migration in the South
Edited by Jigna Desai and Khyati Y. Joshi

Undercover Asian: Multiracial Asian Americans in Visual Culture
Leilani Nishime

Islanders in the Empire: Filipino and Puerto Rican Laborers in Hawai'i
JoAnna Poblete

Virtual Homelands: Indian Immigrants and Online Cultures in the United States *Madhavi Mallapragada*

Building Filipino Hawai'i *Roderick N. Labrador*

Legitimizing Empire: Filipino American and U.S. Puerto Rican Cultural Critique *Faye Caronan*

Chinese in the Woods: Logging and Lumbering in the American West
Sue Fawn Chung

The Minor Intimacies of Race: Asian Publics in North America *Christine Kim*

Reading Together, Reading Apart: Identity, Belonging, and South Asian American Community *Tamara Bhalla*

Chino: Anti-Chinese Racism in Mexico, 1880–1940 *Jason Oliver Chang*

Asianfail: Narratives of Disenchantment and the Model Minority *Eleanor Ty*

Becoming Refugee American: The Politics of Rescue in Little Saigon
Phuong Tran Nguyen
The Work of Mothering: Globalization and the Filipino Diaspora
Harrod J. Suarez
Discriminating Sex: White Leisure and the Making of the American "Oriental"
Amy Sueyoshi
Muncie, India(na): Middletown and Asian America *Himanee Gupta-Carlson*
The Labor of Care: Filipina Migrants and Transnational Families in the Digital Age *Valerie Francisco-Menchavez*
Disrupting Kinship: Transnational Politics of Korean Adoption in the United States *Kimberly D. McKee*
Raced to Death in 1920s Hawai'i: Injustice and Revenge in the Fukunaga Case *Jonathan Y. Okamura*

The University of Illinois Press
is a founding member of the
Association of American University Presses.

Composed in 10.5/13 Adobe Caslon Pro
by Jim Proefrock
at the University of Illinois Press
Cover designed by Dustin J. Hubbart
Cover illustration: Myles Fukunaga, 1928
(Oahu Community Correction Center)

University of Illinois Press
1325 South Oak Street
Champaign, IL 61820-6903
www.press.uillinois.edu